AF531780

As I Please

As I Please

K. Natwar Singh

Rely on yourself! Bore down with your drill as deeply as you can, without fear or mercy, but into yourself. And if you do not find the people, the earth and the sky there, then give up the search-in that case there is nowhere else to go.

Boris Pasternak
1890-1970

HAR-ANAND
PUBLICATIONS PVT LTD

HAR-ANAND PUBLICATIONS PVT LTD
E-49/3, Okhla Industrial Area, Phase-II, New Delhi-110020
Tel.: 41603490
E-mail: info@haranandbooks.com/haranand@rediffmail.com
Shop online at: www.haranandbooks.com

Reprint, 2022

Published by Ashok Gosain and Ashish Gosain for
Har-Anand Publications Pvt Ltd

Printed in India

To
Michael Foot
Amaury de Riencourt
Han Suyin

Note on China

by Natwar Singh, an Officer in the Prime Minister's Office and submitted to the Prime Minister

13 May 1970

As China watching is a whole time job I submit this note to PM and Secretary with some hasitation. My own experience in China is limited to the post Bandung era-1956-58. This was followed by a brief interlude when I was attached as Liaison Officer to Chou En Lai in April 1960 during his visit to Delhi for talks with Prime Minister Nehru and other leaders.

The China of 1956-58 seems very far off. Our relations at that time were so good that the Chinese authorities allowed me to join Peking University to study Chinese. I even managed to pass the advanced examination in Chinese conducted by the University.

In those days Chou En Lai was a frequent visitor to the Indian Embassy and even junior members of the Embassy could dine and wine with the great Mao Tse Tung himself. I am, therefore, not unduly excited about our Charge d'Affaires brief encounter on May 1 with Mao Tse Tung at the Tien An Men.* It was not an earth shaking event. At the same time I am aware that it would be wrong to dismiss it as a casual encounter and to ignore what Mao Tse Tung said. On the other hand I do feel that it is equally important not to exaggerate the import of this meeting and read too much into it.

What should then our response be to Mao's four short sentences, which were uttered in the presence of several other

*Document No. 2267.

diplomats. Neither the Chairman nor Prime Minister Chou En Lai sent for our Charge d'Affaires. As a matter of fact Chou En Lai has never received any of our Charge d'Affaires since 1962. At the same time I appreciate Shri Misra's point of view. It is an event in a diplomat's life in China when Mao says something and even a mature person like Misra can be subjective about it.

Our relations with China have a long and difficult history and I for one feel that there are no easy or dramatic solutions for our problems. Mao himself thinks in terms of centuries and we would be ill advised to consider a hasty response to his remarks. We must give a measured, cautious and sober response. Any action which involved announcements in Parliament or direct messages to Chairman Mao should at this juncture be resisted. It would be premature. A part of our troubles in the past arose from Government permitting Parliament to get the initiative in this matter. Government was gradually compelled to taking a rigid stands in Parliament thus making it difficult for quiet diplomatic activity to achieve results. We have now started practicing Parliamentary Diplomacy which is a dangerous game. The publication of the official report (Jagat Mehta and Gopal) in the face of Chinese opposition is one of the serious errors committed by us. That report should never have been made public. Its publication made quiet negotiations impossible.

Chou En Lai's visit to India in April 1960 also got out of hand as he was exposed to far too many people who had little understanding of the complexities of the problem or of the working of the Chinese System.

I mentioned to PM yesterday that it had fallen to my lot to be present and take notes of Chou En Lai's meeting with Shri Morarji Desai, who treated the Chinese Prime Minister as if he was the Chairman of the Broach or The Nasik Municipal Committee.

My own submission, therefore, would be as follows:

(i) We consider the possibility of raising the level of our

representation in Peking to that of Ambassador after sounding the Chinese both in Delhi and Peking. If they react favourably other things could follow. After all, the Yugoslavs and Russians have been cooling their heels for a long time and the Chinese have not yet given firm commitment about the exchange of Ambassadors with the Soviet Union and Yugoslavia. The Americans have been talking to the Chinese in Warsaw for 15 Years.

(ii) We could probe the Chinese about this here in Delhi and through our c.d.a. on his return to Peking. We should then find the right man to be our Ambassador in Peking. I for one would put my money on Dr. Shelvankar.

(iii) We should set up a cell which should carefully study all the material on the Indo China border dispute. With due respect I submit that under the present dispensation in the MEA a serious and non-publicised study of the matter is hardly possible. We should have competent, dedicated and self effacing people to study these documents including the "officials report."

(iv) We might show a little more interest in the Chinese c.d.a. in New Delhi and I would go as far as suggesting that at some airport function PM might exchange a few words with their new man. That is a gesture the Chinese would understand.

I have collected some of the relevant documents and shown them to Secretary. I shall submit them to P.M. after May 20th 1970.

K. NATWAR SINGH
13.5.1970

P.M.

Contents

Part I: Essays

I	Gandhi and Tolstoy	17
II	Jawaharlal Nehru and Winston Churchill	23
III	Nehru as a Man of Letters	29
IV	Charles de Gaulle, 1890-1990: Soldier, Hero, Statesman	37
V	Indira Gandhi, Margaret Thatcher, Mother Teresa and Queen Elizabeth II	41
VI	Radhakrishnan: A Centennial Tribute	43
VII	Nelson Mandela: A Tribute	48
VIII	In Namibia with Rajiv Gandhi	53
IX	Farewell, Brave and Beloved Leader	56
X	Nirad Chaudhuri at 85	59
XI	P.N. Haksar at 75	66
XII	Sonny Ramphal	70
XIII	A Memorable White House Lunch	72
XIV	Living Dangerously: Non-Aligned Summit 1983	76
XV	The Limits of Diplomacy	87
XVI	Li Peng's Passage to India	92
XVII	Count Your Blessings But...	96
XVIII	Let's Talk Peace, Not War	101
XIX	India and Her Neighbours	105
XX	Count Down begins in Kabul	114
XXI	Wither Foreign Policy?	119
XXII	Interview for Celebrity	122
XXIII	50th Anniversary of 1947 Lonely in a Crowded Beach	130
XXIV	The Widening Inequality Gap in India	151
XXV	A.I.C.C Plenary and not Evoke Emotions	153

XXVI Engaging Ideas, Picking Best Title for Book 156
XXVII Nehru Transformed Commonwealth 159
XXVIII Bypoll Results have Altered Political Landscape 162
XXIX Necessity of Order and Laws for Citizens 164
XXX The Art of Love and Hate—The Hindu Contradiction 167
XXXI A Visit Enveloped in Controversy 170
XXXII Shame as Statues are Defaced, Pulled Down 173
XXXIII Martin Luther King Jr's Legacy Lives On 175

Part II: Speeches

I Indira Gandhi Conference 1991 181
II Remembering Indira Gandhi 186
III Address at International Publishers Convention 188
IV A Plea for Peace 192
V Introducing Nobel Laureate Wole Soyinka 198
VI Address of Foreign Ministers Conference on Cambodia, Paris, August 1989 202
VII Thank you Dr. Sagan, Teen Murti Auditorium 207
VIII Homage to Rajiv Gandhi 209
IX Happy Birthday Gamini 210
X A London Dinner 214
XI India and Islam 216

Part III: Among Books and Authors

I Selected Works of Jawaharlal Nehru 235
II Two Alone, Two Together 238
III Jawaharlal Nehru: Letters to Chief Ministers 1947-64 241
IV Don't Spare Me Shankar 244
V The Golden Oriole: Childhood, Family and Friends in India 247
VI Tigers, Durbars and Kings: Fanny Eden's Indians Journals 1837-1838 250
VII No Full Stops in India 252

VIII	Thy Hand, Great Anarch! India (1921-1952)	255
IX	Clive of India by Nirad C. Chaudhuri	258
X	A Sparrow's Flight	261
XI	The Diaries of Lord Louis Mountbatten: 1920-1922	263
XII	City that Rose from the Dead/Review of 'Traders and Nabobs: The British in Cawnpore 1765-1857'	266
XIII	Among Books	268
XIV	Sardar Patel	271
XV	Scholar Extraordinary	274
XVI	Andrei Sakharov	276
XVII	Zia-Ul-Haq	279
XVIII	Tricky Dick	281
XIX	Gandhian Capitalist	284
XX	Maulana Azad	287

Part I:
Essays

Aum Sahanavavatu
Sahanau bhunaktu
Sahaveeryam Karvavahai
Tejasvi navadhitumstu
na vidvisovaki
May we be protected
May we be nourished
May we excell in creative vigour
May we be bestowed with illuminating knowledge
May we be free from envy and hatred.

1

Gandhi and Tolstoy

George Orwell's essay on Gandhiji begins, "Saints should always be judged guilty until they are proved innocent." Tolstoy and Gandhi in their different ways fall into the category of sages and saints and Orwell must also have had the author of War and Peace in mind when he wrote that sparkling sentence.

Two men who in their different spheres of activity should have got the Nobel Prize but did not get it are, Tolstoy and Mahatma Gandhi. Tolstoy died in 1910. The Nobel prize was instituted in 1901. But he was not considered fit to be given the prize while obscure writers got it. Gandhiji should have got the Nobel Peace Prize every year from 1920 onwards.

Worldly goods meant nothing to these two extraordinary men, the parallels in their lives have just been brought home to us in a book published in New York late last year. Martin Green's *Tolstoy and Gandhi, Men of Peace* carries forward the work of Dr. Kalidas Nag, who had published a book with a similar title in 1950. Mr. Green gives us new insights into the lives of Tolstoy and Gandhi.

The anniversary of Gandhiji's assassination invitably evokes a mood of introspection. It really was a perfect death for him. He went out like a flame with the name of God on his lips. I sometimes wonder if the great and good man did not and seek martyrdom. He had read the Bible carefully. Like Tolstoy he considered the Sermon on the Mount among the greatest pronouncements of all time. If ever anyone lived the Ten Commandments, it was Mohandas Karamchand Gandhi. The Christian ethic was deeply ingrained in him.

In his autobiography, Gandhiji tells us that, apart from the great religious books of the world, the two books that made the deepest, the most profound and lasting impression on his mind were Ruskin's *"Unto This Last"* and Tolstoy's, *"The Kingdom of God is Within You."* Although Tolstoy and Gandhi came from very different backgrounds, there were striking similarities in their message and approach to life. Tolstoy was an aristocrat, an intellectual, a landowner who in later life considered property a kind of theft. He was born a Christian but did not die one. He had been a bit of a rip in his youth who was transformed into a kind of Russian rishi in the final decades of his life. As a young man he was a lover of the good things of life but became a believer in non-violence and renunciation.

Both thought simple people were the best. Both idolised the peasent. Both lived like peasants. They taught humility, loved manual labour. Gandhiji went to the extent of cleaning laterines and Tolstoy took to boot-making. Both were teachers and preachers. Gandhiji had his *"nai taleem"*. Tolstoy in his middle age started a school for peasant children on new and original lines. Both had their fads. Dress comes to mind. Gandhiji wore too little. Tolstoy too much. Both were outraged by the materialism they saw around them and were critical of western civilization. When a European correspondent asked Gandhiji during his visit to London in 1931, "Mr. Gandhi, what are your views on Western civilization?" Gandhiji's subtle reply left him dumbfounded. The Mahatma said: "It would be nice".

It is obvious that Gandhiji had read almost all of Tolstoy's non-fictional works by the time he came to correspond with him. There is no evidence to show that he read any of Tolstoy's fictional works. By an odd coincidence Tolstoy's greatest novel. *"War and Peace"* appeared in 1869 the year of Gandhi's birth.

It was not surprising that Gandhiji was drawn to the teachings of the sage of Yasnaya Polyana. There is evidence to show that when Tolstoy turned 80 in 1908, Gandhiji sent him his greetings and felicitations from Tolstoy Farm near Johannesburg.

The first reference to Tolstoy in, *"The Story of My Experiments with Truth"*, is on page 55. It is characteristic that it should be related not to any spiritual subject, political principle or to non-violence, but to one of Tolstoy's aversions. Gandhi as a student in London visited Paris in 1890 for the Great Exhibition. The newly built Eiffel Tower was a major attraction. Gandhiji was not impressed by it. He writes, "I must say a word about the Eiffel Tower. I do not know what purpose it serves today, but I then heard it greatly disparaged as well as praised.

"I remember that Tolstoy was the chief among those who disparaged. He said that the Eiffel Tower was a monument to man's folly, not to his wisdom. Tobacco, he argued, was the worst of all intoxicants in as much as a man addicted to it was tempted to commit crimes which a drunkard never dared to do. Liquor made a man mad, but tobacco clouded his intellect and made him build castles in the air. The Eiffel Tower was one of the creations of a man under such an influence." One is left speechless, tobacco, Eiffel Tower, but then strange are the ways of savants and sages.

The next reference to Tolstoy is on page 65, "three moderns have left deep impression on my life and captivated me. Rayehand Bhai by his book, *"Living Contract"*, Tolstoy by his book, *"The Kingdom of Goo is Within You"*, and Ruskin by his *"Unto This Last"*.

The third reference is on page 98 and again refers to the impact Tolstoy's book, *"The Kingdom of God is Within You"* made on him. And finally on page 115 he writes, "I made an intensive study of Tolstoy's book, *The Gospels in Brief, What to Do,* and other books made a deep impression on me, I began to realise more and more the infinite possibilities of universal love."

In 1909 Gandhiji was in London for discussions with the Colonial office about the problems of the people of Indian origin in South Africa. From London he wrote to Tolstoy on the first of the month. He drew Tolstoy's attention to the plight of the Indian population who laboured under rampant colour bar. Gandhiji said that there was no question of his yielding to such outrageous laws and that he intended to fight against them. Gandhiji also in his letter asked Tolstoy's permission to translate the great Russian writer's, "Letter to a Hindu", which Tolstoy had written in the previous year in response to a letter that he received from some Indian revolutionary living in London. Before writing that letter, Tolstoy had made an extensive study of ancient Indian literature and familiarised himself with Indian traditions.

Tolstoy knew nothing about the Indian community in South Africa, but what Gandhiji wrote to him interested him. He felt that Gandhiji was a kindred spirit and on 24 September 1909, he noted in his diary, "1 have received a letter from an Indian in Transvaal," and a few days later he wrote to a friend, "The letter of the Transvaal Hindu has touched me very much." On 8 October, the 81 year-old Tolstoy replied to Gandhiji's letter expressing his sincere sympathy for the oppressed Indians and wishing them success in the struggle for their human rights. He wrote "I have just received your very interesting letter, which gave me much pleasure. God help our dear brothers and co-workers in the Transvaal. Among us, too, this fight between gentleness and brutality between humility and love and pride and violence, makes itself ever more strongly felt especially in one of the sharpest conflicts between the religious duty and the state laws."

Tolstoy also gave Gandhi permission to translate his 'Letter to a Hindu', saying that the translation, "in circulation of my letter in an Indian language can only be a matter of pleasure to me." Gandhiji was encouraged by Tolstoy's reply and wrote again from London. This time he sent a copy of J.K. Doke's biography of himself and observed that in his opinion, "This struggle of modern times, as it has been idealised both as to the goal as also to the methods adopted to reach the goal ... I am not aware of a struggle in which the participants are not to derive any personal advantage at the end of it and in which 50 per cent of the persons affected have undergone great suffering and trial for the sake of a principle. It has not been possible for me to advertise the struggle as much as I should like.

"You command, possibly, the widest public today. If you are satisfied as to the facts you will find set forth in Mr. Doke's book, and if you consider that the conclusions I have arrived at are justified by the facts, may I ask you to use your influence in any manner you think fit to popularise the movement? If it succeeds it will be not only a triumph of religion, love and truth over irreligion, hatred and underformed by false interpretation. Love is the aspiration for communion and solidarity with other souls and that aspiration always liberates the soul. That love is likely to serve as an example to the millions in India and to people in other parts of the world, who may be down-trodden and will certainly go a great way towards breaking up the party of violence, at lease in India."

In April Gandhiji wrote again to Tolstoy and sent him a copy of his book, *Indian Home Rule.* Tolstoy, now 82 years old, replied on 8 May 1910, and addressed the 41-year-old Gandhi as "Dear Friend". He praised Gandhiji's book, adding that "The question you have therein dealt with is important not only for Indians but for the whole mankind." Tolstoy was old and unwell and said he would be writing at greater length after his recovery. He signed the letter, "your friend and brother, Leo Tolstoy." Gandhiji replied on 15 August from Johannesburg and sent the Count some numbers of *Indian Opinion* which he was then editing.

Tolstoy's final letter was written on 7 September 1910, a few weeks before his death. It is the longest and the most significant and I shall quote from it at some length.

"I have received your journal Indian Opinion and I am happy to know all that is written on non-resistance. I wish to communicate to you the thoughts which are aroused in me by the reading of those articles. The more I live and specially now that I am approaching death—the more I feel inclined to express to others the feelings which so strongly move my being, and which according to my opinion, are of great importance. That is what one calls non-resistance, is in reality nothing else but the discipline of love supreme and unique law of human life, which everyone feels in the depth of one's soul. We find it manifested most clearly in the soul of the infant. Man feels it so long as he is not blinded by the false doctrines of the world.

"The law of love has been promulgated by all the philosophies—Indian, Chinese, Hebrew, Greek and Roman. I think that it had been most clearly expressed by Christ, who said that in that law is contained both the law and the prophets. But he has done more; anticipating the deformation to which that law is exposed, he indicated directly the danger of such deformation which is natural to people who live only for worldly interests.

"The danger persists precisely in permitting one's self to defend those interests by violence; that is to say, as he has expressed, returning blow by blow, and taking back by force things that have been taken from us, and so forth. Christ knew also, just as all reasonable human beings must know, that the employment of violence is incompatible with love, which is the fundamental law of life. He knew that once violence is admitted, doesn't matter in even a single case, the law of love is thereby rendered futile. That is to say that that law of love comes to exist. The whole Christian civilization, so brilliant in the exterior, has grown up on this misunderstanding and the flagrant and strange contradiction, sometimes conscious but mostly unconscious."

Later in his letter, Tolstoy says, "Socialism, communism anarchism, Salvation Army, the growing criminalities, unemployment and absurd luxuries of the rich, augmented without limit, and the awful misery of the poor, the terribly increasing number of suicides—all these are the signs of that inner contradiction which must be there and which cannot be resolved; and without doubt, can only be resolved by acceptation of the law of love and by the rejection of all sorts of violence. Consequently your work in Transvaal, which seems to be far away from the centre of our world, is yet the most fundamental and the most important to us supplying the most weighty practical proof in which the world can now share and with which must participate not only the Christians but all the people of the world."

This was the first time that a world figure had assessed the importance, the originality, the significance and the value of Gandhiji's satyagraha movement which was to play so vital a role in the independence struggle of India and to inspire people in Africa, Latin America and the United States.

I must now come back to the theme of martyrdom which Mr. Green applies both to Tolstoy and Gandhiji. He points out, "One might say that Tolstoy and Gandhi made it their work to rediscover a negative vocabulary, to re-introduce no and not into our moral syntax... Tolstoy and Gandhi rooted their negations in their own lives and deaths and thus completed a set of terms for their contemporaries which could be compared with the moral vocabulary of classical civilization."

2
Jawaharlal Nehru and Winston Churchill

Why an article on Churchill and Nehru? My answer is, Why not: Aren't both super stars? Aren't both arresting characters? How do so many one dimensional greatmen (so called) look in the Churchill-Nehru league? Both left something more than footprints on the sands of time, both enriched the impoverished stock of human courage and decency. Yet in so many ways they were poles apart. To me the most sensible way to tackle this fascinating, exciting subject is to let the two principles speak for themselves. Nevertheless, it is necessary to give a brief background to this relationship in order to put it in a historical framework.

The beginnings were anything but propitious. Churchill, 15 years Nehru's senior in age was a self proclaimed pillar of the British Empire. He was also a dedicated racist. Jawaharlal Nehru was its most uncompromising, outspoken opponent. While Churchill held high office, Nehru spent lonely years in British Indian prisons. Churchill was a child of the House of Commons. Jawaharlal Nehru was a child of the Indian Freedom Movement. The author, producer, director and chief actor of that unique movement was Mohandas Karamchand Gandhi.

Churchill's pre 1947 India record is notoriously bad and does him no credit. He Vigorously opposed Indian freedom. He employed his considerable eloquence and mastery over words to denigrate and belittle Indian leaders and the Freedom Movement. (There is a silver lining here too. He spoke against Lt. Gen. Dyer of Jallianwallah Massacre ill fame in the House of Commons debate on 8 July 1920, calling the shooting, "a monstrous event").

When Lord Irwin (later Lord Halifax) invited Gandhiji for talks at Viceregal Lodge in Delhi, Churchill denounced the meeting in words which did Gandhi no harm but showed Churchill in poor light. Even today I read that passage with rage. This is what Churchill said, on 23 February 1931 speaking at the Council of the West Essex Conservative Association.

"It is alarming and also nauseating to see Mr. Gandhi, a seditious Middle Temple lawyer, now posing as a fakir of a type well-known in the East, striding half-naked up the steps of the Viceregal Palace, while he is still organising and conducting a difficult campaign of civil disobedience, to parley on equal terms with the representative of the King-Emperor. Such a spectacle can only increase the unrest in India...."

In 1941 he declared that the Atlantic Charter he and Roosevelt had signed, granting the Four Freedoms to all and sundry, did not apply to India! About the same time he declared that he had not become, "the King's First Minister to preside over the liquidation of the British Empire." Five years later his successor, Attlee did precisely that. One more instance of Churchill's verbal overkill will suffice. He asserted that Attlee's government was handing over India, "to men of straw" Gandhi, Nehru, Patel, Rajagopalachari, Azad, Rajendra Prasad, Pant. Some men. Some straw.

There are over a hundred references to Churchill in Jawaharlal Nehru's Selected Works. Characteristically the first appearance of Churchill is in Vol. 4. Nehru asks his father, Pandit Motilal Nehru to read Churchill's "World Crisis". The letter is dated l0th September, 1930. "The Discovery of India", has a sub-chapter headed, "Mr. Winston Churchill." The amazing fact is that while on Indian freedom Churchill and Nehru were on opposite sides of the barricade, on the rise of the European Dictators, Nazism and Chamberlains' policy of appeasement, they held very similar views.

Jawaharlal Nehru was in London in September 1938. He heard a debate in the House of Commons. He was not impressed by Chamberlain, "Though Prime Minister of Britain, he is not used to these high tasks, and the intoxication of the adventure (meeting with Hitler) fills him. A Palmerston or a Gladstone or a Disraeli would have risen to the occasion. A Campbell Bannermann would have put fire in what he said. A Baldwin might have gripped the House, so would Churchill in a different way."

Reporting on his travels on his return to India in November 1938

Nehru remarked that, "Mr. Churchill is the ablest politician in England today." In Vol II of the Selected Works, he writes thus about Churchill, "I admire Winston Churchill for his ability and courage and determination and I admire the British people for the spirit they have shown in the defence of their own freedom. But that admiration does not lead me to accept the British Prime Minister's dictation in regard to India."

In, *The Discovery of India,* Nehru writes, "But the person who really counted was Mr. Winston Churchill, the new Prime Minister. Mr. Churchill's views on India's freedom were clear and definite and had been frequently repeated. He stood out as an uncompromising opponent of that freedom.... The gulf between Mr. Churchill and us was vast indeed.

"We remembered his words and knew him to be a stout and uncompromising person. We could hope for little from England under his leadership. For all his courage and great qualities of leadership, he represented the nineteenth century, conservative, imperialist England, and seemed incapable of understanding the new world with its complex problems and forces, and much less the future which was taking shape. And yet he was a big man who could take a big step. His offer of a union with France, (1940) though made at a time of dire peril, showed vision and adaptation to circumstances and had impressed India greatly. Perhaps the new position he occupied with its vast responsibilities, had enlarged his vision and made him outgrow his earlier prejudices and conceptions. Perhaps the very needs of the war situation, which were paramount for him, would compel him to realize that India's freedom was not only inevitable but desirable from the point of view of the war. I remembered that when I was going to China in August, 1939, he had sent me, through a mutual friend, his good wishes for my visit to that war-racked country."

But, as we have seen, there was no change in Churchill's outlook. Nehru spent his longest prison term (1942-45) during Churchill's first term as Prime Minister.

Now see how the wheel of fate can change the scene so dramatically and light the candles. India's independence produced unexpected results. The past was to be buried. A new beginning made.

Jawaharlal Nehru, after consulting his colleagues, decided that India even after becoming a Republic should remain in the Commonwealth. Churchill admired Nehru's realism and used his considerable knowledge of history to find a precedent in Roman history for the presence of a Republic in a Commonwealth. Dr. S. Gopal in his biography of Nehru writes, "In 1949, he had welcomed India's continuance in the Commonwealth. When Smuts, then out of office, cabled him deploring the decision, Churchill replied, "When I asked myself the question, would I rather have India in, even on these terms, or let them go altogether, my heart gave the answer, I wanted them in. Nehru has certainly shown magnanimity." But it was not until Churchill's second tenure as P.M. (1951-55) that Nehru's relations with Churchill took a wholly unexpected turn-of mutual admiration, cordiality and warmth.

Michael Brecher, Nehru's Canadian biographer, describes at some length the Churchill-Nehru reconciliation meeting.... "And so, a group of old Harrovians arranged a dinner in Nehru's honour during one of Nehru's many visits to London early in 1953.

"Churchill consented to attend and to propose Nehru's health.... Churchill was at his best. He paid tribute to Nehru's courage and integrity. He spoke rapturously about Nehru's magnanimity in remaining within the Commonwealth after the experience of subjection. Nehru accepted the gesture and the formal reconciliation took place."

I remember Mrs. Indira Gandhi telling me the story of her encounter with Sir Winston Churchill at the time of the Coronation of Queen Elizabeth II in 1953. When the service at Westminister Abbey was over, Churchill, Nehru and Mrs. Gandhi found themselves together waiting for their cars. Churchill said to Mrs. Gandhi, "You must have hated the British for the treatment meted out to your father. It is remarkable how he and you have overcome bitterness and hatred." Mrs. Gandhi replied, "We never hated you." Churchill looked at her and said, "I did, but I don't now."

Churchill valued Nehru's views on Africa, Portugal, Korea, Egypt etc. Nehru refers to all these issues in his letters to the Chief Ministers. Churchill took Nehru into confidence about nuclear testing in the Pacific in 1954. The British Prime Minister wrote to his Indian counterpart:

"I am sure that you will share my feeling and anxiety on the momentous issues involved. We are indeed at a turning point in the world's history and very grave responsibility rests on those of us in authority. I wish that at this moment it had been possible for us all to take consul together—as we did at the time of the Coronation. I am devoting my mind as to how best any words of mine can help, conscious as I am, of all that is involved for the future of mankind."

Nehru responded immediately sharing Churchill's concern. Nothing came of this as, Nehru says, "The next day, Sir Winston Churchill spoke in the British House of Commons and I must say that his speech was a great disappointment. It did not fit in with the message he had sent me."

In one of his earlier letters to the Chief Ministers, Nehru had written touchingly about Churchill. "Sir Winston Churchill naturally played a great part in all these functions. He is, I believe, about 78 years of age. He was particularly friendly to me personally although we were differing on many matters from day to day. His recent indisposition, no doubt due to the heavy burden he had undertaken as well as the coronation, is very unfortunate. He appears to be determined to do his utmost to give a lead for peace in the world." Jawaharlal Nehru's world influence was at its peak during this period. "The Economist," of 1 May 1954 observed, "at the moment Labour's attitude to the Indian Prime Minister falls little short of canonization. Most Labour questions to Sir Winston imply that he should not move a step in Asia without Mr. Nehru's approval."

Churchill, even in extreme old age did not minimise the pre-eminent role that Nehru played at the world stage. On 21 February 1955 he wrote to Nehru:

"I am so obliged to you for sending me the fascinating book of paintings taken from the Ajanta Caves. The reproduction is beautifully executed and I am indeed happy to possess such a wonderful book. It also gives me great pleasure that it should have come from you, and that our personal relations, after all that has happened, are so agreeable. I hope you will think of the phrase, 'The

Light of Asia'. It seems to me that you might be able to do what no other human being could in giving India the lead, at least in the realm of thought, throughout Asia, with the freedom and dignity of the individual as the ideal."

Nehru wrote back on 8 April thanking Churchill for his generous remarks. Churchill wrote back on 30 June 1955. The letter is marked 'Private', it reads:

"My dear Nehru,

I hope you will forgive the lapse of time in replying to your letter of 8 April. Events following upon my resignation, and the General Elections here, have delayed my correspondence greatly.

I was much touched by what you said. One of the most agreeable memories of my last years in office is our association.

At our conferences your contribution was a leading and constructive one, and I always admired your ardent wish for peace and the absence of bitterness in your consideration of the antagonisms that had in the past divided us. Yours indeed is a heavy burden and responsibility, shaping the destiny of your many millions of countrymen, and playing your outstanding part in world affairs. I wish you well in your task. Remember "The Light of Asia!"

With my personal regards,
I remain,

Yours sincerely,
Winston Churchill

These civilized and memorable exchanges continued. In 1956 Vol. I of Churchill's "A History of the English Speaking Peoples" appeared. He sent a copy to Pandit Jawaharlal Nehru, who replied on 22 October 1956, "It is a delight to read this book and I am very grateful to you for sending it."

The two kept in touch in the years that remained. Mutual respect, warmth of feeling combined with shared literary interests, gave this extraordinary relationship a perpetual imaginative freshness. There is after all much else to life besides politics. Nehru and Churchill showed the world that it was possible to transmit private decencies to public affairs.

3

Nehru as a Man of Letters

Jawaharlal Nehru belonged to that small company of statesmen who were also men of letters. Lenin, Churchill, De Gaulle, Mao Tse Tung, Kennedy. Nehru's books were read the world over. His Autobiography became required reading for freedom fighters in all colonial territories. It gave them hope. It provided much needed inspiration. Through his writings Nehru made politics reach out to touch history.

Of Nehru's Autobiography, John Gunther wrote in his best selling book, *Inside Asia:* 'Nehru's Autobiography is subtle, complex, discriminating, infinitely cultivated, steeped in doubt, suffused with intellectual passion. It is a kind of Indian "Education of Henry Adams," written in superlative prose, Hardly a dozen men alive write English as well as Nehru and it is not only an autobiography of the most searching kind, but the story of a whole society, the story of the life and development of a nation.'

Without a Jawaharlal Nehru, the Indian Freedom Movement would have lacked the vital intellectual dimension. Also an aesthetic one. It was Nehru who saved it from aggressive philistines getting the upper hand.

His writings radiate with vitalising freshness. Almost all his serious writing was done during prison terms. In his famous and brilliantly drafted statement at his Gorakhpur trial in 1940, Nehru said, 'I am a lover of words and phrases and try to use them appropriately. Whatever my opinions might be, the words I use are meant to express them intelligently and in ordered sequence.'

In *Glimpses of World History* in the last letter dated 9 August 1933, he wrote to Indira Gandhi thus:

'Benjamin Disraeli, the great English statesman of the 19th century has written, "other men condemned to exile and captivity, if they survive, despair; the man of letters may reckon those days as the sweetest of his life." He was writing about Hugo Grotius, a famous Dutch jurist and philosopher of the seventeenth century who was condemned to imprisonment for life.... "There have been many famous literary gaolbirds, the two best known perhaps being the Spaniard Cervantes, who wrote Don Quixote, and the Englishman. John Bunyan, the author, *THE PILGRIM'S PROGRESS*." We can without hesitation add Jawaharlal Nehru's to list of famous literary gaolbirds.

Nehru used his time in prison to keep himself intellectually informed and mentally active. He kept his mind in training. He did not allow it to go to seed. He knew that the human brain is a muscle and if it is not to become flabby and lethargic then it needs constant nourishment. Nehru made sure that his brain remained a sharp and sensitive instrument for receiving, absorbing and generating new ideas. Nehru was rather fond of making self-deprecatory remarks. In the letter quoted above he was being unduly modest, when he said, 'I am not a man of letters, and I am not prepared to say that the many years 1 have spent in gaol have been the sweetest in my life, but I must say that reading and writing have helped me wonderfully to get through them. 1 am not a literary man, and I am not a historian; what indeed am I?" In fact he was both and much more.

Nehru's knowledge of English literature, world history, Greek Drama and poetry was deep and wide. His writings are replete with quotations from saints and sages of all ages and countries. 'The Discovery of India,' which he wrote in five months in Ahmednagar jail, carries on the page preceding the title page this quotation from Shakespeare—'When to the sessions of sweet silent thought I summon up remembrances of things past....' One can open any of his books at any place and derive wisdom and pleasure. That Nehru enjoyed writing is quite obvious. Take his remarkable anonymous article about himself, which appeared in 'The Modern Review' around Nehru's 50th birthday. It is a shrewd bit of self-analysis:

'From the Far North to Cape Comorin he has gone like some triumphant Caesar, leaving a trail of glory and legend behind him. Is all this just passing fancy which amuses him ... or is it his will to power that is driving him from crowd to crowd and making him whisper to himself, 'I draw these tides of men into my hands and wrote my will across the sky in stars.' The quotation is from T.E. Lawrence's "Seven Pillars of Wisdom."

Nehru's literary style, literary form and sensibility and literary talent never deserted him. Not even after he became Prime Minister. One has only to read his notes dictated each day on mundane matters to notice this fact. I have read many thousands of them. Not a cliche', nowhere the dead hand of dreary dullness which is the hall mark of most administrative and bureaucratic work.

Jawaharlal Nehru was a voracious reader and a prolific writer. 21 volumes of his Selected Works (Ed. S. Gopal) have appeared. Each is over 500 pages. 9 more are yet to appear. Then there are his books - *Glimpses of World History, An Autobiography, the Unity of India, The Discovery of India, A Bunch of Old Letters.* Add to this his speeches and we have something monumental.

I shall give just one example of Nehru's dedication to reading and writing. During his imprisonments he read several thousand books on all kinds of subjects ranging from Astronomy to Marxism. From May 1922 to January 1923 Nehru was in Lucknow Jail. He read 131 books including, the Gita, the Bible, the Koran, Symond's Italian Renaissance, 6 Volumes, Manuchi's Storie de Mogor, 4 Volumes, Berneir's Travels, Jadu Nath Sarkar's Shivaji, Vincent Smith's Akbar, Havell's Aryan Rule in India, Memoirs of Babar, Poems of Keats and Shelley, Tulsi Dasji's Ramacharitmanas, Economic Consequences of the Peace by J.M. Keynes, Human Nature in Politics by Graham Wallas, Outline of History by H.G. Wells, Decline and Fall of the Roman Empire by Edward Gibbon, 7 Volumes, several plays of Shakespeare. The French revolution by Carlyle, Les Miserables by Victor Hugo, Anna Karanina by Tolstoy, to name just a few.

For each book he read, he kept a notebook to take down passages that stirred his mind and heart. During all his imprisonments he filled many notebooks and kept a diary. These diaries are also beautifully written and we get a glimpse of Nehru's inner most feelings and thought. We get to know his moods, his meloncholy, his ebulliance, his extraordinary resilience and profoundly impressive detachment as far as the less important activities of mortals were concerned.

Many of Nehru's public speeches were made without much preparation, but when the occasion demanded he always rose to the occasion. I shall give just three examples each, worthy to be included in any anthology of the world's best speeches. I shall quote from his statement at his Gorakhpur Trial. It cannot be bettered. It is as perfact as such a statement could be.

"I stand before you, Sir, as an individual being tried for certain offences against the State. You are a symbol of that State. But I am also something more than an individual-I, too, am a symbol of Indian nationalism, resolved to breakaway from the British Empire and achieve the independence of India. It is not me that you are seeking to judge and condemn, but rather the hundreds of millions of the people of India, and that is a large task even for a proud Empire. Perhaps it may be that, though I am standing before you on my trial, it is the British Empire itself that is on its trial before the bar of the world. There are more powerful forces at work in the world today than courts of law; there are elemental urges for freedom and food and security which are moving vast masses of people and history is being moulded by them. The future recorder of this history might well say that in the hour of supreme trial the Government of Britain and the people of Britain failed because they could not adapt themselves to a changing world. He may muse over the fate of empires which have always fallen because of this weakness, and call it destiny. Certain causes inevitably produce certain results. We know the causes; the results are inexorably in their train.

"It is a small matter what happens to me in this trial or subsequently. Individuals count for little; they come and go, as I shall go when my time is up. Seven times I have been tried and convicted by British authority in India and many years of my life lie buried within prison walls. An eighth time or ninth, and a few more years, make little difference. But it is no small matter what happens to India and her millions of sons and daughters. That is the issue before me, and that ultimately is the issue before you, Sir. If the British

Government imagines it can continue to exploit them and play about with them against their will, as it has done for so long in the past, then it is grievously mistaken. It has misjudged their present temper and read history in vain."

Next, is his unforgettable, "Tryst with Destiny" speech at midnight 14-15 August 1947. The third followed Gandhiji's assassination on 30th January 1948. "The light has gone out of our lives." All three are supreme examples of the high combination of eloquence strengthened by literary flavour. I heard the last two and I can never forget them. Reading them produces a kind of intoxication. In each case, the man made the hour. Each is a unique utterance, each captures the spirit of the moment and we are transported into higher regions of thought, introspection, reflection, even prayer.

In The *Unity of India,* he writes thus about the loveliness of Kashmir: "Like some supremely beautiful women, whose beauty is almost impersonal and above human desire. such was Kashmir in all its feminine beauty of river and valley and lake and graceful trees. And then another aspect of this magic beauty would come to view, a masculine one, of hard mountains and precipices, and snow capped peaks and glaciers, and cruel and fierce torrents rushing down to the valley below. It had a hundred faces and innumerable aspects, ever-changing, sometimes smiling, sometimes sad and full of sorrow. The mist would creep up from the Dal Lake and, like a transparent veil, give glimpses of what was behind. The clouds would throw out their arms to embrace a mountain top, or creep down stealthily like children at play. I watched this ever-changing spectacle, and sometimes the sheer loveliness of it was over-powering and I felt almost faint. As I gazed at it, it seemed to me dream-like and unreal, like the hopes and desires that fill us and so seldom find fulfilment. It was like the face of the beloved that one sees in a dream and that fades away on awakening."

He wrote marvellous letters. In march, 1939 Subhas Chandra Bose wrote Nehru an angry. vituperative and acquisitory epistle. Nehru's reply was gently and sophisticatedly crushing. It was an artistic political put down of the formidable Bose.

Nehru wrote to Bose.

"It is not easy to answer a letter which runs into 27 typed sheets... Your letter is essentially an indictment of my conduct and an investigation into my failings. It is, as you will well realise a difficult and embarrassing task to have to reply to such an indictment. But so far as the failings are concerned, or many of them at any rate, I have little to say. I plead guilty to them, well realising that I have the misfortune to possess them ... but I am a dull subject to discuss, especially at the tail end of an inordinately long letter. Let us leave it at this that I am an unsatisfactory human being who is dissatisfied with himself and the world, and whom the petty world he lives in does not particularly like."

Now we come to another letter. This time to George Bernard Shaw. Nehru was now Prime Minister. Shaw was 92. Time. September, 1948.

Prime Minister Nehru wrote... "Forty years ago, when I was 18 and an undergraduate at Cambridge, I heard you address a meeting there. I have not seen you again since then, nor have I ever written to you. But, like so many of my generation, we have grown up in company with your writings and books. I suppose a part of myself, such as I am today, has been moulded by that reading. I do not know if that would do you any credit.... There is a chance of my going to England for two or three weeks in October next. I would love to pay you a visit, but certainly not if this means any interference with your daily routine. I would not come to trouble you with any questions. There are too many questions which fill the mind and for which there appear to be no adequate answers, or if the answers are there, somehow they cannot be implemented because of the human beings that should implement them. If I have the privilege to meet you for a while, it will be to treasure a memory which will make me a little richer than I am." Nehru was a big enough man to write a fan letter at age 59 to a literary giant. The two met the next year, a few months before Shaw's death in 1950.

I had several intimate occasions to be with Pandit Nehru. There was a touch of the divine about him and I certainly felt mesmerised. I now regret not drawing him out on literature and history. He seemed indestructible and eternal. What was the hurry. There would be many more intimate encounters. There weren't.

My two strictly literary run ins with him were brief, yet memorable. I have written about them elsewhere. So I shall mention them here en passant.

In March 1961 R.K. Narayan came to Delhi to receive the Sahitya Akademy Award for his novel, *The Guide.* I took him to see Panditji at Teen Murthi House. This was R.K. N's first ever visit to Delhi and this tickled Jawaharlal Nehru very much. It was a pleasant meeting but nothing earth shakeing happened. R.K. Narayan gave the P.M. his latest novel, *A Tiger from Malgudi.* J.N. said he had unfortunately not read any of Narayan's book but his "daughter had." We were then handed over to Mrs. Gandhi.

A few months later I ran into him in the Ministry of External Affairs. I greeted him with folded hands with a book between my palms. When he discovered the book was Amoury de Riencortis the *Soul of China,* he said he had read his "Soul of India." "So have I, Sir." I said. "Rather Spenglarian, I thought." I gave a nervous smile, and having never read Spengler, did not respond.

He then walked on and as he was walking down the steps he looked around and said with a beautiful smile and twinkle in his eyes, "Nehru, Imperator, hm!"

The great man was sharing a little joke with me, as I had read *The Soul of India,* which has a chapter entitled "Nehru Imperator."

His will and testament is yet another literary gem. Generally such documents are dry as dust wherein the legal jargon dominates, but in Nehru's will poetry and prose and refinement of feeling run through like a golden thread.

"My desire to have a handful of my ashes thrown into the Ganga at Allahabad has no religious significance, so far as I am concerned. I have no religious sentiment in the matter. I have been attached to the Ganga and Jamuna rivers in Allahabad ever since my childhood, and as I have grown older this attachment has also grown. I have watched their varying moods as the seasons changed, and have often thought of the history and myth and tradition and song and story that have become attached to them through the long ages and became part of their flowing waters. The Ganga, especially, is the river of India, beloved of her people, round which are intertwined her racial memories, her hopes and fears, her songs of triumph, her victories and her defeats. She has been a symbol of India's age long culture and civilization, ever-changing, ever-flowing, and yet ever the same Ganga ... as my last homage to India's cultural inheritance, I am making this request that a handful of my ashes be thrown into the Ganga at Allahabad to be carried to the great ocean that washes India's shore...."

Who else but a man of letters would have kept Robert Frost's final lines from his poem "Stopping by Woods on a Snowy Evening" on his working desk:

The woods are lovely, deep and dark,
    But I have promises to keep,
And miles to go before I sleep,
    And miles to go before I sleep.

4

Charles de Gaulle, 1890-1990: Soldier, Hero, Statesman

"All my life I have thought of France in a certain way .... In short, to my mind, France cannot be France without greatness." I have quoted the first and last sentence of the opening paragraph of the first volume of *The War Memoirs of Charles de Gaulle* "The Call to Honour 1940-42."

It is now conceded even by his severest critics that Charles Andre' Marie de Gulle was the greatest Frenchman since Napoleon. His enduring monument is the France of today, prosperous, peaceful, stable and influential.

France and the world celeberate his centenary on 22 November 1990.

In his biography of De Gualle, Bernard Ledwidge wrote, "De Gaulle is both a historical and a legendary personality. Because of the heroic stature he acquired relatively early in his historical career, he was able to imbue his historical achievements with symbolic significance. This duality is an essential feature.

"To become a hero it is not enough to have heroic qualities, one must also live in times fit for heroes. One must suffer great misfortune and be called upon to overcome it."

This is as good and perceptive a summing up of the life, legacy and achievement of Charles de Gaulle as I have come across.

His hour came in June 1940 when France suffered the most overwhelming military disaster in her history. A puppet French regime was set up at Vichy under Marshal Petain. de Gaulle had been a subordinate of Petain in World War I. In June 1940 de Gaulle was 49, unknown except for his four books on military matters. But in that fateful month Brigadier General de Gaulle was appointed Deputy Minister in the crumbling Daladier government. When France surrendered to Hitler de Gaulle just managed to get on the last plane that left Paris for London.

From London, de Gaulle made his famous 18th June appeal on the B.B.C. Like Churchill and Nehru, de Gaulle was a great man and a great writer. Like the two he was a lover of words and phrases, had a profound sense of history. His literary style was gravely dazzling. His eloquence moved the hearts and minds of men and women, just as did his defiance in the face of defeat. There is a grandeur about his life which cannot but make a deep and abiding impression. On 18 June 1940 De Gaulle.

"But has the last word been said? Must hope be abandoned? Is our defeat complete? NO!

"Believe me when I tell you that nothing is lost for France. I speak in knowledge of facts. The same means which have defeated us can bring us victory one day. France is not done. She is not alone. She is not alone.... I General De Gaulle, now in London, call on all French officers and soldiers now present on British Territory to get in touch with me.

"Whatever happens, the flame of French resistance must not and will not be extinguished."

For the next four years be kept that flame burning against odds that would have overwhelmed a lesser man. De Gaulle quarreled with Churchill, got on the nerves of Roosevelt, kept on at Stalin, till free France was given a place at the high table. It is an epic tale which de Gaulle has recorded in his war memoirs.

After the war he headed the French government in 1945-46 and again from 1958 to 1969. It was during his second tenure that de Gaulle restored the pride, honour and dignity of France. He made her economically strong, politically stable and militarily independent. The Socialists under Mr. Mitterrand railed at him. Francois Mitterrand, his socialist opponent called the Fifth Republic, "a permanent Coup." Then in April 1969, he quit because in the referrendum on the draft law he did not get a majority. On 28 April 1969, a two line communique issued from the Elysee, the official residence of the French Head of state said, "I am ceasing to exercise my functions as president of the Republic. This decision takes effect at midday today." And off he went to his beloved home in Colombey Eglises. Eighteen months later he was to die there.

De Gaulle is the 20th century European I admire most. In January 1989, I was leading the Indian delegation to the Chemical Weapons Conference in Paris. I took half a day off to visit the modest de Gaulle home, La Boisserie, in the village of Colombey-Les-Deux-Eglises. My French hosts were mildly surprised. Why should an Indian Minister drive 250 Kms on a cold, grey day in winter to pay homage to a man who had never been to India and in whose dramatic life India had not figured in any significant way. But the village appreciated my visit and the local paper wrote approvingly.

Yes, De Gaulle had met Nehru. He had got on well with Indira Gandhi. He was charmed by Mrs. Vijayalakshmi Pandit and if one is to believe K. M. Panikkar, the French President quite enjoyed the Indian envoy's conversation. Andre Malraux was another important link between India and de Gaulle.

I had read what Nehru had written about de Gaulle's return to power in May 1958. Nehru was unenthusiastic and feared the return of Bonapartism in France. Neither did he see de Gaulle putting an end to the civil war in Algeria and leading that country to Independence. On both counts Nehru revised his assessment: de Gaulle's return did not prepare the ground for Bonopartism and de Gaulle displayed amazing political skill, vision and courage in presenting a solution for Algeria in 1962. He risked his life and outwitted the reactionary Generals and led Algeria to independence. So, when Nehru and de Gaulle met in the early sixties, there was mutual respect and admiration. Mrs. Indira Gandhi on becoming Prime Minister in January 1966, visited Paris in March 1966 to meet president de Gaulle. He liked her. A week before his death on 9 November 1970, de Gaulle sent her an inscribed copy of his book, *Memoirs of Hope* 1958-1962. The moment she heard of his death she decided to fly to Paris for his memorial mass at Notre Dame Cathedral. I accompanied her. De Gaulle was a private citizen when he died. But France and the world did him proud and gave him a hero's farewell. The world's leaders poured into Paris to pay respects to a genuine man of destiny. The French African leaders wept openly.

As I sat through the service at Notre Dame, my mind went back seven years to President John F. Kennedy's funeral. I had gone to

Washington with Vijaylakshmi Pandit who was representing India at the funeral. After the burial at Arlington Cemetary all Heads of Delegation were invited to a White House reception given by Jacqualline Kennedy. President De Gaulle spotted Vijayalakshmi Pandit and walked over to her. After greeting her he asked. "How's your brother keeping? Well, I hope." Mrs. Pandit said he was well but, "had his problems." The 6' 4" tall de Gaulle said with grave courtesy. "Who does not have troubles, Madame. Tell Mr. Nehru, I have mine and give him my best wishes."

General de Gaulle's funeral was in essentials different from Kennedy's. It was the most public private burial. He was not buried at the Arc de Triumph or at any grand spot but in the village cemetary at Colombey. A simple, unadorned grave.

In his will, written on 16 January 1952, de Gaulle gave clear instructions for his funeral. Just as Nehru had done. de Gaulle's wishes were carried out in every detail. Nehru's only partially. Kennedy had died so unnatural a death at 46 that he had left no instructions. He got the standard head of state ceremonial funeral.

De Gaulle wrote.

"I desire my funeral to take place at Colombey-Les-Deux Eglises. If I die elsewhere my body must be taken home without any public ceremony whatever.

"My grave shall be that in which my daughter Anne lies and where one day, my wife will also rest. Inscription.

Charles de Gaulle (1890-)

"The ceremony shall be arranged by my son, my daughter, my daughter-in-law, assisted by members of my personal staff, in an extremely simple manner. I do not wish for a state funeral. No President, no Ministers, no Parliamentary delegations, no representatives of public bodies. Only the armed forces may take part officially, as such, but their participation must be on a very modest scale, without bands, or fanfares or trumpet calls.

"No oration shall be pronounced, either at the church or elsewhere. No funeral oration in parliament.... The men and women of France may, if they wish, do my memory the honour of accompanying my body to its last resting place.

5

Indira Gandhi, Margaret Thatcher, Mother Teresa and Queen Elizabeth II

In November 1983 over 40 Heads of State and Government came to Delhi for the Commonwealth summit. So did Queen Elizabeth II in her capacity as the Head of the Commonwealth. She does not participate in the deliberations. She meets each head of delegation and hosts a banquet for them. While the Queen and her husband, Prince Philip stayed at Rashtrapati Bhawan, the Heads of delegation were put up in hotels.

On the second day of the Summit, Mrs. Gandhi asked me to quietly enquire from Rashtrapati Bhawan if the Queen was holding an "Investiture" at R.B. for bestowing on Mother Teresa with the highest British award, the O.M. The Rashtrapati Bhawan confirmed what the Prime Minister had heard. Invitations for the "Investiture" had apparently been issued, that too on "Buckhingham Palace" stationary, without consulting the Secretary or the Military Secretary to President Giani Zail Singh.

I conveyed this to Mrs. Gandhi, who did not like what she heard. In the meanwhile H.N. Bahuguna had written to the Prime Minister saying that he had from his own sources gathered the Queen was to hold an "Investiture" at R.B. for Mother Teresa. He hoped that what he had heard was incorrect. Only the President of India could hold an "Investiture" at R.B. If the Queen was to go ahead with the "Investiture" then he and other opposition leaders would be compelled to raise the matter in the Lok Sabha.

It was quite evident that H.N. Bahuguna, who was a Lok Sabha M.P., was right and the British, who are known for being specialists on ceremonial had, in good faith, erred. That error had to be rectified. It fell to my lot as Chief-Co-ordinator of CHOGM to sort this quite unprecedented and spectacular protocol cock up.

Mrs. Gandhi asked me to get in touch with Mrs. Thatcher and get back to her. The British High Commissioner Robert Wade-Gary was an accomplished and skillful diplomat. I asked him to convey to Mrs. Thatcher and Her Majesty the Queen that the proposed "Investiture" could not be held at R.B. It could be held either at the U.K. High Commission or the residence of the High Commissioner. I added that we held the Queen in high esteem and Mother Teresa was a very special person. At the same time we could not countenance anything that violated a well established convention. We were surprised that we had not been consulted. Gently I reminded Wade-Gary that Her Majesty was Queen of Australia, Canada and New Zealand but not of India.

Within two hours he rang back to say that his Prime Minister felt it was too late to change the venue. Invitations had been sent and above all the Queen would be inconvenienced. The U.K. press too were aware of the "Investiture". This was bad news. I told Wade-Gary that I would pass on Mrs. Thatcher's response to Mrs. Gandhi, but I wanted to make it quite clear that my recommendation to Mrs. Gandhi would be that we could not agree to a formal "Investiture" at R.B.

Here was high grade protocol dynamite. The dramatis personae consisted of four world famous ladies. Two powerful Prime Ministers, one Queen and the fourth something more than a Saint. What, if the Indian press got hold of the story. What a diplomatic bon fire they would light!

I reported to Mrs. Gandhi what her British counter-part had said. A fleeting irritation, a moments pause and then a masterly diplomatic googly. "Natwar, go back to Mrs. Thatcher and tell her from me that the Queen can have the "Investiture" at Rashtrapati Bhawan. But leave her in no doubt about the matter being raised in Parliament the next day. Critical references would be made and the Queen's name would be dragged in. It was only fair the Queen be made aware of this."

No "Investiture" was held at Rashtrapati Bhawan. The Queen invited Mother Teresa to tea in the Mughal Gardens where she handed the O.M. to the Nobel laureate, who was blissfully unaware of the diplomatic upheaval, she had caused. The finale was entirely satisfying to me personally. Prime Minister Thatcher in the concluding session singled me out for praise. Before leaving India, the Queen received me. She could not have been more gracious, she even had a royal gift for me.

1992

6

Radhakrishnan: A Centennial Tribute

YEAR: 1957. Place: Chung Nan Hai, Peking. Time: Late evening. Vice-President Radhakrishnan is entering Chairman Mao Tse-Tung's residence. The mighty Mao walks up to greet his distinguished guest midway in the courtyard leading to his study. They shake hands. Then the unimaginable happens. Radhakrishnan pats Mao on the cheek. If it had been the cultural revolution Mao's guards would have drawn their guns. But this was 1957. There was not a cloud on the Sino-Indian horizon (or so we thought). Before the Chairman could show surprise or annoyance and his staff their outrage, Dr. Radhakrishnan broke the tension by an exit line which would do any great actor proud: "Don't be alarmed, Mr. Chairman, I did the same thing to Stalin and the Pope."

One more example of his wit. Early in 1962 the King of Greece came on a state visit to India. Dr. Radhakrishnan welcoming him said, "Your Majesty, you are the rust King of Greece to come as our guest. Alexander the Great came uninvited."

As these examples show, all philosophers are not crushing bores, insufferable, self-righteous pomposities with encyclopaedic pretensions. I had the good luck to come into contact with Dr. Radhakrishnan at a very young and starry-eyed age. His son, S. Gopal, would from time to time take me to see him. In July 1961, I had undergone an appendicitis operation at Safdarjung Hospital. On the second day, when one feels as miserable as one possibly can, I noticed a lot of activity around my ward. Why can't they give me a pain killer and leave me alone, I said to myself. A little later I heard commotion in the corridor. I thought some blasted VIP was being admitted. Then through a haze I saw Dr. Radhakrishhnan walk towards my bed. Gopal was with him. I was a 30-year-old Under Secretary in the M.E.A. (a lower type of bureaucratic species does not exist) and here was the Vice President of India coming to see him!!

What a totally overwhelming gesture of gracious concern for a young man? How can I ever forget it?

Sarvepalli Radhakrishnan began life as a teacher. He became a world famous and respected philosopher and free India's second Head of State. He did not seek high office. If one is to judge from what he wrote in 1950 in, "Fragments of a Confession," he neither aspired to it nor expected it. He writes, "No particular good fortune has lifted me above the sphere in which our common humanity struggles along, and I have had my own share of the burdens and anxieties of life. Although these are of immense importance to me, discretion forbids me to speak of them. Besides they are of no particular interest to the philosophical public...."

Dr. Radhakrishnan and Pandit Nehru had known each other since 1928, but could not be said to be close or particularly intimate. Each was aware of the other's eminence. They read each other's books. The bond was intellectual, not political. They shared an outlook which laid supreme stress on right ends, those that really count because they give meaning to our lives. They shared a lofty common vision of India. They sought harmony, they practised humanism, they had a horror of hedonism. Tagore, Gandhi, Radhakrishnan and Nehru were a galaxy representing the spiritual, moral, literary, philosophical and political panorama of modern India. I have excluded Swami Vivekananda and Sri Aurobindo from this list. Their inclusion would enlarge the scope of this article.

Sending the Spalding Professor of Eastern Religion and Ethics at Oxford as India's Ambassador to the Soviet Union in 1949 was an imaginative decision. It was Nehru's. The move from Oxford to Moscow could not have been without its hazards. During her two years in Moscow—1947-49—Mrs. Vijaya Laxmi Pandit could not meet Stalin. But Stalin received the author of *The Hindu View of Life, Eastern Religion and Western Thought, Religion and Society.* Radhakrishnan was not unfamilier with Marx. In, "Fragments" he makes a startling observation: "When however, the study of philosophy became my life's work, I entered a dominion which sustained me both intellectually ami spiritually all these years. My conception of a philosopher was in some ways similar to that of Marx. who proclaimed in his famous thesis on Feuerbach that philosophy had hither to been concerned with interpreting life, but that the time had come for it to change life. Philosophy is committed to a creative task. Although in one sense philosophy is a lonely pilgrimage of the spirit in another sense it is a function of life."

In "Fragments", he also made the wise and true assertion that, "any sensitive man who takes life seriously is somewhat inaccessible to the public...." Little did he then know that the sensitive philosopher would look back on the inaccessible years with longing.

His election as Vice President in 1952 was widely acclaimed. Radhakrishnan became a public figure. He presided over the Rajya Sabha with verve and unchallenged authority. No excess went unchecked. His admonishments were not lightly taken. He travelled widely conveying the message of India to the four corners of the world. His eloquence, his lucidity, articulation, invited attention and respect. He sought understanding. He generally received it. While speaking of great philosophical and political abstractions and realities he never talked down to people, who were not endowed with an equally formidable intellect, intuition and communicator's skills. Deep down he felt that to transform was far greater than to inform. He combined clarity of thought with purity of heart. His sensibility was all embracing. He was teaching philosophy to politicians and politics to philosophers. He was interpreting Hindu philosophy, Indian culture and civilization, yoga, and mystical experiences to his world-wide reading public, "when the personality of the mystic rises to a level which is disconcerting to his normal, self-centered life, certain disorders show themselves ... when new wine is poured in old bottles, they burst. Man must become a new vessel, a new creature, if he is to bear the spiritual light. That is why the Hindu system of yoga insists on the development of healthy nerves."

I would be straying into deeper waters if I were to deliberate on his religious and philosophical writings. What interested me was his life-long attempt to knock some sense of history into the minds of his supremely a historical people. He gave us a philosophy of history and a history of philosophy. In "Eastern Religion and Western Thought," he writes, "The historical process is not a mere external chain of events, but offers a succession of spiritual opportunities.... History is something organic, a phase of man's terrestrial destiny as essential for him as memory is for personal identity."

His passage from Vice President to President was not all smooth sailing. Many eminent persons raised their eyebrows. Had he not been knighted by the British? His roots were not in the Congress. He had not participated in the Freedom Movement and so on. Jawaharlal Nehru finally had his way. The two came much closer to each other after the Sino-Indian conflict. During these dark weeks Radhakrishnan kept Nehru's morale up when all around him was falling apart, but he left Nehru in no doubt that Krishna Menon had to go. Even during that sombre and nerve-wrecking winter Radhakrishnan did not lose his sense of humour. American Ambassador Galbraith ran into the President at some function. He enquired if the rumour of Lt. Gen. B.M. Kaul being taken prisoner was true or not. President or Radhakrishnan replied: "The rumour is unfortunately untrue"!

His five years as President were a rather depressing half decade. The Chinese invasion left the country bewildered and shaken; Pandit Nehru passed away; the conflict with Pakistan in September 1965 put a huge burden on the country's resources; the drought of 1966 caused widespread misery. Lal Bahadur Shastri's unexpected death at Tashkent was another body blow. Radhakrishnan's relations with Indira Gandhi lacked warmth. He became openly critical. That created strains. While Dr. Radhakrishnan retained his philosophical detachment, his tenure ended in 1967, not on a triumphant but on a melancholy note.

His writings, not the offices he held, are his monument. What set him apart from others was that by education he was a larger man, by temperament a forgiving one, by training a disciplined one. He was modern India's greatest philosopher. Politics was not his domain. He once wrote: "A meditative frame of mind is perhaps responsible for my love of loneliness." One regret he certainly nursed. For several years he was a serious candidate for the Nobel Prize. Bertrand Russel, his friend and fellow philosopher beat him to it. Without casting aspersions on Russell, all I can say is that Radhakrishnan was in the very great non-recipient company of Tolstoy, Mahatma Gandhi and Pandit Nehru.

The Times of India
1987

7

Nelson Mandela: A Tribute

If one were to use a racing term, one would call Nelson Mandela a thorough bred of the highest order.

At his trial known as the Rivonia trial, Nelson Mandela made his historic statement on 20th April, 1964. It invites comparison with two other unforgettable statements, one by Mahatma Gandhi at his trial on March, 1922 and the other by Jawaharlal Nehru at his trial on 3rd November, 1940.

Nelson Mandela conducted his own defense and concluded on this soul stirring high note:

"During my lifetime I have dedicated myself to this struggle of the African people. I have fought against white domination and black domination, and I have fought against Black domination. I have cherished the ideal of the democratic and free society in which all persons live in harmony and with equal opportunities. It is an ideal which I hope to live for and to achieve. But if needs be, it is an ideal for which I am prepared to die."

After twenty one years in prison, on 10 February 1985, he said he would never accept his release under, "humiliating conditions."

"I cherish my own freedom dearly, but I care even more for your freedom (the Black Africans). Too many have died since I went to prison. Too many have suffered for the love of freedom. I owe it to their widows, to their orphans, to their mothers and their fathers who have grieved and wept for them.

"Not only have I suffered during these long lonely wasted years. I am no less life loving then you are. But I cannot sell the birth-right of the people to be free.

"Only free men can negotiate, prisoners cannot enter into contracts. Your freedom and mine cannot be separated."

This is the man the imbecile racist mafia has kept locked up for 27 years. When Mandela was arrested in 1964, Nehru, Khruschev, Macmillan, Nasser, Mao, de Gaulle were heading the governments of their countries. Three fourths of black Africa was still under British, French, Spanish and Portugues colonial rule. How long ago that was.

The first 15 years were spent in solitary confinement doing hard labour at Robben Island. He never despaired, never compromised, never asked favours. His exemplary serenity of spirit, his moral courage and his devotion to a great and noble cause won the admiration, nay the adulation of the world. The Commonwealth Eminent Persons Group, after meeting him in May, 1986 returned profoundly impressed. The group consisted of, Malcolm Fraser, former Prime Minister of Australia, General Olusegun Obasanjo former President of Nigeria, Lord Barber, former British Chanceller of the Exchequer, Dame Nita Barrow, President of the World Council of Churches, John Malacela, former Foreign Minister of Tanzania, Sardar Swaran Singh, Former Defence and Foreign Minister of India and The Most Rev. Edward Scott, Primate of the Anglican Church of Canada.

In their report, published by the Commonwealth Secretariat, London they wrote "Nelson Mandela has indeed become a living legend. Just as the gaoling of nationalist leaders like Mahatma Gandhi and Jomo Kenyatta invested them with a unique aura and helped galvanise resistence to the colonial power, so, we believe, the imprisonment of Nelson Mandela is a self defeating course for the South African Government to take." Their report goes on to say, "we were first struck by his physical authority by his immaculate appearance, his apparent good health and his commanding presence. In this manner he exuded authority and received the respect of all around him, including his gaolers. That in part seemed to reflect his own philosophy of separating people from policy.

A little later they add, "In our discussions Nelson Mandela also took care to emphasise his desire for reconciliation across the divide of colour. He described himself as a deeply committed South African nationalist but added that South African nationalists came in more than one colour they were white people, coloured people and Indian people who were also deeply committed to South African nationalism. He pledged himself to work for a multi racial society in which all would have a secure place." And they concluded thus, "our judgement of Nelson Mandela has been formed as the result of the lengthy discussions with him, spanning three meetings. He impressed us as an outstandingly able and sincere person whose qualities of leadership were self evident. We found him unmarked by any trace of bitterness despite his long imprisonment. His over-riding concern was for the welfare of all races in South Africa in a just society; he longed to be allowed to contribute to the process of reconciliation. We all agreed that it was tragic that a man of his outstanding capabilities should continue to be denied the opportunity to help shape his country's future, especially as that is so clearly his own profound wish."

I have quoted from the report of the Eminent Persons Group at some length because here we have a most authoritative assessment of the personality of one of the great heroes of the 20th century, whose indomitable will and strength of character are an inspiration for all freedom loving people throughout the world. This is the man successive South African regimes have incarcenated for over a quarter of century. Human kind will neither forget nor forgive this crime. When will the South African ruling racist mafia realize that imprisonment does not silence ideas whose time has come.

We in India have always honoured Mandela. Some years ago the Jawaharlal Nehru International Prize was awarded to him. He hoped that the South African authorities would allow Winnie Mandela to come to India to receive the prize. She was denied permission and her daughter received the prize from Rajiv Gandhi.

Our 90 years old association with South African is widely known in the world, particularly Gandhiji's 21 years stay there and our unsurpassed anti-apartheid record at the United Nations.

Nelson Mandela read the books of Gandhi and Nehru. His autobiographical book takes its title. 'No Easy Walk to Freedom' from an article Jawaharlal Nehru wrote in his, *Unity of India. Nelson Mandela quotes these lines from Nehru's essay. From Lucknow to Tripuri.*

"There is no easy walk to freedom anywhere and many of us will have to pass through the valley of the shadow of death again and again before we reach the mountain tops of our desires."

Bearing this in mind I was naturally surprised and distressed to note the absence of an Indian contribution in a volume of literary tributes to Mandela published in Paris in 1986 under the title *Pour Nelson Mandela* by Gallimard and in New York in 1987, as *For Nelson Mandela.* The editors are Jacques Derrida, who teaches at the Ecole des Haute Etudes en Sciences Social in Paris and the Tunisian Novelist, Mustapha Tlili.

Among the contributors are Samuel Beckette, Susan Sontag, Nadine Gordimer, Allen Ginsberg, William S. Burroughs.

Tilli in his preface to the American edition writes, "Nelson Mandela is an exceptional political prisoner meriting exceptional tribute—a literary monument not to the glory of the man but to the moral figure he has year by year become, a tribute in the way that Plato invoked the memory of Socrates. It matters little, ultimately whether Socrates was a real individual. He is the Great Witness, and that is the critical thing, just as Gandhi and Martin Luther King Jr. are witnesses for our own time."

Dominique Leco editor of *Ajourdui L' Afrique* looks at the tributes in a different way. For *Nelson Mandela* is not a collection of texts entered on a passing topic, but literature, connected always, with evil and death.... Lodged in this book, in a certain way, is the solution to the engima which, in the end, carries the day and remains unchanged. Nevertheless, something will have changed, like a subtle deepening of conviction apartheid will have one face, and freedom another that restores Africa to its universal calling. Freedom will henceforth wear the face of Nelson Mandela."

Mandela won the moral battle long ago. If he dies in detention he becomes a martyr. If he is released, he will have the authority and power few have at their command. Hero or Martyr that is his destiny.

Without Mandela the A.N.C. might not have made it. His release is not in doubt, but Mandela will accept nothing short of unconditional release. Once out, he can pull off a miracle.

Mr. de Klerk is an improvement on Mr. Botha, but the whites in South Africa present a case of schizophrenia on a vast scale. Morally paralyzed; facing administrative chaos, financial ruin and isolation they are groping. Mr. de Klerk should help Mandela and the A.N.C. to find a negotiated political settlement that will ensure the establishment of a democratic multi-racial South Africa. Mandela is not averse to talking to other Black leaders like Buthelezi to find a solution. Only the A.N.C. and Mandela can bail them out and help them to right one of the most damnable moral obscenities of the 20th century.

The Bible, if I am not mistaken says, that one final act of goodness can obliterate all previous wrong doing. Can Mr. de Klerk and his colleagues rise to the occasion. The civilized world asks them to get on with it and release Nelson Mandela so that South Africa can get ready to bathe in a heavenly light. The alternative is a blood bath that is too aweful to contemplate.

1990

8

In Namibia with Rajiv Gandhi

For over a week from 18 March to 26 March 1990, I, spent almost 18 hours each day with Rajiv Gandhi. Although, no longer Prime Minister he was invited by President Sam Nujoma to participate in the celebrations to mark Namibia's independence on 21 March. He asked me to accompany him. Pradeep Gupta, who perished with Rajiv Gandhi at Sriperambadur was also with us as his Security Officer.

We travelled economy class from Delhi to Lusaka via Bombay. All attempts by the Air India and Zambian Air Ways to upgrade us were politely but firmly turned down. It would be putting it mildly if I were to say that R.G.'s presence in that part of the plane created a management crisis. The autograph hunters disregarded all regulations, unfastened their seat belts and zeroed in on the ever obliging former Prime Minister. He signed on air line tickets, odd bits of paper, bank notes, on even the palm of a young boy who just would not take 'no' for an answer. A large number of ladies descended on him to pay their respects or to just stare at him. He blushed, he smiled and won their hearts.

The Bombay Lusaka flight is a long one. After about an hour, the Zambian Air hostess came to me and said that if Gandhi, remained in the economy class then neither he nor anyone else could sleep as every passenger wanted to meet him, talk to him. Meals could not be served.

I told R.G. if he had any notion of the upheaval he was causing. He smiled, oh; that devastating smile and said, "you deal with it." The only solution I could think of was to tell him that he must move to the first class. The answer was, "No way." I then said with mock, seriousness, "I know, you do not need sleep, but the other passengers do and so long as you stay here no one is either going to eat or sleep. That is hardly fair." Answer "I have an economy class ticket and economy I shall travel." The Cabin staff pleaded, so did I and Gupta. Finally he agreed, provided Gupta and I too shifted with him. "Gupta yes, but there is no need for me to be upgraded. You need rest and we have busy days ahead of us." All three or none. And that was that. The Cabin staff were so relieved. They almost carried us out of the economy cabin. The first class was almost empty. I cannot say I had any remorse leaving our humbler perch.

At Lusaka we stayed with President Kaunda. He had his hands full. The Presidents of Egypt, Mozambique and Tanzania were in town, all three put up in hotels. Not Rajiv Gandhi. I had served in Zambia in the late seventies when the Janata Government 'banished' me there from London. I enjoyed my posting immensely as I had known President Kaunda intimately since 1962, when he had come to the Committee on de-colonization as a petitioner pleading his country's case. So, I took Rajiv Gandhi round the Town and we spent an hour with President Mubarak, who had with him Boutros Boutros Ghali.

Next day we flew to Windoek with President Kaunda in his plane.

No Indian VIP had ever set foot on Namibian soil. Windoek is a small town, with a distinct colonial look about it. Rajiv Gandhi was given a double room in Kalahari Sands Hotel. I, in a luxurious house of a family three kms. away.

Rajiv Gandhi loved every moment of his 'freedom' and we walked the streets. Every few yards he was stopped – "You. Rajiv Gandhi, Really." Then out came a camera – "Can we have a photo with you"? When he entered a restaurant, there was clapping. In the lift, people stared in disbelief. Pakistanis, Bengla Deshis, the Irish, Norwegians, Nigerians, members of the U.N. Peace Keeping Force all wanted to be photographed with him. Jessie Jackson, the black leader sought him out and the two together caused a traffic jam.

The evening we arrived - 20th - he had a meeting with Nelson Mandela, who was the most sought after individual in Windoek. A Rajiv Gandhi-Nelson Mandela meeting had tremendous symbolic significance - much more than the Vishwanath Pratap Singh-Mandela one, which was a formal protocol exercise. The Gandhi-Mandela meet had great emotional overtones. Mandela had grown up admiring Mahatma Gandhi and Jawaharlal Nehru. He was only a few months younger than Indira Gandhi. She and Rajiv Gandhi had done all they could to help Mandela and the A.N.C.

When Nelson Mandela was arrested in 1962 R.G. was 18 years old. When the two met they embraced each other and were speechless for a few moments. Winnie too was there. Mandela used Rajiv Gandhi's first name, the latter called him "Mandela."

Rajiv Gandhi's opening words were, "When my daughter Priyanka learnt that I was to meet you, she asked me to think of her when I shook your hand. I am now doing so." That was a wonderful opening line.

Mandela was at his avuncular best. He did most of the talking. Rajiv Gandhi said he and the Congress would continue to do all in their power to help the A.N.C. He also invited Mandela to give the 1990 Nehru Memorial Lecture.

That day we witnessed the lowering of the South African flag and the hoisting of the Namibian flag amidst unforgettable enthusiasm. The beginning of the end of colonialism commenced with the independence of India. The end of that beginning we witnessed at Windoek on 21.3.1990.

What was heart warming and pleasing was to witness the high esteem Rajiv Gandhi was held in the world. In Namibia he was treated both as a friend and the future Prime Minister of India. He met a large number of world leaders who were present in the Namibian capital - many more met him then Vishwanath Pratap Singh who was also in Namibia and for some odd reason missed one of the main functions on the 21st.

We returned via London. For me the most rewarding aspect was the opportunity I got to talk about substantial national and international issues with Rajiv Gandhi at length and leisure, undisturbed. One also discovered sides of his character which were not generally known. For example - I observed he disliked being alone for any length of time. He would get restless if he had some moments to himself. He was good with his hands and quickly fixed the aerial of his pocket radio in his room and we were kept upto date on world news.

9

Farewell, Brave and Beloved Leader

The country weeps. The world mourns. I feel a terrible emptiness within and there is no drowning this sorrow. At the moment our consolations are few, our torments many. When the tears have dried, the anger subsided, the horror diminished, the scar will remain. The shame will remain. So will the heart ache.

I ask myself, shell-shocked and benumbed, is this the land of the Buddha and Gandhi. We were in my own life time an example to be emulated Today we are a warning.

Rajiv Gandhi was at the peak of his vigour. He died standing on his feet in the midst of the people he loved. He had a natural way of entrancing people, of offering affection, consolation. He had that rare and genuine gift to lift his followers up and provide them inspiration and hope. What scored on my mind was his composure, but even more appealing and refreshing was his youthful passion and engaging warmth of spirit.

Fate holds all the cards. Against fate there is no armour. The Nehrus are a star crossed family. They attract the lightening. Only Motilal Nehru and Jawaharlal Nehru died peaceful deaths. Sacrifice, supreme sacrifice comes to them naturally. That is why this country responds to them as to no one else. There is no parallel for this in modern history. It is unique.

The philosopher, Kierkgaard has written that life must be lived forward but can only be understood backwards. So let me change gear and turn from the public aspect to the personal and the private. At least the past provides a procession of lively, fragrant memories.

When did I meet Rajiv Gandhi first? 1949 or was it 1950? I was still at St. Stephen's College. I had gone to Teen Murti to see Mrs. Krishna Hutheesing whom I had known since my school days. There was Rajiv Gandhi playing with a large toy motor car. Years pass and then he comes to the Ministry of External Affairs to go with me to the

British Council Office at Raft Marg to get information on his future studies in England. Then his grandfather asks me to take a tin of "Rasgoolas" for Rajiv Gandhi's 17th birthday to London.

On 21 June 1980 I was in Delhi for consultation from Islamabad and went to Ladakh with Mrs Gandhi. Next day Sanjay Gandhi died. R.G. held his grief stricken mother's hand and was a tower of strength. Both fitted Hemingway's definition of courage, "Grace under pressure."

Early in 1981 I had, written to Rajiv Gandhi saying that it was both his duty and destiny to enter the political arena. When I came to Delhi next l had a long talk with him. His candour was so refreshing, "I am not cut out for politics. I am not Sanjay." He also spoke about my letter in which I had quoted Niccolo Machiavelli :

"Pray follow your star, and give up not an iota of it for anything in the world, for I believe, have believed, and ever shall believe in the truth of Boccaccio's saying that it is better to act, and be sorry, then not to act, and be sorry." Act he did.

I saw much of him during the 7th Non-Aligned and the Commonwealth Summits. It is not widely known that, behind the scenes he played a role in making these Conferences the success they were. I know, I was Secretary General of the NAM Summit and Chief Co-ordinator of the Commonwealth Summit. All world leaders wanted to meet him and size him up.

Rajiv Gandhi kept a relaxed stance and was at his best in a crisis. How spontaneously effective he could be, he showed at a meeting of U.S. Senators in Washington in 1982 during Mrs Gandhi's visit. Suddenly and without warning Senator Percy asked Rajiv Gandhi to say a few words on how he looked at Indian problems. There was a deadly silence. Mrs Gandhi smiled and asked her son to reply. He did and won the day.

I could go on and on, but will end with summing up his historic achievement. A man's true character is shown in times of adversity. Here Rajiv Gandhi scores ten out of ten. He never despaired, never wavered, never showed ran-cour. His international standing remained very high. The presence of so many foreign dignitaries at his funeral is evidence of that.

He made his mark early. I accompanied him to the Commonwealth Summit at the Bahamas in October 1985. I was then Minister of State for Fertilizers, but he asked me to accompany him. On the opening day he was the second speaker after Mrs. Thatcher, who was at her combative best. Gandhi excelled her. He had not a piece of paper with him and spoke off the cuff. I had been to several such summits before, but what followed was unprecedented. More than a dozen Presidents and PMs walked over to Rajiv Gandhi to congratulate him. I distinctly remember what Lee Kuan Yew said, "Listening to you, I was reminded of your grandfather. He had brought a new vision before the world. Lately I was beginning to despair. But now I am reassured. In you we now have a new voice on the world stage and I can go home unworried. Congratulations." When he appointed me Minister of State for External Affairs, I saw much of him and shall write about it later, but none can deny his quick grasp, understanding and articulation of our foreign policy. On the domestic side his achievement is equally impressive and enduring. After the 1989 set back not one member of the Party deserted him. There can be no greater tribute. He was the one strong, imaginative young figure standing against unending, dismal, defeatist tides of drift and surrender and feeble impulses. It took him time to sort his gifts out and to choose his path. Once at the helm, he served this country with style and panache. He held it together. He moved it forward. He gave youth inspiration and hope.

Farewell, beloved friend, brave leader, gentle soul, who 'drew these tides of men into his hands and wrote his will across the sky in stars.'

Farewell.

May 1991.

10

Nirad Chaudhuri at 85

The twentieth century has another 18 years to run. It is, therefore, not too early to draw up a preliminary list of literary masterpieces that have been written by Indians in the last 82 years. Judging from past performance it is safe to say that the remaining decade and a half is unlikely to throw up a Kalidas, Shakespeare or Tolstoy. No new and blinding insights into the human predicament are likely to be offered. No new morality will emerge. Here and there a patch of light might unravel some minute mystery of the universe. That I think is about it.

What books by twentieth century Indian authors are likely to survive the next 100 years. Any listing must necessarily be arbitrary. However, some works do stand out. Five non-fiction books which, to my mind, would still be read in the year 2082 are:

1. GITANJLI by Tagore

2. THE STORY OF MY EXPERIMENTS WITH TRUTH by Gandhiji

3. AN IDEALIST VIEW OF LIFE by Radhakrishnan

4. AN AUTOBIOGRAPHY by Jawaharlal Nehru

5. The AUTOBIOGRAPHY OF AN UNKNOWN INDIAN by Nirad C. Chaudhuri

Of these five, only Nirad Chaudhuri's book was published after 1947. It is possible to admire a book without agreeing with its philosophy. I have serious reservations about Nirad Chaudhuri's analysis, interpretation and understanding of our freedom movement under the leadership of Mahatma Gandhi. Nevertheless, he has made an exceptionally persuasive case for his own point of view. The first half of the book is of classic proportions and should find a permanent place in the history of English literature.

Nirad Chaudhuri has been living in Oxford with his wife for the last 11 years. They have been married 50 years. She is a lady of great charm and strength of character. I have seen them a number of times in the past few years. Over the years we have had our differences, Nirad Babu and I. I think highly of his scholarship and respect his intellectual integrity. I also find him exasperating and at times impossible. He is undoubtedly one of the most original characters I have ever met.

Early in July this year a Seminar on Indian Writing in English was organised by the Commonwealth Institute in London, as a part of the Festival of India. Among those who participated were Mulk Raj Anand, Raja Rao, Anita Desai, Salman Rushdie, Maria Couto. Nirad Chaudhuri was the senior member present. He was the first speaker. His opening sentence was, "I am a chihuhua among literary Alsations." Original, provocative, witty. Born 23 November 1897, he is in full control of his intellectual faculties. His memory is sharp and dependable as ever. His health is good.

He is the only living Indian writer who combines the classical with the contemporary, a master of style and form, yet not one of his books has sold more than 5,000 copies. He ekes out a living in Oxford. Strange as it may seem but he is finding it hard to place Volume II of his autobiography with a publisher. Printing costs are prohibitive and a book of 200,000 words has no takers. Nirad Chaudhuri is hoping to divide the book into two Volumes, the second carrying the story of his life from 1921 to 1937, and Volume III from 1937 to 1947. In Volume II he has argued that independence could have come to India in 1922. His view is that the final break with British association, psychologically had taken place in 1919 at the time of the Jalianwala Bagh tragedy. But I must not dwell on this since I have not read the manuscript.

When we last met I put him a few questions. I thought it might be a good idea to publish his answers on the eve of his 85th birthday. I only hope I have not distorted what he said.

Natwar: You will be 85 years soon. Looking back on your life, do you have any regrets?

Nirad Chaudhuri: No. I have gone through problems, want, poverty, which were horrible; worse than probably even a peasant in India experiences. All this out of free will. That is a choice I made. I have chosen a hard way of life. I never applied for a job in my life.

Never. In five places I have taken salaried jobs but no application form has ever gone to anyone. I have had to pay for this pride. I have sat at home waiting for somebody asking me to do a job. But all the degradation has been worthwhile. I should never have been what I am had I not passed through these problems, because adversity gives you two things – a larger and more generous view of life for the simple reason that luxury never really gives one true satisfaction. What a struggle life is! What a sad thing it is! what a glorious thing it is! So I have no regrets whatsoever.

Natwar: You said that you do not have any regrets in life but do you ever fed dissatisfied with yourself?

Nirad Chaudhuri: In this sense, had I more physical strength, which of course I have never had, as I was born prematurely. I could foreseeably have done at the age of 30, what I did at the age of 50. I was not given a chance before then, but I do blame my own weakness. Also I was not given anything due to lack of perception of any kind of talent in India. They could have made use of me, given me enough to live when I was 30. They never gave me anything. It was only when Englishmen came in contact with me that they were ready to give me something to live on. But I never accepted any kind of work in which my convictions were not involved. That is why I would not work for the British Empire in India unless I was convinced that the British Empire was something good for India. I did not work for the British Empire in India. I worked for the Allied cause.... I have also my perversity to blame. After all if you have to deal with the world, you will have to accept the world's terms, I won't accept those terms. Had I been physically stronger, it could have perhaps quickened my pace of achievement 10 to 15 years. That is the only qualified regret I have. I should have started writing a book at the time when I was 30, I could have easily done so, because my ideas were already formed by 1930. I did not start to write a book till I was 50, six months short of 50 in 1947. I did not publish it till 1951, when I was nearly 54. The main thing I wanted to write was the cultural history of modern India, social and cultural history. I have been collecting material since I came out of college. I could perhaps have 15 books to my credit, and not the 10 that I actually produced.

Natwar: Which is your favourite book?

Nirad Chaudhuri: None. My books are so different I can hardly choose. The most valuable or retainable permanently as a documentation, as a testimony to Indian life; it will be the First Volume of the Autobiography and the Second Volume. But in regard to interpretaton of Hinduism, I take my stand on *"Circe"* and my *"Hinduism."*

Natwar: What do you see is the future for India and England?

Nirad Chaudhuri: Decadence of different kinds. There is some justification for the decadence of the British today. After all they have done great things in history. They have played their part and if they are aged now, I can regret that, but I cannot blame them. But what of us? We got our opportunity after 700 years of servitude in 1947 and are in greater decay than even the British people. So there is no future. But I am writing for the future and I have faith in the future. I have greater hopes for the future than for the present. I have faith in humanity. At the same time, I feel we are passing through a phase of humanity in which she will greatly decay. We are passing through one cycle, which can go on for two, three or four hundred years. I believe that nothing of the past will be allowed to be forgotten. We have not forgotten Greece, ancient India, ancient China. So this age will also be remembered.

Natwar: You say that you stand or fall as a Hindu. What part does religion play in your life?

Nirad Chaudhuri: I lost my faith in traditional Hinduism by the time I was 20. I have not gone into a temple since then. I have not gone to any other religious place. I have no faith whatsoever in established religions, because they are, I believe, fundamentally wrong in their view of the Cosmos. I was without faith for about 25 years and suffered greatly. I have now evolved a faith of my own, it might be called my own religion. It is very personal.

Natwar: You have regained faith and lost hope.

Nirad Chaudhuri: I have lost faith in the present age, I have not lost faith in humanity. There was a Frenchman who said he had one disillusionment; mankind, and one illusion; France. It is the other way with me. It have one disillusionment; India, and an interim illusion still left about mankind. I don't think that mankind will be destroyed by nuclear war. I do not at all believe that a nuclear war will take place. I am a student of military affairs. I have given considerable thought to the possibility. And even if nuclear weapons are used, they will not result in destruction of mankind. Exactly the same thing was said about aerial bombardment in 1920 and 1931. Nothing happened. Gas was used in the First World War. Gas was not used in the Second World War. So mankind somehow has an instinct for self preservation and that will always prevent it from committing suicide. But nuclear weapons could be used tactically. That is another matter.

Natwar: You have been living in England for a number of years. Will you stay here for the rest of your life or return to India?

Nirad Chaudhuri: I do not know. In my whole life I have never been able to plan from the practical point of view. I have not extended my lease here beyond six months. I have never planned for 2, 3 or 4 years. But as things are, and I am now 85, how long can I live - 2 or 3 years. If I go back to India, the problem of livelihood will arise, which has been solved here. I can now live here modestly, a civilised life. In India till 1970, I paid a rent of Rs.125. Shall I get a rented house for that price now? So I may live here three or four years. There is another very interesting thing about my life and this looks like superstition. Whenever I have moved West, I have never gone back to the East. I left East Bengal after my family had lived there for 14 generations. I left in 1927. I never went back. Even I left Calcutta after living there for 32 years, I have never returned to Calcutta. I lived in Delhi for 30 years, and have come to England, and have not gone back to Delhi. So it looks the same. My westward journey will be a re-told westward journey as that of an Englishman going west.

Natwar: Does the theory of Karma have any meaning for you?

Nirad Chaudhuri: No, none whatsoever. Karma has no meaning. I have no belief in previous birth. I do not believe in future life. It ends here. I have talked to you about my religion, my faith. These are based on a fundamental existence of death, of death as a final end of an individual's life. All religions have been based on belief in another world, belief in survival after death. My personal religion is not based on that at all. We end with death. Every individual ends with death. We are parts of universal energy.

Natwar: Do you believe in the existence of a Supreme Master or a Cosmic Intelligence?

Nirad Chaudhuri: I believe in purpose being eminent in the universe. Certainly there is a force which is driving the cosmos in a certain direction. It cannot be accidental. Scientists who say it is permutation, combination are to my thinking fools. A definite intention seems to be there. There is some force some where in the universe, not out side it, which is effecting every thing, a force and a power. This is a very personal view. I can watch and see that force which takes l care of those who are least free or capable of taking care of themselves. Otherwise I cannot explain anything. Otherwise, I cannot explain anything in my life. How, I, at all got some money, some job because I could not predict it 5 minutes before the thing came.

Natwar: So, like Thomas Hardy, you believe in Chance.

Nirad Chaudhuri: Let me explain. It seems chance to me for the simple reason that I have no fore knowledge, but it may not be chance. It may be part of a design, who knows. Now, I do believe in Hardy. Hardy is very perverse in this sense. The things that happened to Hardy would never happen to me. But my case is very curious in this sense every step seems to be a chance. Why did not I perish by chance instead of surviving by chance. So, my survival seems to be purposive towards, some end.

Natwar: At the end of the day, at the end of the innings is there going to be a thanks giving given by you. If so to whom?

Nirad Chaudhuri: It seems to me to be Inevitable that I was to adopt a particular kind of life, that of a writer. I shall certainly be thankful that I have been able to do little things, something I wanted to do. But I have been thankful for giving up all vain desires and ambitions.

Everybody asks me why I did not go into politics. I tell them I have not the least political aptitude.

Natwar: When fame suddenly came, were you surprised.

Nirad Chaudhuri: No, fame did not come suddenly. I thought I would get it when my "Autobiography" appeared. I expected recognition. So, in a way I was not surprised. Certain things pleased me very much. I, somehow, very foolishly having lost faith in the immortality of the soul, retained faith in the immortality of my mind as perpetuated in my books. Only writers can be assured immortality for themselves. Not Princes. Because wherever they have lived, their minds remain with future generations. Only a writer gets that kind of immortality, Nobody else.

11

P.N. Haksar at 75

On 4 September 1988, P.N. Haksar completes 75 years. To mark this event friends and admirers have brought out a book of tributes.

This is perhaps the first time that a former civil servant has aroused such affectionate passion. But P.N. Haksar was no run off the mill civil servant. Endowed, with a first rate intellect, a deeply analytical mind, a fine command over Hindi and English, a flinty sense of humour, strong nerves, a love of truth, fearlessness, compassion, detachment, a horror of humbug, enormous moral stamina, he has today a place in our national life which many holders of high political office must envy. His pronouncements on national and international subjects invite attention, stimulate serious debate, revive hope. He has a national constituency among the truthful, the sensitive and the reflective.

P.N. Haksar gave up a promising legal career at the Allahabad Bar to join the Indian Foreign Service in 1947. His name had been recommended to Pandit Jawaharlal Nehru by Sir Tej Bahadur Sapru who said to Panditji that, "Haksar is the coming man at the Allahabad Bar." Jawaharlal Nehru has made generous references to P.N. Haksar at several places in his Selected Works.

From 1948 to 1967 his career in the I.F.S. was a steady progression up the ladder. He was our first High Commissioner to Nigeria – 1960-64. Then Ambassador to Austria. He was Deputy High Commissioner, London during the 1965 Indo-Pak conflict. When Smt. Gandhi succeeded Shastriji she decided to ask P.N. Haksar to head her Secretariat. I was a middle level member of that establishment at the time (1966-71), the first I.F.S. Officer to be selected to serve in the PM's Office. P.N. Haksar had been my boss in 1959-60. But I really got to know him well in the late sixties. I admired him immensely. Most personal relationships do not remain constant. This one has, with just one short, shadowy spell in the mid 1970s.

P.N. Haksar attracted national attention when he presided over Smt. Indira Gandhi's secretariat from 1967 to 1973. It was a small, compact, functional faceless team of rather exceptional individuals. P.N. Haksar was the undisputed Captain. He inspired both affection and awe. Awe of the right kind. One never sent up anything slip shod to him. When sent for, one was slightly tense. He soon made the impact of his powerful personality felt in the corridors of power. In the process he changed the character of the PM's Secretariat, its relationship to other Ministries and Departments of Government. Civil Servants are required to be anonymous, unseen, to be heard behind closed doors. No member of Smt. Gandhi's staff sought publicity till P.N. Haksar was there. P.N. Haksar least of all. He considered self-advertising, unseemly and vulgar. His direction of policy, his conceptualising of it, his penetrating analysis of events, his deep understanding of the dynamics of national and international events, could not but attract attention. It also aroused envy. The I.C.S. were the most afflicted. He thought poorly of most of them.

Till 1973, Smt. Indira Gandhi had implicit faith in Haksar's judgement and full confidence in his tactical and strategical planning. She knew what the country wanted. He knew how to produce well thought out, integrated relevant policies. On four major events his role was crucial and his advise decisive. Many have taken credit for each but those who know, know that Haksar alone held the key. The 1969 Congress split, the Indo-Soviet Treaty, the birth of Bangladesh and the Simla Agreement cannot be mentioned without acknowledging P.N. Haksar's monumental contribution. There was no dithering, no directionless paralysis. No loss of nerve or national purpose. He never got into a flap. What impressed one and all was his composure. He had no time for calculated ambiguity, for phoney meddlers in serious undertakings, or for congenital amatures who passed judgement on matters that even wise men found complicated.

It was during these years (1969-72) of Smt. Gandhi's tenure that the Government and the Congress Party appeared as a vehicle of history and change. Haksar had much to do with this. He had a philosophy of Government and administration which was informed by a passion for justice, freedom, uprightness and an awakening of our consciousness. He understood that, "Societies did not die from contradictions but from their inability to remove them." He wanted to change and renew society, but by the right means, right ideas, moral purpose, and at the same time avoiding distortions of reality.

In his two books, *Premonitions: Imperatives of Change* and, *Reflections on our Times,* P.N. Haksar's personal and political credo is spelt out with clarity and courage.

His powerful critical intellect and his integrity are outraged by the virus of vulgarity, the bacteria of bad taste, the cancerous spread of the political pollution, the mushrooming of frauds and upstarts, the spurious, the pretentious, the hawking of pseudo-profundities, the moral back sliding, the crass opportunism, the pretentious silliness, the lowering of standards of rectitude.

In the introduction to Premonitions, he writes:

"When I was enlisted in the Foreign Service, I was thirty five years of age. I was not a stranger to life. And yet when it came to dealing with images of our country so universally and tenaciously held even by the educated and the informed, the task of explaining India to other people and governments with widely differing history, traditions, preoccupations and interests was baffling ... since the human mind yearns for simplicity, India became Hindu and Pakistan a Muslim State. And the Kashmir question became an example of India perversely resisting the logic of position. Kingsley Martin, who was friendly and normally rational, died in the belief that Nehru's ethnic origin was the cause of the trouble in Kashmir. I endeavoured to counter this particular piece of Martinion superstition by facetiously suggesting that on this reasoning the hastening of the liquidation of the British Empire by Lord Mountbatten could be perhaps explained by his Battenberg ancestory and was thus a subconscious and genetically induced revenge of Germany's defeats in the two world wars." Here you have humour mounted on logic destroying a myth.

Later he flattens another holy cow:

"That we are inheritors of an ancient civilization which shares with China the distinction of continuity in its survival over several millennia gave me no satisfaction. While the Chinese humiliation was a matter of textbook knowledge, the deep sense of humiliation of having been conquered and ruled from the distant island had scared my consciousness. I discovered later in West. Africa how slavery had deeply scarred the racial unconscious of the Africans. And when one found that the distant island race conquered India by, enlisting Indians I began to ask myself – what makes a country into a nation, more specially a country like ours with its diversities. I can write an ode in praise of our diversities, but I knew too that such compositions combined with our attempts to take refuge in the Golden Ages of the past were merely an ex-postfacto rationalisation of our past humiliation and an attempt to escape from our present concerns."

Historical amnesia among the sons and daughters of Bharat is chronic and widespread. No other people is so supremely indifferent to history as the Indian. We disregard time. We invoke eternity. We leap, Hanuman like, from Ashok to the Guptas, from Harsha Vardhan to Akbar from Akbar to Nehru, paying no heed to disagreeable and degrading events in between. 41 years after independence we are unwilling to face upto our shortcomings. Does anyone ask why Babar with less than 10,000 men could conquer North India? Why a callow young scribe of the East India Company triumphed at Plassey? Why a 1,00,000 Englishmen ruled India with such ease? To ask such inconvenient questions would involve soul searching, self-criticism, maturity and historical detachment. P.N. Haksar does precisely that. He is not a comfortable writer to be with.

He concludes his Introduction to his book *Premonitions,* not on a stale negative note, but on a constructive, positive one:

"I hope these themes and ideas will stimulate the urge to comprehend in all its baffling complexity, the realities which we Indians might wish to change one way or another. And change we must ignore are not to be left behind once more. Our country has had its devotees of Prem Marg and Bhakti Marg. Perhaps, our salvation lies through the much more difficult Jnana Marg. And this Jnana Marg must of necessity adopt the methodology of Vignana." Saluti
P.N.H.
1988

12

Sonny Ramphal

When it comes to the Commonwealth my motto is: when in doubt do as Ramphal does. It is impossible to exaggerate the value of the great services Shridath Ramphal has rendered to this unique organisation. Without his total commitment to the Commonwealth ideal, without his outstanding diplomatic skills, wide sympathies, generous heart, brilliant intellect, engaging personality and the utter absence of airs and his exceptional administrative ability, the Commonwealth would have run into rough and deep waters. It could even have been rendered irrelevant.

Jawaharlal Nehru is the father of the new multiracial monarchical/republican Commonwealth. Naturally, India attaches importance to its Commonwealth link Minus India the Commonwealth might carry less weight in the scheme of things. From time to time voices have been raised in Parliament and the press questioning the utility of our continuing in the Commonwealth. During the Suez crisis in 1956 Pandit Nehru seriously asked whether India could, in the given circumstances, continue her association. The crisis passed. Another surfaced in 1971. That too passed. That was the pre-Ramphal era.

When Shridath Ramphal was elected Secretary-General at Kingston, Jamaica in 1975, I recall Smt. Indira Gandhi telling him, "Put some life into it." During the last 14 years this is precisely what Ramphal has done, put life into the Commonwealth.

The supreme crisis the Commonwealth faced and overcame was over Rhodesia. A number of people have taken credit for resolving the Rhodesian problem but if I were to name one man who navigated the Commonwealth craft with wisdom and exemplary diplomatic flexibility, it was the Commonwealth's dynamic Secretary-General. It was an achievement of world significance. I hope that Sonny Ramphal will one day write his version of the drama of Zimbabwe's tortured journey on the road to independence.

In November 1983, the Commonwealth Summit was held in Delhi. Smt. Indira Gandhi presided. Sonny Ramphal was by her side, while I was in the wings as Chief Coordinator. Sonny had her full confidence. She held him in very high regard. She ensured his unanimous election for a third term. Thus we made up for the embarrassing folly that we were made to commit at the Lusaka Summit in 1979 when we put up a thoroughly undeserving candidate to challenge Ramphal.

Normally collections of speeches unless they be those of Lenin, Churchill, Jawaharlal Nehru, De Gaulle, Kennedy and Gorbachev, do not hold together, date early, remain unsold, because they offer a limited shopworn store of non-ideas. Ramphal's statements, musings, reflections, utterances are lively, serious, well-written, well spoken. They touch upon the great issues of our era. He articulates these through a rich vocabulary, a free and analytical mind. His deep commitment to democratic values, his lothing of racism and his genuine concern for the less fortunate are manifestations of his humanism. The link between events and decisions is the exciting arena of history. In these speeches Ramphal provides that link.

The world has now fortunately run out of colonies. Namibia shall soon be independent. Change will come in Sou th Africa. What will the Commonwealth do then? How will it respond to new post-colonial challenges? The CFTC programme will not be enough, "Inseparable Humanity," provides some of the answers.

For me it is both a delight and an honour to write the foreword. Sonny and I have been friends for over 20 years. He is an entrancing companion, a marvellous friend. He has illuminated and enlarged my horizons in more ways than one. With him around, the world becomes less menacing.

1988

13

A Memorable White House Lunch

I first set foot in the White House, the official residence of the President of the United States, in November 1963. It was a sad day. The world was in mourning. The sun set abruptly and cruelly on Camelot. Vijay Lakshmi Pandit represented India at President Kennedy's funeral. I accompanied her.

The next time was in the summer of 1982, with Indira Gandhi. My role then was of an official who was inconspicuous by his presence. The last time was with Rajiv Gandhi. I had moved up. Instead of being seated at the end of the table, I was now sitting next to the Indian Prime Minister. The date: Tuesday 20 October 1987. It has come down in history as Black Tuesday. The financial markets took a nose dive. It caught every one unawares.

Rajiv Gandhi, after participating in the Commonwealth summit in Vancouver, flew to Washington D.C. to parley with President Ronald Reagan. We were received at Andrews Base by Secretary of State George Schultz. The formal, ceremonial reception was in the south portico of the White House. Reagan and Rajiv Gandhi made brief statements. These broke no new ground. Controversy has no place in so public an occasion. The established rules of diplomacy are respected. These include calculated ambiguity, avoidance of any commitment, no humour, no new ideas.

The President, although 33 years older than the Prime Minister asked Gandhi to call him Ron and the P.M. asked the President to call him Rajiv. Indira Gandhi was very selective in this regard. No question of her being on first names with either Reagan or Nixon. Always President. They too stuck to Madame Prime Minister,

Ron and Rajiv got an very well. They were comfortable in each others company. Both enjoyed irreverent jokes. President Reagan was an accomplished raconteur. Their sophisticated informality broke down the barriers put up by unimaginative ceremonial and conventional and deadly tedious protocol. This did not entail short circuiting well established proprieties.

At the plenary session the two leaders were assisted by their principal advisers. On the American side, Vice-President Bush, General Judy Powell, Whitehead (My counter part) Ambassadors Armacost and John Gunther Dean.

On the Indian side, apart from me, Pratap Kaul, K.P.S. Menon, Sarla Grewal, P.K. Singh, Sharda Prasad and Ronen Sen. The atmosphere was pleasant. No discordent note. No tension. The unwritten but well respected practice for these meetings is for the two leaders to do the talking. Detail is avoided. They can if they feel necessary ask one of their advisors to elaborate a point or recall a U.N. resolution or give a trade figure. In other words the supporting casts listen attentively and respectfully. The junior most take copious notes. The others are attempting to conceal their unemployment. The Americans are less deligent in taking notes. Reason. The conference room is probably bugged and everything said is recorded.

The plenary was followed by lunch. As we were going into the dining room, President Reagan went into a huddle with messers Bush and Whitehead. There was nothing for the Indian side to do except to hang around. What had happened that was so vital for the President to abandon his Indian guest? We didn't have to wait too long. Reagan walked up to Gandhi, apologised, then informed him that the market had crashed, the Hong Kong stock exchange had stopped transactions. Reagan was asked whether Wall Street should follow suit. For the time being he had decided against (his and would wait and see. Bush asked Gandhi to excuse him for a few minutes to speak to the Treasury Secretary. He would join us as soon as hc could.

It must be said for Reagan that, not for a moment did he appear worried or pre-occupied during lunch. His sang-froid was impressive. Mr. Bush joined us. Whitehead then left. More suited for finance than foreign affairs (he had been a stock broker) to keep track of the financial earth quack. The menue was not ducal, but neither was it austere. Of course, wine, red and white was verbotten for the Indian side. The waiters were all black. The pantry was very close by and it comforted me no end to hear the din and racket emanating from that quarter. Since President Reagan was a little hard of hearing, it did not really matter.

Despite Wall Street the mood at lunch was relaxed, even jovial. The President was in good form. We were aware of his impressive stock of amusing anecdotes and jokes. Many were his own creations. He told them with effortless ease and an actor's verbal skill. Anyone with a sense of humour delighted Rajiv Gandhi.

After the first course President Reagan was in his element. His jokes about Gorbachev and Mrs. Thatcher were out of the top drawer. It was obvious that he was the author of these excruciatingly funny anecdotes. Gandhi nudged me. I produced one, K.P.S. Menon another about the Romanians. Score: two all. Reagan then changed gear.

He mentioned his meeting earlier in the week with a very remarkable and courageous Chinese lady. She had suffered and survived the Cultural Revolution. Her daughter had been driven to her death. This lady was now living in Washington. She had written a book about her hair raising experiences. Reagan paused. That gave me an opening.

I said, "President, the lady's name if I am not mistaken, is Nien Chang. Her book, "Life and Death in Shanghai" is a deeply moving account and indictment of the Cultural Revolution. Her book is a triumph of the human spirit." The President hadn't expected this. K.P.S. Menon referred to the lady having appeared at the Indian Consulate General in Shanghai. This was one of the crimes she was accused of. She has written about it in her book. Our American friends began to look at us rather incredulously. Next P.K. Singh also pointed to another incident in the book. Three out of six members of the Rajiv Gandhi team had read the book. Not one among the Americans!

President Reagan thereafter left Mrs. Chang and pulling out a note from his pocket sprang a surprise on us. His friends in California wished him to ask Gandhi why India was not buying more Californian almonds ? One for the Americans.

After the lunch John Gunther Dean, the American ambassador in Delhi caught me by the elbow, "How the hell did you guys know that the President was going to speak about that ... Chinese female." With a near smug look on my face I said, "As good diplomats we had come prepared for all eventualities, except Californian almonds."

14

Living Dangerously: Non-Aligned Summit 1983

"If the creator had purpose in equipping us with a neck, surely he meant us to stick it out"

Arthur Koestler

1983 was an exceptionally rewarding year for Indira Gandhi. Her international prestige was as high as it was in 1971-72 after the birth of Bangladesh. This was to a considerable extent due to her presiding over the Non-Aligned and Commonwealth Summits. No country had hosted both summits in the same year. The two summits, held in March and November 1983 were spectacular and flawless successes. They boosted national morale. They put India on the conference map of the world. The Retreat of Commonwealth leaders in Goa was an organisational wonder. Indira Gandhi was riding the crest of the wave. She had to a great extent created the wave. On a purely personal level I might record that these conferences made me widely known. No civil servant had ever received the cudos I did, or the national and international exposure I experienced. Mrs. Gandhi awarded me the Padma Bhushan. At the investiture she took me aside, "Congratulations, Natwar, but don't let this go to your head."

Commonwealth Summits are held every two years, NAM summits every three. At the Melbourne Commonwealth summit in 1981 it was decided to allot the 1983 summit to India. Mrs. Gandhi returned from Australia much taken by the Melbourne CHOGM - Commonwealth Heads of Government Meeting (the irreverent acronym is HOGS).

While not doubting our ability to organise a summit efficiently, she did harbour some doubts about our surpassing the Australians. Within a few days of her return from Melbourne she was on the look out for a suitable Chief-co-ordinator for CHOGM 1983. The aspirants were many, including one or two who qualified for membership of the club of upward failures.

In May 1980, I took over as Ambassador of India in Islamabad. Prior to that I had spent two and a half years as High Commissioner to Zambia and Botswana. I was the only member of the Indian Foreign service to be singled out for "punishment" by the Janata Government, for being an "Indira Gandhi favourite." As soon as the Janata Government took office in March 1977, I was asked to hand over charge as Deputy High Commissioner, London and proceed on leave. B.K. Nehru was the High Commissioner. We were both considered soft on the Emergency. The truth was that both of us were deeply disturbed and outraged at the promulgation of the Emergency on 26 June 1975. It was almost impossible to "sell" it or Sanjay Gandhi to the British people, Parliament or the Press. B.K. Nehru in no uncertain terms told his cousin the Prime Minister, that the sooner she lifted the Emergency the better. I too had written to her— "I know what to say to our critics, but I do not know what to say to our friends." But to no avail.

While I was transferred to Zambia, B.K. Nehru was denied the Governorship of Maharashtra, following the death of Ali Yavar Jung. During my enforced leave I saw the less attractive side of my colleages, both in London and Delhi. It really was sickening. Three years later the same toadies and time servers were crawling allover the place to prove their loyalty to Indira Gandhi when she got back to power in January 1980. Self-abasement and moral degradation came to them naturally. One couldn't even feel sorry for them because they knew what they were doing.

I took up my post in Lusaka in September 1977. I thoroughly enjoyed myself in Lusaka. Had the Janata Establishment been aware of my close links with President Kaunda, they would not have sent me to Zambia. I had known President Kaunda since 1962—two years before he became President. He had come to the U.N. as a petitioner in the spring of 1962 and made a deeply moving and persuasive appeal to the Committee of 17 for Northern Rhodesia being granted freedom. Two years later when he returned to New York as President, he sent for me to "thank you for the support you gave me and Zambia, in our independence struggle." I saw Kaunda many times between 1966 and 1977.

He received me at State House soon after my arrival and said that his doors were always "open to Natwar." This cheered me no end. I wrote Mrs. Gandhi about K.K. wishing her well and that he and the Zambians still considered her the leader of India.

I had a lot of time on my hands. I read a great deal, wrote my biography of "Suraj Mal". Played tennis five times a week and made no effort to hide my under employment. I also wrote reports and despatches on Zambia and Southern Rhodesia. These were largely ignored by the Ministry of External Affairs. Lusaka was not on the diplomatic highways and no one in the Janata Government showed the slightest interest in Zambia or Africa.

Mrs. Gandhi, to right a wrong sent me to Pakistan. It is a coveted post, combining responsibility with influence. Tension is a constant companion. The pleasures are few, the pitfalls many. It is the most important and the most difficult job in the service. One is in the diplomatic mainstream, a semi-celebrity. The Indian Ambassador to Pakistan is not just a diplomat. He is in a position to influence the making of policy. He is therefore selected with care. He must have the full confidence of the Prime Minister and unhindered access to her or him.

I took to my job right away. It was challenging, stimulating and professionally immensely satisfying. I got on well with President Zia-ul-Haq. I established contact with the Bhutto family and other opposition leaders. Life in Islamabad was comfortable but restricted. This was not so in Lahore or Karachi where people were only too keen to establish contact with their Indian friends. Additionally, Mani Shankar Aiyer, our Counsel-General in Karachi had the city eating out of his hand.

Among the many perks' that the Pakistan job offers, is the necessity to frequently go down to Delhi for "Consultations". These are useful only if the Ambassador is well prepared and the

P.M., F.M. and the F.S. have the time, not only to receive him but also to have meaningful discussions. The Ambassador also meets Ministers in other Ministries and briefs them on what is taking place in Pakistan. In turn he gathers information on what is happening in India, what is the political temperature, what are power equations, etc. He meets important newspaper editors, leaders of business and trade.

On each trip I saw Mrs. Gandhi. She kept a close eye on Indo-Pak relations and expected her Ambassador in Islamabad to send her something more than tedious routine reports. So, one had to go well prepared. At the top there is no room for error. Its a greasy pole. You come down faster than you go up.

During one of these "consultations" the P.M. brought up the Melbourne CHOGM. She was not easily impressed. Melbourne had quite obviously left a lasting impression. She said she had so far not found a Chief-co-cordinator. I suggested a couple of names. No bid. I took leave and roamed the corridors of power, in the Ministry of External Affairs. Here and there I picked up a pebble or two of information about who was up and who was down. Snakes and ladders, we called it. I was aware that the snakes were on the whole not out of business. While the ladders needed constant repairs, the snakes had no shortage of venum. The grape wine told me that I too was in the running for the CHOGM job.

Early next day I got a call from R.K. Dhawan. The P.M. wanted to see me before I left for Islamabad. Even those who knew her well, were a triffle tense when they went in to see her. She come straight to the point. "You better pack your bags in Islamabad. You will be incharge of CHOGM 1983."

I was not entirely taken by surprise, but her directness was unusual. Normally she used an indirect procedure. I am not generally at a loss for words, but on this occasion I chose my words with care. Long years with her had taught me that it was unwise to triffle with her will or question her judgement. No one took any liberty with her. When she was cut of humour, she could be chilly; without uttering a word she could freeze and snub. Me, she treated with considerable affection. Charming, beautiful, amusing and amused she drew a sharp line between the personal and the public, the formal and the informal. This was quite clearly not an informal occasion.

The human brain is capable of thinking at various levels almost simultaneously and about several matters. One part of my brain told me that this was a great opportunity Which I should embrace with alacrity. It was not every day that Indira Gandhi offered such bounties to mere Ambassadors. The other part said, 'Stay in Pakistan. A bird in hand is worth two in the bush.'

I thanked her for placing so much confidence in me. It was a great honour. Out come the platitudes, drip, drip. Then I changed gear. I had never organised even a foreign minister level meeting, let alone a Heads of Government Summit. My only exposure to summitry was when I accompanied her to the Lusaka 1970 NAM Summit and the Commonwealth Summit in Jamaica in 1975. Finally, that I had done only 18 months in Islamabad. I liked the job and had reason to believe that I was not doing badly.

She heard me out and continued signing papers. Many, who did not know her well found this most disconcerting. In fact she missed not a word. Hard pressed for time, she drove herself hard and did several things at a time. All she said was, "Go and see, Alexander." End of meeting.

I returned to South Block in April 1982 after a gap of eleven years. I was chief Co-ordinator CHOGM 1983. No one had the foggiest idea how to run a Summit, which would bring 45 Heads of states and Government and Queen Elizabeth to New Delhi. The more one thought about it the more one became aware of the scale and complexity of the undertaking. What had I let myself into!

I was just beginning to get on top of my new job, when an entirely unexpected diplomatic hydrogen bomb was hurled at me. I had accompanied. the P.M. in July to Washington. On our return journey via the Pacific we stopped for 24 hours in Tokyo. The New Ottani Hotel is something to rave about. The waiters do not accept tips. They are paid three times the salary of an Indian Ambassador. G. Parthasarthi and P.C. Alexander were the senior Mandarins on this trip. We were sitting in the hotel lobby waiting for Mrs. Gandhi who had an appointment with Prime Minister Sato. From these two heavy weights, I learnt that the 7th Non-aligned Summit could not be held in Baghdad on account of the Iraq-Iran war. President Fidel Castro the current chairman, had enquired if India would be interested in holding the 7th Summit in March 1983. My reaction was - Thanks, but no thanks. Nam Summits took nearly 3 years to prepare. Vigyan Bhawan, even for CHOGM needed major repairs and alterations, it simply could not cope with a NAM Summit.

When we got to Delhi, serious consideration was given to President Castro's soundings. There was more to a NAM Summit besides the organisational aspect, and security and bandobast and protocol. Political considerations took precedence over every other consideration. If we refused, then who else? The Yogoslavas were only too willing. Comrade Castro was not likely to oblige them. He and Tito had fallen out at the 6th Summit in Havana. Indonesia? Too much in the American camp. Algeria, Egypt, Sri Lanka had already held NAM Summits. If Mrs. Gandhi accepted the Castro suggestion then India would be presiding over the largest peace movement in history. The other side of the NAM was less tempting. The Iran-Iraq war, Kampuchea, the Arab-Israeli question, inter Arab rivalry, Arafat's scarcely disguised allergy to King Hussain. Having looked at the pluses and minuses the decision was taken to hold the 7th summit in New Delhi, provided the majority of NAM members favoured New Delhi as a venue. President Castro ensured that. As the Chairman of NAM he had a lot of diplomatic elbow room, and being the forceful individual he is, he made sure that Mrs. Indira Gandhi should follow him as NAM Chairman. By early October it was as good as decided. It was to be in the first week of March 1983.

The NAM Summit edged CHOGM out. We turned our thoughts and energies to the colossal undertaking. NAM Summits are less informal and the friendly atmosphere of CHOGM is missing. The main reason for this is—language. All commonwealth HOGs speak English. All NAM HOGs don't. For NAM we had to get some of the best and highly paid simultaneous interpreters—French, Spanish, Arabic.

Unlike CHOGM, NAM Summits have a Secretary General, who is provided by the host country. Also, unlike the Commonwealth, NAM does not have a permanent Secretariat. Broadly speaking such institutions end up having vast bureaucracies which invent work to hide their unending leisure. These secretariats also become dumping grounds for the unwanted of member states, the fired, the retired and the rejected get lucrative jobs. So, India has Vigorously opposed the setting up of a permanent NAM Secretariat. How long we will get our way is a moot point.

NAM Summits have a Chairman, half a dozen Vice-Chairmen, a Rappoteur and a Secretary General. Regional groupings elected the Vice-Chairmen and the Rappoteur. The Secretary-General is selected by the host govt and that is approved by the NAM Bureau, consisting of the Chairman, past Chairmen, the Vice Chairmen.

The search for a Secretary-General began. Almost all senior members of the I.F.S. had their eye on the job. I did not for the simple reason that I already had the CHOGM post.

Once again Mrs. Indira Gandhi's choice fell on me. She went against the advice of all her advisers. Some of them rather over did their running down of Natwar Singh. The argument against me was, that I was the junior most secretary in the MEA and already had a full time CHOGM position.

There comes a time in our lives when luck plays a decisive role. Napoleon, before selecting his generals, asked, "Is he lucky." For me it was the opportunity of my life. The common view was that I would not be upto the job and would fall flat on my face and Mrs. Gandhi's confidence in my organisational abilities was, to say the least misplaced. It was for me to prove these merchants of doom's wrong. I did.

I do not like people who have never stumbled or fallen. The important thing is to get up and get going after each stumble or fall. I am allergic to dedicated frauds who thrive on envy and jealousy, two of the commonest and vilest of human emotions. Mercifully I am afflicted by neither. I have many faults and shortcomings but the Cosmic Master has spared me these two monsters.

From October, 1982 to 1 March, 1983 five months was all we had to prepare for the 7th NAM Summit. Real work could only begin after the Asian Games which wound up on 4 December 1982. Many agencies and departments involved in the Games were also required for the NAM Summit.

The Asian games were well planned and organised. Rajiv Gandhi for the first time received national exposure. It was well deserved. His eye for detail, impatience with the slothful, his commitment to punctuality, his preference for the elegant and the stylish and his being utterly himself, did not go unnoticed. Something else was also noticed. His extreme discomfiture when faced with crawling sycophancy and demeaning servility. This endeared him to large numbers of people throughout India. The Games were seen live on T.V.—that too in colour.

There was, however one jarring note. While Rajiv Gandhi recoiled from toadism and flattery some upstarts in his entourage relished the attention paid to them by skilled ji hazoors. In the months to come I had to battle with this despicable tribe of shameless professional cheer leaders. The young friends of Rajiv Gandhi had never had so much attention paid to them in their lives by people in high positions.

The first encounter came within a couple of days of the closing of the Games. From 4 December, I went full steam ahead with preparations for the NAM Summit. We had not a moment to loose. To use a space flight phrase—all systems were A O.K. Then suddenly a thunder bolt from the blue.

Mrs. Gandhi asked me why the NAM Heads of State and Government and their delegations could not be put up in the Asian Village, where the athletes had stayed. Not only would it save us expense but would be most welcome to the security people to have the VVIPs staying in one place. The Asian Village at Siri Fort had an excellent dining room, a modem media centre, parking space etc. I was dumfounded. After I had recovered I rather thoughtlessly blurted out, “Madame, you can’t be serious.” The moment I had said this I realized I had more than shot myself in the foot. The Prime Minister, very deliberately closed the file she was studying, took off her reading glasses and fixing me with her eyes said, "Natwar Singh, I am very serious," and banged, the table with her right hand. Pause. "Where do you think the money is coming from? Why can't we do this in an austere way?" Having known her for 33 years and worked on her staff for five I had learnt that it was fatal to say anything when she was worked up. I said nothing. Within a few minutes the temperature lowered. She went back to her files.

"Madam, may I say something?" She nodded. I reminded her of the accommodation provided for her and other HOGS by host governments at past summits. I had recently been to Baghdad, Belgrade and Havana to see for myself the facilities provided for the Nam summits. They were breath takingly impressive.

"My accommodation in Lusaka was nothing to write home about,"the P.M. said.

"New Delhi is not Lusaka. The Zambians did the best they could. You were given a villa, so were other HOGS. I was with you. The delegates were put up in hotels, not in university hostels."

She listened. Then, in her usual warm way asked me to discuss this problem with, 'Alex and G.P.' the two benign peas in the Prime Ministerial pod. This I did. It was decided that G.P. Jagmohan, Lt. Governor of Delhi, I and the security people should visit the Asian Village to see if the accommodation and other facilities were adequate.

I asked these wise men a simple question, "Who put this idea into the P.M's head? If we continued to pursue to it, we would have no King, President, Prime Ministers to participate in the New Delhi summit." Both agreed with me but were unwilling to go back to the P.M. at this stage. Certainly not before a tour, of the Asian village.

So off we went to the Siri Fort—G.P. Jagmohan and I, plus fifty others including representatives of a dozen Ministries and departments. On reaching our destination I spotted one of the more bumpteous "boy scouts" who was a close friend of Rajiv Gandhi and had been among the more visible members of his Asian Games outfit. Then the penny dropped. It was this boxwalla who had sold the idea to P.M. and to Rajiv Gandhi.

Within ten minutes it was clear that the Sri Fort would not do. How could world leaders be expected to stay in flats which were no better than C.P.W.D. structures with a common bathroom, no telephone etc. In the evening we all joined Rajiv Gandhi for dinner in the Asiad village dining room. With him were several "boy scouts" including the one whom we had seen earlier in the day. G.P. in his measured tone murmured to Rajiv that perhaps the village was not the ideal place for HOGS, but Foreign Ministers and other delegates could be put up in the village. By this time I was doing my best to camouflage my anxieties and worries. This was getting us no where. Till he become Prime Minister, I called him by his first name. I said, "Rajiv, I must be candid No Foreign Minister, not even a lowly Deputy Minister would agree to spend ten minutes in this complex. The only use we can make of the village is to put up the large numbers of press persons who will be descending on us from all parts of the world to cover the NAM Summit."

He was surrounded by the Boy Scout Brigade. These smart alees were responsible for selling this idea to the P.M. and Rajiv. I ignored their disapproving looks and stuck to my guns. Rajiv Gandhi was non-commital, but G.P. and I had made some head way. While negotiating one must go step by weary step, and then ask for more. At the end of the dinner it was agreed that we meet the next day for taking a final decision. I insisted on this. Each day, each hour was precious. We just could not afford to loose time.

We had for several weeks been in close touch with the Heads of Mission of Non-Aligned countries posted in Delhi. Each made quite certain that his Leader of Delegation secured the best possible accommodation. Nothing in Delhi remains a secret. In spite of our best efforts, word got round that there was a possibility of Heads being put up in the Village. As soon as I got home my wife informed me that several Ambassador had telephoned. They wished to speak to me at whatever hour I got back. I went straight to bed.

The next morning the telephone made its presence felt with a vengence. Nearly a dozen Heads of Mission announced they had heard about our Asian Village scheme. They hoped what they heard was not true. The question of their President, King or Prime Minister staying in the village did not arise. This strengthened my hands.

When we met later in the evening I informed P.C. Alexander and G. Parthasarthy and others, on the NAM Summit Task Force how agitated some Ambassadors/High Commissioner were on this accommodation mess. To me it was abundantly clear that we would be making a laughing stock of ourselves if we persisted in offering boarding house facilities to world leaders. Later in the day I saw Rajiv and the P.M. and told them how impractical the Asiad idea was for putting up HOGS. It was ideal for media persons. They both agreed but we had lost four days and raised the blood pressure of a number of senior diplomats. I too had made myself unpopular with the boy scouts. In the months to come, they were to cause no end of confusion. They really believed that having successfully run Asiad they could run India.

Since I had the full backing of the P.M. and Rajiv Gandhi, these over zealous upstarts were to a considerable extent kept in check. On 7 March 1983, 77 Heads of state and Government attended the opening ceremony. Nothing comparable had been seen in Delhi's troubled and majestic history. When President Fidel Castro handed over the Chairmanship to Indira Gandhi on the morning of 7 March, every individual in the Great Hall of Vigyan Bhawan spontaneously stood up. The ovation lasted nearly ten minutes. No one who was present at the opening ceremony is likely to forget it. As I stood on the dias with Prime Minister Indira Gandhi and President Fidel Castro, I felt my spirit soaring. Yes, it was a great time to be alive.

15

The Limits of Diplomacy

Diplomacy provides hope, not salvation.

We set great store by legend and myth. So, let me begin at the beginning. Diplomacy got off to a bad start at the time of the Mahabharat. Sri Krishna was the first Hindu diplomat. When Yudhister requested him to go as a special envoy to the Kaurvas, Draupadi asked Krishnaji, what the purpose of his mission was, since it was doomed to fail. Sri Krishna gave the Pandav consort an exquisitely diplomatic reply. He said he was going to the Kauravs to present the Pandav case in the best possible light. He would invite them to accept the reasonable demands of the Pandavs. If, however, he failed and war become inevitable, then the world would know who was right and who was wrong, "So that the world may not misjudge between us."

His mission was unsuccessful. Diplomacy, creative and eminently reasonable diplomacy, suffered its first set back. Nevertheless, Sri Krishna obtained one very special privilege, diplomatic immunity for himself. Thus was born the concept, which made the person of the emissary sacred. This is no longer so. In the last 25 years every outrage has been visited upon diplomats, including cold-blooded murder.

The other name that comes to mind when we examine the origins and roots of our political thinking is that of Kautilya, better known as Chanakya. The T.V. Serial has also helped in popularizing the name of the author of the Arthashastra.

The Arthashastra is not an easy read. It offers practical advice to Princes, Rulers, Statesmen and Diplomats, on a multiplicity of subjects relating to the theory and practice of government.

This undoubtedly original book was written anytime between the 4th century B.C. and 2nd century A.D. The startling fact IS that it remained unknown to India and the world till 1904, when it was accidentally discovered in a village in Mysore State. The first English translation appeared in 1909. That established the fame of Dr. Shamashastry. Prof. Kangle's translation was published in 1960. In between, the Arthashastra appeared in several European languages. Most recently, 1990 L.N. Rangarajan has brought out an excellent English translation for Penguin Classics.

Kautilya, although he lived fifteen hundred years before Machiavelli has often been called the Indian Machiavelli. This is not meant as a compliment. Both have had a 'bad press'. Their precepts are regarded as synonymous with unscrupulousness. The epithets used for them are, patron saints of the devious and the underhand. Their sinister reputation obscures the fact that both possessed sharp and powerful minds. Both understood the power game—in short how to attain power and how to retain it. The end justifies the means. Politics is not an arena of morality but interests.

Kautilya's philosophy of state craft (including Diplomacy) can be summed up in four words—SAMA, DANA, BEHDA and DANDA.

SAMA is conciliation, DANA is concession, BHEDA is rupture and DANDA is force. These, Kautilya calls the four UPAYAS. Kautilya judged a policy by the results it produced not by its idealism or morality. If the actions of king or a State produce unfavourable results, then that policy is harmful.

Kautilya divided State policy under six headings—peace, war, neutrality, war preparedness, alliances and separating enemies. The lengthy seventh book of the Arthashastra is a comprehensive treatise on foreign policy and diplomacy. Kautilya is in some ways remarkably modern. Relations and negotiations between States were to be conducted by the Duta i.e. ambassador or envoy. There are three types of Duta.

Nisrstartha, the *plenipotentiary, Parimitartha,* an envoy with limited powers for negotiations and the *Sasanathera,* who was a message carrier. Kautilya, visualises the posting of permanent envoys, whose person is to be regarded as inviolable.

What if any, impact has Kautilya made on independent India's foreign policy? Neither our freedom movement under Gandhiji, nor our diplomatic relations under Pandit Nehru, considered him as our patron saint. Nehru had read the Arthashastra and is rather taken by Chanakya. How well, I remember his reaction in March 1953, to my answer to his question on the future of Sino-Indian relations. मुझे चाणक्या नीति सिखा रहे हो।

He said this with a twinkle in his eye.

In the Discovery of India, Nehru is on the whole generous to Kautilya.

"Chanakya has been called the Indian Machiavelli, and to some extent the comparison is justified. But he was a much bigger person in every way, greater in intellect and action.... Bold and scheming, proud and revengeful, never forgetting a slight, never forgetting his purpose, availing himself of every device to delude and defeat the enemy.... There was hardly anything Chanakya would have refrained from doing to achieve his purpose; he was unscrupulous enough ... he never forgot that it was better to win over an intelligent and high-minded enemy than to crush him." The odd fact is that Emperor Ashok followed not one precept of Chanakya. It is doubtful if he was ever aware of his existence. Nehru, who attached the highest importance to right means to achieve right ends, never practised Chanakya Niti.

So let us now leave the learned and wily Kautilya and turn our gaze to more recent times and to note the subtle difference between foreign policy and diplomacy. Foreign policy is what you do. Diplomacy is how you do it.

The Oxford English Dictionary defines diplomacy thus "Diplomacy is the management of international relations by negotiations; the method by which these relations are adjusted and managed by ambassadors and envoys; the business or the art of a diplomatist."

Hans J. Morgenthau in his book, *Politics Among Nations,* has much to say about diplomacy. Most of it is sensible. Some of it far too theoretical and academic. So often scholars disregard the practical aspects. Theory and practice must go hand in hand. Learned professors, with notable exceptions, are for ever catching diplomacy by the tail and spinning it around in the class room. Morgenthau from time to time provides interesting insights into art, craft and theory of diplomacy. He writes, "Diplomacy of a high quality will bring the ends and means of foreign policy into harmony with the available sources of national power."

Only sovereign and independent nations can have a foreign policy. Only the plenipotentiaries of these nations can conduct diplomatic negotiations. It is possible for a country to have a good foreign policy and poor diplomacy or vice versa. A bad home policy cannot produce a coherent, meaningful, influential, creative foreign policy. No amount of diplomatic agility or brilliance could make the Anglo-French-Israeli Suez misadventure acceptable either to their allies or their adversaries. The 1961 Bay of Pigs fiasco of the United States made American diplomats hang their heads in embarrassment and shame. No diplomatic genius of the Soviet Union could 'sell' their invasion of Afghanistan to the world. Pakistani diplomats were helpless in the face of the disastrous course adopted by their President Yahya Khan in East Pakistan in 1970-71. No amount of sophistry by Indian diplomats could 'sell' to the world, the emergency imposed by Mrs. Indira Gandhi in June 1975. The Cultural Revolution of Mao Tse-Tung left Chinese diplomacy in tatters. The U.S. involvement in Viet-Nam created serious domestic and international problems for America. In all these crises, diplomats could do very little.

The most glaring example of the limits of diplomacy has been dramatically highlighted by the disappearance of the Soviet Union. The Russian and C.I.S diplomats are not to be envied. What can they do when confusion prevails. Gromyko was Foreign Minister for 27 years. Now they do not last even 27 weeks.

The worst example is that of South Africa. Apartheid could never make good foreign policy and South African diplomacy almost and deservedly perished for almost two generations. One Nelson Mandela was worth more than a 1000 South African diplomats.

The communications revolution has also led to the decline of conventional diplomacy. So has the demise of reticence. The media intrusion is irreversible and diplomats have to live with it. Ideological diplomacy is all but dead. Media, shuttle, Conference and Summit diplomacy are there to stay. Diplomats of the future will be of a totally different breed and figure lower in the pecking order. They will, to survive, have to become experts in finance and trade, drug control and terrorism, environment and ecology, science and space, interest rates, balance of payments, debt rescheduling.

Thus diplomacy in the decades to come will assume a different character, a substantial shift from the diplomacy we have known. The maintenance and creation of new institutions and procedures to tackle the new problems and protect the common interests of human kind will be high on the agenda of the New Diplomacy. This is a challenge for all diplomats. Indian diplomats, accustomed to the Soviet Union exercising its Veto in the Security Council on Goa and Kashmir, will no longer be so complacent. They will have to work very hard *to rebuild* our relations in the post cold war era. A great deal of new thinking is needed, not only by us but all major countries. The New International Order cannot be imposed by anyone country. There are limits even to the influence the diplomacy of anyone power can weild to shape tomorrow's world. There are limits even to the diplomacy of the most powerful superpower. The U.S.A. is not all powerful. It recognizes its limits.

1992

16

LI Peng's: Passage to India

At the end of his trail blazing visit to China in December 1988, Rajiv Gandhi invited Prime Minister Li Peng to India. Today, he is not with us physically, but his legacy is very much with us and Mr. P.V. Narasimha Rao must carry it forward.

Rajiv Gandhi's discussions with Mr. Li Peng were frank, forthright, pleasant and substantial. Even when deliberating on the border and their respective formulations—mutual interest, mutual benefit and mutual acceptability versus mutual understanding and mutual accommodation—goodwill and warmth reigned. Both leaders invoked the five principles of Panchsheel. They talked as statesmen, not as politicians, out to score unrewarding debating points. The stakes were too high. New ground was broken, when Mr. Deng Xiaoping said to Rajiv Gandhi, *"My young friend, let us forget the past. We should look forward."* Anyone remotely familiar with China will grasp what this meant. But, it had taken a very long time to get there and we would not have got there but for Rajiv Gandhi.

Although human beings have been around for several million years. systematic thinking is only three to four thousand years old. Even today, people who organise their thinking is relatively small. Mostly, humankind lives by passion. emotion, prejudice, impulse, anger and suspicion. The tenor of life, its creativity and refinement are strengthened by those who combine action with thought, justice with liberty, freedom with equality. With their efforts. human society has advanced.

This applies forcefully to the conduct of foreign policy. Rajiv Gandhi broke the fossilised mindset of 28 years. As soon as he appointed me Minister in the Ministry of External Affairs. I had several frank and lively discussions with him on the static state of Sino-Indian relations. There had been some movement, but it was peripheral. There had been too much diplomatic shadow boxing. It was the single most important foreign policy question confronting his government. If he, with over 400 MPs in the Lok Sabha, did not take the initiative to break the impasse in a bold and dramatic manner, no one else could. His credentials were impeccable. The Chinese too realised that precious time had been lost during the insane Cultural Revolution. The temper of the times had altered. Confrontation and conflict were going out of fashion. They had been taking soundings and more than hinted that a visit by the Indian Prime Minister was long overdue. Neither did they neglect to remind us that while Zhou En-Lai had visited India thrice, Jawaharlal Nehru had been to Beijing only once.

Zhou En-Lai last came to India in April 1960 to discuss the border issue with Jawaharlal Nehru. Having served in China: I was attached to him as Liaison Officer. Consequently, I spent several hours each day for a week in his company. As the days passed, Zhou En-Lai, who was an outstandingly patient, clever and quick-witted diplomat showed visible signs of irritation.

Pandit Nehru suggested to him that he might meet some of his senior colleagues like Pandit Govind Ballabh Pant and Mr. Morarji Desai. Zhou En-Lai's unexpected response was that he would call on them. This was an amazing gesture by the Prime Minister of a major country.

Zhou En-Lai and Foreign Minister Chen Yi met Vice President Radhakrishnan, Pandit Pant and Mr. Morarji Desai. I was present at all three meetings. It was even for me, a bewildering and disquieting experience. The Zhou-Morarji encounter was a disaster. Zhou En-Lai actually walked out of the meeting. He was obviously very upset. On our way to the Rashtrapati Bhawan, he told me in the car that as a matter of courtesy and to show friendly feelings towards India, he had put protocol aside. But, wherever he went, he was being lectured in unacceptable language on the border dispute. When he was discussing this matter with the Prime Minister, why was he being subjected to this treatment.

I was then a 29-year-old Under Secretary. I listened in respectful silence. During a two-year posting in China, I became familiar with the influence and power Zhou En-Lai wielded, not only in his own country, but worldwide. Faithfully, I told Mr. Nehru what the Chinese Prime Minister had said. Mr. Nehru obviously spoke to Pandit Pant who during his return call absolutely charmed the Chinese Prime Minister by his vast knowledge of a variety of subjects which included his familiarity with the current year's coal production in China. Mr. Morarji Desai was denied a return call.

V.K. Krishna Menon was publicly kept out of the talks, but did meet the two leaders. Next day, all hell broke out in Parliament. That is another story. Pandit Pant did not have high regard for Menon and picked Sardar Swaran Singh to have talks with Marshal Chen Yi.

The visit ended on a very sour note. There was no joint communique. A joint statement took days to be agreed upon and said almost nothing. At Nehru's banquet for his Chinese guest, the atmosphere was near funeral, although we all put up a brave face.

I gave all this background to Rajiv Gandhi and said he must seriously consider going to China. That needed political will. Secondly, if he did decide to embark on so crucial a journey, then it must be preceded by a most exhaustive and comprehensive exercise in the Ministry of External Affairs and Ministry of Defence to work out options. Additionally, Parliament and leaders of political parties should be taken into confidence. This was done over a period of 12 months, quietly and methodically, Mr. P.N. Haksar went to Beijing on a secret visit. He had important talks with the then Chinese Prime Minister. He brought back encouraging news.

Rajiv Gandhi's response was, "I have no hang-ups. I have no 1962 complex. The visit is on. Go ahead and start the homework."

It is today possible to look at 1962 in a less emotive, more balanced and mature manner. Even in 1962, Pandit Nehru said that ultimately this question would have to be settled through negotiations.

For 37 years, I have been involved in Sino-Indian relations. Looking back, I do conclude that there was no inevitability about the 1962 conflict. The derailment of history by accident is a recurring phenomenon in the annals of recorded time. In many ways, the 1962 conflict was a product of vast disinformation about the alleged Indian and Chinese intentions. Nevertheless, 1962 has remained with us a painful memory. However, against the memory of that episode, there is also the memory of peaceful interaction between Indian and Chinese civilisations over two millennia. The traditional concepts of balance of power and real politik sometimes tend to ignore the presence of the past and how it intrudes on the future. If one carefully looks around the world today, one cannot fail to notice that everywhere human upsurge derives its nourishment and support more from the roots of civilisation rather than theories of economic development, class struggle, perceptions of military arsenals, this or that 'ism'. Ideology is receding.

If this view is accepted, then the renewal and restructuring of Sino-Indian relations in its *totality* is the task facing the two countries. Rajiv Gandhi had the wisdom, the foresight, the courage to recognise this. The question of defining the border attracts its due place in the totality of our relations—political, economic, cultural, scientific. Mr. Li Peng in his extraordinarily, frank interview to H.K. Dua (The Hindustan Times, 7 December 1991) has pointed in this direction.

It is not beyond human ingenuity to find ways and means of defining and delineating the frontier. This is the task of creative statesmanship which faces Prime Minister Narasimha Rao and Prime Minister Li Peng. This is the great legacy Rajiv Gandhi has left. Besides, what is the alternative? War?—Forget it. Status quo?—For whose benefit? Negotiate?—Certainly.

The refashioning of India-China relations should not be viewed in terms of narrow domestic partisanship. In fact, in the arena of foreign policy, there should be no partisanship. Given this understanding, all our problems with China, including the border question can be resolved on the basis of objective criteria, rather than subjective factors. The world is watching how the leaders of two billion human beings go about it and how these two great countries will cope with the challenges of the 1990s jointly.

Welcome, Mr. Li Peng.

December 1992

17

Count Your Blessings But ...

15 August and 26 January are occasions when we lapse into what I might call, a tiresome, ritualistic, self-conscious, self-righteousness. It is easy to be cynical about these anniversaries. Yet they serve a national purpose and are points of reference for annual stock taking. On these days, rightly, our thoughts turn to our spiritual, political and social landscape.

As we pass through a period of unease and uncertainty, India bashing has become fashionable. This is orchasterated by frustrated politicians, chronic grumblers and those foreign and Indian journalists who trivialize serious and grave issues. In such an atmosphere the temptation to snipe at P.V. Narasimha Rao is almost irresistible. P.V. Narasimha Rao possesses two unusual qualities which do not make exciting 'copy' for journalists. He lacks charisma and he lacks *indiscretion*. The former he has turned into an asset. The latter into a potent non-violent weapon. He gives nothing away. His silences have been reduced to art form. He has put the country on a steady course. He runs a minority Government with the skill of a Chanakya and the studied detachment of a sage.

It is short sighted of India bashers to write Narasimha Rao's India off as an irrelevance and throw the Indian democratic secular baby out with the muddy bath water of Ayodhya. One seventh of humanity can never be irrelevant.

No one knows better than Narasimha Rao that politics is the art of the possible and that human beings throughout history have behaved irrationally, impulsively, emotionally, and follishly. Even if one subscribes to Darwin, one finds that the evolutionary process has produced startling results. Sinners have always outnumbered the saints. With all humility it can be stated that the Cosmic Creator dispenses intelligence, wisdom and virtue somewhat arbitrarily and selectively. So far no disinfectant has been invented to cleanse or repair our malfunctioning mental equipment.

What in fact has been happening in history all the time is that imperfect human beings take imperfect decisions on devilishly complex questions in an imperfect world. There are no chosen people. There are no final solutions. Only eternal values. The BJP would do well to remember that. Our aim should be to make our imperfections less imperfect. Anything beyond that is like chasing ever receding mirages.

As we approach our 45th independence day introspection is permissible. Our ideals have been harmony, a civilized religious tolerance and a disdain for the allurements and temptations of the material world. That we have forsaken these ideals is our shame and tragedy. Gandhiji, no starry eyed idealist, showed the world that a political struggle could not be conducted with moral back sliding. He tried to prove that despite deep seated differences and conflicts Indian societies shared a national consensus about a scale of values which encompassed certain ground rules—an undefined *Lakshman Rekha*—for our political, social and spiritual conduct. Such a scale of values and ground rules ensure order in society. In their absence, families, institutions and nations loose their bearings. False gods appear, promising political moksha and economic salvation.

What are the blessings that I have in mind? Blessing One: Look at the list of the tyrants and dictators of the 20th Century. Stalin, Hitler, Tojo, Pol Pot, Idi Amin, and Malan, to say nothing of fundamentalists and fanatics of one hew or another. No Indian appears on this list. Blessing Two: Nothing stood in the way of Nehru (except Nehru himself) on 15 August 1947 from declaring India a one party State with himself as P.M. for life. Instead he put us on the path of democracy, humanistic socialism and secularism. Such an experiment on so large a scale has not been tried in history. That it works is one of the political miracles of the 20th Century.

Blessing Three: No other country in the so called third world could have emerged from the trauma of the mid-election assassination of a young leader, in the orderly and mature manner we did.

While no Indian should forget all this, complacency would be a cruel joke. Our democracy is under very severe strain. The electoral process is increasingly dominated by money and muscle, not the mind. Reasoned debate has all but disappeared from our legislatures. The judiciary inspires little confidence. The bureaucracy is being mauled and corrupted.

It is worrying to see Chief Ministers treating the democratic process with the delicacy of an earth remover and getting away with it. It is demoralising to witness the leakage of UPSC examination question papers. It is shattering to hear open talk of the highest in the judiciary being accused of graft. It is heart-breaking to come across boys and girls with 95% marks not finding a place in engineering colleges and I.T.T.s.

Corruption is no longer on the 'retail' scale. It is beginning to assume 'wholesale' proportions. The grip the political industrial-bureaucratic combine has on our system is alarming. This powerful combination has its faithful agents to ensure that no one steps out of line.

And who are the sufferers? The innocent, the underprivileged, the low paid, the poor farmer, the landless labourer, the destitute widow, the retired army officer, and the over worked teacher. The harassment the common man has to endure to get his legitimate due is quite extraordinary.

The ones who are best off complain the loudest. They are, for ever seeking grounds for their luxurious discontent. They spend half their time deceiving themselves and the other half justifying that deception.

Mere theorizing and verbalising is not enough. Do I have any practical remedies to offer? While I am only too conscious of the ultimate futility of all human arrangements and plans, I cannot take shelter behind such fatalism an give up.

Family Planning: Our present growth of population is the greatest barrier to economic growth and well being of our people and quality of life. In 1970 the population of the world was 3.5 billion. Today it is 5.4 billion. India's population in that period rose from 565 million to 850 million. An increase of nearly 60%. We may be winning the family planning battles here and there, but we are losing the demographic war.

All major political parties must collectively decide and decide now that family planning will not be exploited as an electoral issue. On the contrary every *candidate and party will speak infavour of Family Planning.* It is later than we think.

Electoral Reform: It is a mockery to say that Lok Sabha election can be fought for 1 lakh 50 thousand Rupees. State funding should be tried. The election process from start to finish must not take more than 10 days. Voting machines must be introduced so that booth capturing (a unique Indian contribution to the electoral process) is eliminated.

Jobs: Each year 2.50 crore come into the job market. The best and the brightest are among them. A whole five year plan for job creation should be on our national agenda.

Second States Reorganisation Commission: If the U.S. with 1/3rd of India's population and 2½ times larger in area can have 50 States, why cannot India? U.P., Bihar, Madhya Pradesh, and Rajasthan are a drag on the country. The South is forging ahead, the smaller States are doing much better. Sub-nationalisms have begun to assert themselves. What is happening in the former Soviet Union, Yugoslavia, Czechoslavakia is encouraging new and divisive thought processes. The first sinister sign is talk of the north-south divide.

Education: Our record here, compared with China, Sri Lanka, Indonesia is dismal. After 45 years of independence, only 52% are literate. A complete overhaul by 1997 is absolutely necessary. By 2000 A.D. we should ensure that no more than 10% students go to university. The rest must be put in vocational institutions.

Reservations: How long will we continue putting a premium on backwardness? The economic criteria is the only one that will work. Otherwise descheduling of the richer class of SC/ST will never be possible. The dialectics of Reservations have been turned into a minefield by V. P. Singh and the synthesis will take a long-long time.

Dr. Ambedkar had a tea period limit for the viceroy the clauses of related to reservations.

Defence and Threat Perceptions: Do we really expect a war either with China or Pakistan? Should we not in all earnestness get down to discussing troop reductions with Pakistan? Even a 10% reduction in our defence budget could change the face of education in our country.

I have said nothing about discipline, efficiency, punctuality, political good manners, decency. I have taken these for granted. These qualities are basic. Without them, great heights cannot be achieved.

If we don't wake up, then, our tryst with destiny will continue to elude us and counting our blessings will not be enough.

1992

18

Let's Talk Peace, Not War

Some years ago Barbara Tuchman, the American historiar (She died last year) wrote a book called *The March of Folly.* The first paragraph of that most illuminating book reads:

"A phenomenon noticeable throughout history regardless of place of period is the pursuit by Government of policies contrary to their own interests. Mankind, it seems, makes a poorer performance of government than almost any other human activity. In this sphere, wisdom which may be defined as the exercise of judgement acting on experience, commonsense and available information, is less operative and more frustrated than it should be. Why do holders of high office so often act contrary to the way reason points and enlightened self interest suggests? Why does intelligent mental process seem so often not to function?"

Nothing sums up better Pakistan's current performance on the so called Kashmir question. "Wisdom, judgement, commonsense" all three have been brushed aside. Shrill voices emanate from different power centers in that rudderless and confused country. Tensions have arisen, an atmosphere of crisis has been created. We in India must deal with this verbal saber rattling in a calm, mature and sensible manner. Strong nerves are indispensable. India cannot be pressurised. Surely the Pakistanis must know that. A self-reliant country of 800 million people cannot be pushed around. Have they forgotten 1971? Have they also forgotten that war is out of date and that they can never win a war against India. Their armed forces, their defence budget and Zarb-e-Momin exercise should not hypnotise them into folly. I say to them, please do not overreach yourself. Let me quote President Eisenhower.

"No matter how much we spend on arms, there is no safety in arms alone. Our security is the total product of our economics, intellectual, moral and military strengths.

"Let me elaborate on this great truth. It happens that defence is a field in which I have had varied experience over a life time and if I have learned anything, it is that there is no way a country can satisfy the craving for absolute security but it easily can bankrupt itself, morally and economically, in attempting to reach that illusionary goal through arms alone. The Military Establishment, not productive of itself, necessarily must feed on the energy, productivity and brain power of the country, and if it takes too much, our total strength declines."

Our friends in Pakistan would do well to ponder on this. They should also bear in mind that people living in glass houses should not throw stones. Miss Bhutto's political glass house is very fragile and vulnerable.

Having served as India's Ambassador to Pakistan, I am only too conscious of the fact that Indo Pak relations are accident prone and frequently need diplomatic first aid. The quality of that aid depends on the quality of diplomats on both sides. Unfortunately in Pakistan the diplomat has for long years had to take orders from soldiers, not statesmen. That makes diplomatic intercourse somewhat difficult. The subtleties of the dynamics of international life so often are beyond soldiers to grasp or understand. Why has the Indo-Pak diplomatic temperature suddenly risen in the past few weeks? Did Mr. Sattar take back a wrong impression about our political cohesion (of the present government) or our military capabilities? Did Gen. Yakub Khan come to test Indian waters? Or is it that the internal situation in Pakistan is once again such that an external diversion is necessary. In the past Generals in Pakistan have been responsible for some of the most disastrous foulups that lead to national tragedy on a grand scale. They must learn some lessons from history.

Even accounting for I.K. Gujral's "Noncoersive" approch and V.P. Singh's laconic style, Sattar and Gen. Yakub must know deep down in their souls that regardless of the political colouring of the government in Delhi the Indian people will not permit outside interference in Kashmir, an integral part of India. If however they got the impression that this government was not cohesive or strong enough then we must disabuse Pakistan in no uncertain terms. More likely it is the unstable internal situation in Pakistan that is perhaps responsible for the unbriddled rhetoric that is emanating from Islamabad, Lahore and Karachi.

The economic, political, linguistic, ethnic and leadership problems confronting Mrs. Bhutto are formidable. At no time in its 43 years has Pakistan faced up to its fundamental problem—the problem of identity. For thousands of years they were Hindus and Buddhists. Then they were converted to Islam. For another thousand years they were Indians. Then came 1947. They became Pakistanis. Soon the ruling, establishment was faced with a delicate but unavoidable nagging problem— "yes, we are Muslims, but we are also Sindhis, Baluchis, Pathans and Punjabis." And then there are the Ahmedias, Ismalis, the Muhajirs. Thanks to General Zia-Ul-Haq, Islamic fundamentalism got a big boost. Add to this, Pakistan's uneasy relations with three of its most important neighbours—USSR, Afghanistan and India. If that was not enough, the Americans too have now started to invoke the Simla Agreement and not the outdated and irrelevant U.N. resolutions. Not a comfortable national or international scenario for Pakistan, a country not adapt in crisis management. India's forte is crisis management.

The current internal situation in Jammu and Kashmir is no concern of Pakistan or the U.N. In the first place we should never have gone to the U.N. in 1948. That Pandit Nehru was deeply disappointed and distressed at the anti-Indian stance in the Security Council is abundantly clear from his letters, notes and statements published in full in S. Gopal's *Selected Works of Jawahar Lal Nehru, second series.* Gopalaswamy Ayyangar, the father of G. Parthasarthi, lead our delegation to the Security Council in January 1948. By 21 April 1948 he was so disgusted by the one sided approach of the Security Council and said to a colleague in New York, "I will never advise my government to bring any other case to the security council. Yes, if you have a bad case, bring it to the council." In fact it took India another 17 years to free itself from the U.N. embrace on Kashmir.

It was in October, 1965 that Sardar Swaran Singh lead the Indian delegation out of the Security Council Chamber, never to return again. I was proud to be Part of that delegation. What Krishna Menon could not achieve (his 9 hour speeches made Pakistan better known in America) in 9 years, Swaran Singh accomplished in 9 minutes. All Mr. Z. A. Bhutto could do that day was to resort to street level abuse and the Security Council debate flopped.

But the so-called Kashmir question is still with the U.N. Can Pakistan convene a Security Council meeting? Yes, it can. What should our response be? We should make it abundantly clear to the five permanent and ten non-permanent members of the Security Council that any attempt to discuss internal developments in India would be taken by us as an unfriendly act. If inspite of our protest the Security Council does meet then we should *refuse to participate in the debate.* That will reduce the debate to a farce. But it is my hope that the Permanent Members, USA, UK, USSR, China and France would not wish to be embarrassed and would want to avoid an acrimonious discussion in the Security Council between the USSR and the USA on this subject.

The present situation can be diffused by Pakistan acting in a level headed and responsible manner. To invoke the Umma and look to an Islamic solution is both dangerous and shortsighted. They should resort to diplomacy, which may not offer salvation but does offer hope. We want non-conflitual relations with Pakistan. Both countries need to divert their resources to raise the standard of living of their people. Their welfare, not war should be uppermost in our minds. Three times Pakistan has tried military action. The consequences have been disastrous for Pakistan. Rajiv Gandhi put it quite bluntly to Prime Minister Junejo in Kathmandu,— "if you try any military tricks, we will give you ... nose." I pray and hope that it will not come to that and that wisdom will take precedence over folly in the Pakistani military political establishment.

1990

19

India and Her Neighbours

Having spent almost my entire adult life articulating India's foreign policy, I have come to the meloncholy conclusion that Foreign Ministers, ambassadors and lesser diplomatic mortals have far less liberty of choice than is generally supposed. There are no quick fixes in international relations. The diplomatic pharmacopoeia has no ready made answers. Often the choice is between the bad and the worse. The only anti-dote to dramatic posturing and slogans is to have as realistic a perception as possible of issues and problems and an equally realistic perception of our limitations in dealing with them. In international affairs even modest progress is worthy of profound respect.

The foreign policy of a country is conditioned by many factors – geography, history of course. Next come its economic and commercial needs. Also national character, passions and prejudices. No foreign policy can free itself from the compulsions generated from within each country. Among these internally generated compulsions are complex and shifting perceptions of national interest. These have a history of their own. The past is everywhere with us (no where more than in the Indian Sub-Continent). We cannot bury it. We have to understand it. What part has history played in creating impediments for the growth of friction free, cooperative relations with our neighbours? How to erect a durable edifice of peace and friendship? All these complexities must be analysed. This requires serious study and the necessary intellectual underpinning without which no conceptualisation of our foreign policy concerns or threat perceptions is possible.

In recent weeks there has been much irresponsible talk regarding our relations with our neighbours. Thoughtless expressions like, "India is becoming a regional bully." "Get out of Sri Lanka," etc. have been freely used. In foreign affairs as in most aspects of life, a little knowledge is a dangerous thing. One fact we should never forget, India cannot shed its geo-political responsibilities.

First let us be clear about who our neighbours are. There are some who would confine the list to SAARC countries. I do not go along with this. Our oldest and most important neighbour is China. We cannot exclude Afghanistan and Burma. Anyone familiar with history (alas, the Hindus are supremely indifferent to history and have repeatedly paid the price) knows that the entire area from the Pamirs to the Mekong delta is of intense relevance and importance to us. After all, the name Hindu Kush signifies something, just as the name Indo-China reminds us that two great civilizations meet there.

Nations can choose their friends. They cannot choose their neighbours. Thus geography is the mother of diplomacy. Before 1947 all SAARC countries were controlled or governed from, Delhi and London. This fact cannot be wished away. Even in Afghanistan and China the British were among the leading players. British-Indian armies fought in both countries. Burma was a part of the Indian Empire till 1937.

Today all these countries are independent and sovereign. However, the transition from dependence to independence did not automatically ensure a sound economy, flourishing commerce, social cohesion, progress in science and technology. With the sole exception of India, no other SAARC country has had economic emancipation, planning and self-reliance high on its agenda. But even India economically, scientifically and technologically is not in the category of big powers. We are not yet a Nuclear power. China is. In one vital area India and all her neighbours—China included have failed miserably—population control. We are, if we do not take drastic steps soon going to be drowned in the excess of our own populations. It is a striking comment on our near fatal demographic complacency that not a single political party during the recent Lok Sabha elections, mentioned family planning. Population control should be outside and above the electoral arena. It is a national not an electoral question. Unless we wake to this reality immediately, it may be too late to push back the Malthusian monster.

Immediately after independence we in India were confronted with grave and momenteous internal and external problems. On the one hand we had to preserve our independence and sovereignty and on the other get on with our economic development. We rejected the assumptions of the cold war. If we had taken any other route we would have bartered both our independence and sovereignty. Thus was non-alignment born.

The compulsions of Pakistan. Nepal. Sri Lanka and later Bangladesh were more or less the same as ours. Regretfully the leaders of these countries could not work out the proper balance between their vital national interests and their own private pursuit of power and its retention.

In Pakistan, successive military governments made it their business to promote friction with India. The so-called Kashmir question was and is still being used for acquiring legitimacy at home. Unless it comes to terms with its destiny and goo-political realities and above all discover or create a national identity it must remain an unease with itself. India baiting carries with it the law of diminishing returns.

The Pentagon casts a shadow on Islamabad and other agencies are not inactive. Unless Pakistan stops using India's difficulties as Pakistan's opportunity, a worthwhile or durable relationship is unlikely to be achieved. They must keep their hands off Kashmir and the Punjab. India is willing to discuss force reduction, freer rail, road, sea and air travel, easier visa regimes. greater exchanges between students. scholars. scientists. artists, authors, journalists, parliamentarians and above all unhindered trade. The future of Indo-Pak relations should not entirely lie in the past.

In Sri Lanka no easy options are available either to the Prime Minister of India or to the President of Sri Lanka. For far too long Sinhala politicians have built their political careers by raising the Tamil bogey. The consequences have been disasterous.

The India-Sri Lanka Agreement was rightly hailed throughout the World (except in Pakistan and Nepal). The necessary ingredients for resolving the uncongenial ethnic tangle were incorporated in the Agreement. It saved the territorial integrity of Sri Lanka. It implicity and explicity rejected Elam is a solution. Prabhakaran had accepted the Agreement in his meetings With Gandhi. In his speech at Sudumalai in early August 1987 he agreed to lay down arms and work for the implementation of the Agreement. Then he went back on his word and all but wrecked the Agreement. Repeatedly we asked the LTTE to join the political mainstream but they refused. It they do so even now they can help restore ethnic peace in that beautiful island. Is the LTTE publicly prepared to give up Elam? That is the bottom line.

Rajiv Gandhi's government was not averse to signing a treaty of friendship With Sri Lanka. That will only complement the Agreement. V.P. Singh and Gujral, I notice have accepted the hard realities regarding the Withdrawal of the I.P.K.F. by 31 December 1989. As I said there are no quick-fixes available in foreign affairs. In short no U turns in our Sri Lanka policy.

It is tempting to speculate on how V.P. Singh's government would respond to a future request for military help from Sri Lanka or the Maldives. Or will this government play the diplomatic virgin and look the other way and permit unfriendly countries to replace us? It would be extraordinary if we were not to go to the help of our Indian ocean neighbours.

India's relations with Nepal are unique. Geography, history, language, religion, culture an open border, emotions, sentiments, contribute to this relationship. Pandit Jawarharlal Nehru and His Majesty King Tribuvan laid the foundation of eternal friendship between the two countries. Unfortunately the son and grandson of that far sighted monarch have in the past two and a half decades played the China card against India without seriously contemplating the consequences. Admittedly Indian democracy is presumed in Kathmandu as a threat to the political system evolved there.

Whether we have one, two or three trade and transit treaties is not significant and skirts the real issues. The fundamental question is what kind of a relationship Nepal wants with India. If Nepal wants a MNF relationship with India, then it must forego the economic, trade and transit advantages which the 1950 treaty allows Nepal to enjoy. This would result in over 50 lakh Nepalese living, working, owning property, facing no discrimination over night becoming aliens. Since

Calcutta port is over crowded goods for Nepal would have to off loaded either at Madras or Bombay. Railway freight would go up. Many other benefits would disappear. Nepal wants MNF treatment plus the benefits of the 1950 treaty too. Kathmandu wants to eat the cake and have it too. No responsible Indian government could agree to such an arrangement.

We are accustomed to diplomatic filibustering by the Nepalese royal establishment. Foreign Minister S.K. Upadhyay's coming to Delhi is not likely to produce anything blindingly dramatic. S.K. Upadhyay is a Marxist turned Monarchist who knows that power in Nepal resides in the Palace, and no where else.

I keep hoping, nay praying that some day, in someway our brothers and sisters in the Nepalese establishment will realize that when the chips are down they have only one place to look to for help and that is India. Even an absolute monarchy cannot stand outside geography and above history.

The birth of Bangladesh knocked the two nation theory on the head, besides proving that political and economic compulsions take precedence over religion. We are proud to have participated in the process which lead to the emergence of a new country. So long as Sheikh Mujib was alive our relations were cordial and warm. Alas, it is not the case today anti-Indianism has been turned into a national activity to butteress the quasi military leadership in Dhaka.

It is not a part of my argument to suggest that these problems in our neighbouring countries cannot or ought not to be resolved or overcome. Critics of Rajiv Gandhi's government would be deluding themselves if they think that mere verbalising is the solution. These countries must ask themselves why their relations with India are not as cordial as they might be. We too as the largest neighbour must always be mindful of their sensitivities and fears imaginary and not so imaginary. That is a cross which all big countries have to bear.

SAARC is only five years old. So far its functioning has given the impression of being a somewhat tentative body, not sure of its role or scope of its activities. Its charter is restrictive and needs a review.

Confidence building takes time, national priorities are not the same and SAARC looks different from each SAARC capital. India has land boundaries with all SAARC countries with the exception of Sri Lanka and the Maldives. If SAARC is to get teeth then it ought to produce something less spectacular and more substantial than the annual summit. SAARC must contribute to finding acceptable solutions for our problems, assist in eroding conflictual relations among SAARC countries. Within SAARC serious thought be given to evolving an instrumentality that will ensure cooperation and increase interdependence. The objective should be to ultimately have broad agreement on foreign, defence and financial policies. This is not asking for the pie in the sky. The EEC and ASEAN have shown the way.

The SAARC charter will need yet another amendment for extending its membership to Afghanistan and Burma (or by whatever name its astonishingly insensitive rulers call it). Afghanistan applied for membership at the Kathmandu Summit in November 1987. India supported Afghanistan but Pakistan opposed the Afghan request on the grounds that Soviet troops were still in Afghanistan. Today Pakistan's objection is no longer valid.

Once Burma decides to turn its face towards the world instead of its back, then it too should be invited to join SAARC. During a two hour meeting with Gen. Newin in December 1987 in Rangoon, Rajiv Gandhi did broach the subject. The answer was anything but encouraging. Since then terrible events have occurred in Burma and we must await a change for the better.

China

Soon after assuming charge as Minister of State in the Ministry of External Affairs in October 1986. I put all my weight behind improving, revitalising and restructuring our relations with our oldest and most important neighbour. For almost three decades our foreign policy had been inhibited due to strained relations with China.

I wanted to restore flexibility. I knew China well. I served in Peking from 1956 to 1958. I spent a year at Peking University grappling with a near impossible language. I was Liaison Officer to Prime Minister Chou En Lai when he came to Delhi for his fateful talks with Pandit Nehru in April 1960. If ever a crucial visit was fouled up this was it. In 1984 I lead the official team for the fifth round of talks held in Peking. We carried a negotiating brief which ensured status quo.

The events of 1962 left a hole in our foreign policy. Then the Cultural Revolution in China made it almost impossible to conduct normal diplomacy with China. It was not till 1976 that Indira Gandhi was able to raise the level of our diplomatic representation from charge to Ambassador. For over 15 years we had no resident Ambassador in Peking.

In 1979 Atal Behari Vajpayee's abortive visit to Peking took place. His intentions were honourable but the timing turned out to be disasterous.

In April 1980 Indira Gandhi had a brief meeting with the Chinese Foreign Minister, Huang Hua at Salisbury at the time of Zimbabwe's independence. Huang Hua later visited India and the two countries decided to have official level talks to find a solution to the boundary question. Eight rounds produced volumes of paper and little else. In diplomacy even talks about talks have their place. Diplomatic shadow boxing is not as futile an exercise as it might appear to the uninitiated.

Over the years I reflected deeply and continuously on Sino-Indian relations. The conclusion was inescapable that at least on this front diplomatic paralysis was in danger of becoming chronic. The old mould had to be broken and fresh initiatives taken. Rajiv Gandhi did exactly that: (In my judgement he could have done so in 1985). If Nixon and Kissinger could turn around American policy and public opinion on China, why not we also? If France and Germany could be such good friends after fighting two bloody wars this century; if Japan and China could normalise their relations, if President Sadat could go to Israel then why could not Rajiv Gandhi fly to Beijing? Had not Chou En Lai been to India three times? Nehru, only once to Peking in October 1954.

With the approval of Rajiv Gandhi I sounded people whose judgement and wisdom I respected. Without exception they were for his accepting the Chinese invitation and undertaking the visit. Leading figures of political parties were taken into confidence. Parliament, the Press and the country were, over a period of twelve months prepared for the historic passage to China in December 1988. P.N. Haksar played a silent but crucial role in preparing the ground for the visit. He met the then Chinese Prime Minister in Beijing. The outcome was encouraging.

Many months of quiet preparation went on in South Block. Our diligent China experts worked over-time to produce voluminous documents. Rajiv Gandhi prepared himself most conscientiously. By the time we landed in Beijing he had the briefs memorised. Thus when the visit was officially announced the country was not taken by surprise.

The Prime Minister was accompanied by M/s P.V. Narasimha Rao, B. Shankaranand, Dinesh Singh and myself. The officials included K.P.S. Menon, G.K. Arora and Ronen Sen. But Rajiv Gandhi was very much his own man. The four Ministers were largely under employed. The Chinese leadership attached the highest importance to the Indian Prime Minister's visit.

All that my oath of Secrecy permits me to say is the outcome of Rajiv Gandhi's discussions with Deng Xiaoping and Li Peng was positive. The long shake hand with Mr. Deng was a public gesture and acknowledgement that a new beginning was being made. We have many miles to go but the first step had been taken. For the first time the most sensitive Sino-Indian issues were discussed at the highest level in a friendly atmosphere. The result was that tension on the border was appreciably reduced, the possibility of an armed conflict on the border was diminished or at least became remote. Sino-Indian diplomatic contacts witnessed a warmth and cordiality totally missing for nearly three decades. A joint working group at the official level was set up to deal with the boundary question.

All this did not go unnoticed by the world. An improvement in Sino-Indian relations conveyed its own message to one and all. This was not an insignificant achievement. The credit goes to Rajiv Gandhi and the Chinese leadership for the satisfactory outcome of this visit.

AFGHANISTAN

Rajiv Gandhi's handling of the complex and tragic Afghan situation was extraordinarily deft and skillful. The centrepiece of his policy was support for the P.D.P.A. and President Najib Ullah. He struck an excellent personal relationship with the Afghan President (as he did with so many other foreign leaders) and not for a moment doubted Najib's capacity to hold out. At one time he was almost the only world leader in putting so much faith in his Afghan friend.

The Soviets withdrew on 15.5.1988. Neither Kabul nor Jalalabad fell to the Mujahideens. Consequently a lot of people in Washington, London and in the western media had egg on their faces. Even today neither the U.S.A. nor Pakistan has a viable Afghan Policy. The wisest thing for both would be to cut their losses, swallow their pride (Gorbachev did exactly that) and get on with implementing the Geneva Accords and stop undermining Najib. If Ex-King Zahir Shah could be persuaded to play a role this should be seriously attempted. President Najib has invited the former monarch to come out of his shell and help work out a solution. My 90 minute meeting with the ex-King in Rome in February 1988 was an attempt to sound him out.

Majesty dithered. When President Zia-ul-Haq got to know of my unannounced trip to Rome. He was livid.

20

Count Down begins in Kabul

In happier times Afghans, non-chalantly used to declare, "we are at Peace with ourselves only when we are at war with each other."

Alas! for thirteen tragic, bloodsoaked, brutal years the Afghans have not known a day's peace. One of the monumental blunders the USSR committed was to send its troops into an independent non-aligned country. Worse still they stayed too long, abused and loathed though they were. I vividly remember Indira Gandhi telling the hardly coherent Breznev to pull out of Afghanistan. To no avail. I remember President Castro saying to me in Havana in 1988 how the Soviet invasion of Afghanistan had all but wrecked Cuba's Presidency of the Non-aligned Movement. On the other side Pakistan and the West used the Mujahideen as mercinaries and brought misery to the Afghan people. Some estimates put the death toll at two million. Tens of thousands of children have been orphaned, young brides widowed. The rehabilitation of millions of Afghans, the rebuilding of the country, the reconstruction of the economy, the resuscitation of a viable political and acceptable instrumentality is a monumental task. At long last the process has begun. The count down in Kabul started at a leisurely pace. Now it is progressing at speed.

I was in Kabul as a guest of President Najibullah. I had long conversations with him and my dear friend Foreign Minister Abdul Wakil. I arrived at a most exciting and historic time. Momentous events are unfolding in and around Kabul. It was also a saddening experience. But gloom under any circumstances is a useless emotion. While the past cannot be wished away, the future is far more important.

A very dramatic event occurred in Kabul last month. President Najibullah's statement that he would step down to pave the way for a political settlement sent shock waves in Kabul, Islamabad, Tehran and Washington. The U.S.A. and Pakistan had made

President Najibullah's removal a precondition for discussion on a political settlement. The last U.S.S.R. soldier left Afghanistan on 15.2.89. The West and Pakistan had been certain that Najib would not last more than a month or two after the Soviet withdrawal. Well, he is still there, thirty eight months later. India was almost alone in saying that Najib was no light-weight push over and would hold out.

What the Mujahideen and their powerful backers could not achieve, has been accomplished by Benon Savan, the U.N. Secretary General's energetic and politically astute Special Representative for Afghanistan, through quiet, behind the scene diplomacy. Not only did he succeed in persuading Dr. Najibullah to issue his self-denying statement, earlier he also hammered out the five point U.N. Plan.

The five points are:

1. The necessity of preserving the sovereignty, territorial integrity, political independence and non-aligned and Islamic character of Afghanistan.

2. The recognition of the right of the Afghan people to determine their own form of Government and to choose their economic, political and social system free from outside intervention, subversion, coercion or constraint of any kind whatsoever.

3. The need for a transition period, details of which have to be worked out and agreed upon through an intra-Afghan dialogue, leading to the establishment of a broad-based government.

(a) The need, during that period, for transitional arrangements acceptable to the vast majority of the Afghan people, including the establishment of a credible and impartial transition mechanism with appropriate powers and authority (yet to be specified) that would enjoy the confidence of the Afghan people and provide them with the necessary assurances to participate in free and fair elections, taking into account Afghan traditions for the establishment of a broad-based government.

(b) The need for cessation of hostilities during the transition period.

(c) The advisability of assistance, as appropriate, of the United Nations and of any other international organisation during the-transition period . and in the electoral process.

4. The necessity of an agreement—to be implemented together with all agreed transitional arrangements—to end arms supplies to all Afghan sides, by all.

5. The recognition of the need for adequate financial and material resources to alleviate the hardship of the Afghan refugees and the creation of the necessary conditions for their voluntary repatriation, as well as for the economic and social reconstruction of Afghanistan.

This plan was given tacit support by the West and Pakistan and the Soviet Union. The U.N. General Assembly by its Resolution 45/12 of 7 November 1990 authorised the Secretary General to try and implement the U.N. Plan.

The U.N. Plan could not be fully implemented so long as Dr. Najibullah and the Watan Party remained at the helm. Ever the consumate political strategist, Dr. Najib has put the negotiating process in a tail-spin. This wholly unexpectedtum of events has had a sobering effect in Islamabad and Washington. Both see Najib as a symbol of stability. Alarm bells have now begun to sound, about the emergence of a "Fundamentalist" Afghanistan. If the U.N. peace process was to flounder and with Najib gone, Afghanistan could split on tribal and ethnic lines. That would spell disaster for Pakistan. The demand for an independent Pushtoonistan would be revived with force and vigour. The Baluchis would follow the Pushtoons!

But for the success of the U.N. Plan the co-operation and support of President Najibullah was crucial. Now that this co-operation has been fully extended, Mr. Benon Savan has paved the way for the cessation of hostilities. Additionally he has worked another package which includes a general amnesty, human rights, and U.N. guarantees to ensure the sovereignty, territorial integrity, political independence and the non-aligned and Islamic character of Afghanistan. Kabul, Islamabad, Tehran, Riyadh, Moscow, New York and Washington have all agreed. The Mujahideen too have fallen in line. So has King Zahir Shah.

How is a smooth and peaceful transition to be achieved in a society as violence prone as the Afghan? As I grow older I realise the ultimate futility of all human arrangements and plans. I also realize that to throw up our hands and do nothing would be foolish and unwise. So, go on human beings must and do their best.

After my stay in Kabul I have returned conscious of one stark reality. Every Afghan is tired and exhausted. All yearn for peace. They want the guns silenced and the apparatus of State rediscovered, put together and set in motion. The first step will be to hold an "Ijlass", of about 100. The names apparently have been agreed upon. The "Ijlass" will, if all goes well, and it is a big IF - recommend the establishment of an all party coalition interim government. The "Ijlass" is to provide as wide an expression of the national opinion as possible in the existing circumstances. The "Ijlass" is to be held later this month or in early May in Vienna, Geneva or Kabul. The Interim Government will from the beginning lead the country to free elections. This is a perilous undertaking in a country where war lords and tribal chiefs decide and dispose off. How to get the democratic process moving is a great challenge. Everyone is keen to have a go at it, having tried the dictatorship of the Communist Party.

What happens to Dr. Najibullah and his Watan Party? He steps down. Most likely a collective leadership will emerge in the party, which is the only organised evenly spread political and administrative instrumentality in Afghanistan. It hopes to play an important role in the Interim Government. The Watan party is not faction free but it does have a structure and men of experience.

With the collapse of the Soviet Union, the Afghan problem began to look different to the U.S. and Pakistan. Fears of fundamentalism surfaced. Fears of Afghanistan splitting into three worried all lits neighbours. Afghanistan has to be kept one and secular.

Does India, a traditional and historical friend of Afghanistan, have any role to play at the moment? Frankly, the answer is no. This is mainly due to our keeping aloof from the Afghan problem since 1989. To jump in now would be unseemly, unwise and unwelcome by the U.N., the U.S.A. Pakistan and Iran. All we can do is to support the efforts of the U.N., maintain and strengthen our links with all segments of Afghan Society, seek fresh avenues of trade and aid. Impress upon Pakistan to open the highway from Wagha to Peshwar and beyond. Now our humanitarian assistance goes to Kabul through Odessa on the Black Sea. We should participate in the rebuilding of Afghanistan to alleviate the wretchedness in which a great majority of Afghans live. We must never forget that for India the entire region from the Pamirs and the Hindu Kush to the Mekong is of relevance, My vision of SAARC includes a democratic Afghanistan and a democratic Burma.

Finally let us hope and pray that from now on Afghan history will be written in ink, not in blood. What Afghanistan needs is a reassertion of *douceur di vivre* - the sweetness of life.

The Hindustan Times, 1992.

Authors Note January 1993. Unfortunately Afghanistan's troubles are not yet over. The fate of President Najib remains a mystery. The U.N. seems helpless after the Savan plan misfired at the last moment.

21

Wither Foreign Policy?

Last week the All India Congress Committee met in Delhi for the first time after the November 1989 general elections. The debate on Foreign Affairs had to be curtailed to two hours as a large number of members wished to speak on the Political and Economic Resolutions.

The A.I.C.C. Resolution on Foreign Affairs is an impressive document. It is not simply a severe indictment of the National Front Government's foreign policy (or its absence) but it offers an intellectual, conceptual, historical and philosophical rationale of India's foreign policy over the past four decades. Unfortunately the resolution got smothered is Sardar Swaran Singh's painfully prolix speech. In the absence of P.V. Narasimha Rao, V.N. Gadgil moved the resolution and did a good job. Sardar Swaran Singh, now in his 83rd year asked to second it. From so seasoned, senior, and mature a person, one expected a stimulating tour de horizon, some refreshing in sights and a visionary overview. Alas! this was not to be. In 63 minutes he said what could have been said in 23 minutes. It made me sad because I have both affection and respect for him. One devastating platitude followed another. Everyone was too polite to say anything. Rajiv Gandhi displayed monumental patience and did not press the warning bell. The five speakers who followed Swaran Singhji got 7 minutes each.

Jawaharlal Nehru is the father of India's foreign policy. He pointedly emphasised that there was a vital linkage between a country's domestic and foreign policies. Unless a country had a cohesive, integrated, well thought through and relevant national policy, it could not have a worthwhile foreign policy. To formulate meaningful internal and external policies a country needed a government which had a vision, a well thought through, national and economic charter, a shared point of view, well defined objectives and efficient instrumentalities to attain those objectives.

Even when there was a change of Government in New Delhi in 1977 the Janata Government did not and could not alter even the broad contours of Nehru's and Indira Gandhi's foreign policies. Its implementation was another matter. That left much to be desired. It took nearly three years for the Morarji - Charan Singh establishment to disintegrate. The present dispensation is falling apart within 8 months in front of our eyes in slow motion.

The predicament facing the fragile and increasingly vulnerable NF Government is not a simple one. V.P. Singh is not an Unintelligent man and needs no reminder to tell him that he presides over a minority government, which is all the time at the mercy cf two diametrically opposed political forces—The Left and the Right—CPIM and the BJP. V.P. Singh has shown some agility in running with the hares and hunting with the hounds. Politics does allow for strange bed fellows. That V.P. Singh has accepted this unholy alliance reflects poorly on him.

Add to this the highly original and rurally sophisticated contribution being made by the Haryana School of thoughtlessness, so artfully produced at the Meham School of advanced studies and learning!! All this would be extremely funny if it were not damnably serious and disastrous for India, that is Bharat.

The AICC resolution highlighted the gallop at which our foreign relations are going downhill. India is the great absentee on the World scene. The area from the Hindu Kush to the Mekong is of great relevance to US and yet the present government has paid little need to it. There has been plenty of verbal bombast. The Prime Minister in his recently held Press Conference at Sri Fort said without batting an eyelid that his government's foreign policy was hugely successful. It was inspired banality at its best. We are, entitled to ask V.P. Singhji, "where, pray, where are these much touted successes to be seen?" Afghanistan? Come. Come. Pakistan? Relations have never been worse for the last 18 years. Cambodia. No one mentions us. At one time we are an important and active player. Cambodia has all but seen abandoned by this government. NAM? We should be providing leadership and ideas, but we are not. The G 15 was Rajiv Gandhi's creation at the Belgrade Summit last year. Sri Lanka? This government has no policy worth the name. Will it abrogate the Indo-Sri Lanka Agreement—for what, a treaty of friendship which the previous government welcomed. In the meanwhile the killing fields in the north and east of Sri Lanka multiply. Nepal is trotted out as a great success. All that was done was to carry forward the Belgrade Birendra-Rajiv dialogue. And without the firm stand taken by Rajiv Gandhi in 1989 there was no question of the democratic process surfacing in Nepal.

It gives one no pleasure to catalogue these failures, but this is precisely what the 120 Embassies and High Commissions in New Delhi are reporting to their governments. They are, I have no doubt, telling their governments the grim truth: drift, indecision and confusion and likely to continue.

1990

22

Interview for Celebrity

The period of transition, from career diplomat to politician is very much in evidence at Natwar Singh's government residence, number nine on what is perhaps New Delhi's best-known residential avenue, Safdarjang Road. In the green and pleasant garden, cane chairs are grouped in informal arrangements, all of them occupied; a steady trickle of comings-and-goings (achkans and dhotis are equally represented) adds to the atmosphere of controlled excitement. The curtain is about to go up on what will probably be the most important role of his multi-faceted, event-filled career and Natwar Singh, Congress(1) candidate from Bharatpur; until recently, Secretary in the Ministry of External Affairs, handles his growing number of visitors with the ease and assurance of the born politician. Or perhaps, the born diplomat. He moves from group to group, a word here, a smile there, an intense, low voiced conversation with a few ... the time for waiting in the wings is drawing to a close and with the election fever upon the country, he will be under public security as never before.

A brilliant and seasoned diplomat, closely associated, professionally and personally, with the late Prime Minister and her family, prolific writer and a man of great personal charm, Natwar Singh is a natural for the changing political arena of India. Had he not resigned from the Civil Service (five years before his time) he would have been, inevitably, the Foreign Secretary. Yet, under the soft-voiced, persuasive manner and the quicksilver mind, is the steel of which the enduring political personality is made.

Pandit Nehru: An Early Source of Inspiration

I had my schooling first in Bharatpur, then I went to Mayo College in Ajmer, and, after five years there, to Scindia School, Gwalior. I did my BA honours in history at, St. Stephens, Delhi and then I went to Corpus Christi, Cambridge. In 1953 I qualified for the Foreign

Service. I had no other ambition but to join the Foreign Service, having been so deeply influenced by Pandit Nehru as Prime Minister and Foreign Minister. It was really he who inspired me. And I was rather lucky because Mrs. Krishna Hutheesing's sons, were in school with me so I had known the family since my school days.

Well, in those days, even after one had been selected for the Foreign Service by the UPSC, Pandit Nehru used to interview each candidate individually. It was a great thrill for any young person, to be interviewed by Panditji. In the interview, the first five minutes Panditji used to make each young man or woman feel completely at home by asking about his or her background. He was, you see, aware of the fact that these young men and women in their early twenties were nervous meeting one of the great men of the century: so you see he had that kind of sensitivity and consideration. And when you went into the room, he stood up to greet you: you know, that floored one completely. And when one left, he saw one to the door: I'll never forget how exquisite his manners were.

CHINA: THE 'PROPHETIC' QUESTION AND PEKING UNIVERSITY

I remember two or three questions Nehruji asked me at the interview: one was about our policies on South Africa's apartheid and then—it was prophetic—he asked me "What do you think of India's relations with China? Is there a possibility of conflict?" And I remember I said to him, "Your next door neighbour is your best friend and your worst enemy," and he said, *Kya aap mujhe Chanakya-niti sikha rahe ho?*

I volunteered to study Chinese as my foreign language—it was very common to take French or German, so I decided to take something different. I spent a year at Peking University. The pass marks there were 80 per cent, while the pass marks at the Defence Services School were 40 per cent and I remember, when the first Secretary of the Embassy, Ashok Bhadkamkar, was asked by the ministry of defence to let them have the qualifications of the examiners of Natwar Singh in Chinese he was so outraged, he wrote, "I don't know their qualifications but the names are Mao Tse Tung and Chou En Lai." He was so upset that they were asking the qualifications of Professors of Chinese at Peking University. So I had two years in China, then I came back to Delhi and was Under-Secretary and Private Secretary to the Secretary-General, R.K. Nehru.

New York: Rapporteur at the UN and the Start of a Literary Career

After that, I did five years in New York with the U.N. It was a fascinating experience. I got elected as rapporteur of the Committee on Decolonisation for three years; I started reviewing books for the New York Times, the Saturday Review, and I published three books there, between '64 and '66: one on E.M. Forster, one on Pandit Nehru and one, Tales from Modern India. Yes, I enjoy writing very much. First I write longhand, once, twice, could be even ten times; I could have upto 10 drafts. And, after typing, I may make more changes - so, you see, it's hard work. But I enjoy it.

E.M. Forster and a Host of Literary Figures

I first met E.M. Forster at Cambridge in 1952. The *Hill of Devi* had just come out. I wrote and told him how much I enjoyed it and he said, come and have tea. He was very sympathetic and sensitive to young people. A simple man, and such a genius. I have written a great deal on Forster. He had a profound influence on me, he encouraged me to write. He believed in personal relationships as one of the most important aspects of one's life. Of his books on India: well, *Hill of Devi* was a marvellously entertaining book and, speaking purely from a literary point of view. *Passage to India* was a masterpiece, but most Indians find it biased; they say he knew the Muslims better than the Hindus etcetera etcetera. Well, the man was trying to depict personal relationships.

It. was through Forster that I met a lot of other literary figures, like R.K. Narayan, Narayana Menon, Mulk Raj Anand. Then during the period I was based in New York, I met Raja Rao, Santha Rama Rao.

Han Suyin I met first in China; and I've been meeting her in other parts of the world. I met her recently, in the month of September. Her literary timetable is chalked out till 1990—she's always writing. Last year she wrote *Till Morning Comes;* her next book is going to be about an Indian monk of the 7th century, who took Buddhism to China.

WITH THE PRIME MINISTER'S SECRETARIAT: AN INSIGHT INTO LIFE AT THE TOP

After New York I came back to Delhi and was, for five years, on Mrs. Gandhi's staff, from April '66 to April '71. That was the high mark of my career, really, because, at a very young age I held a position of both professional interest and influence, and responsibility. The Secretariat was very small, obviously one got to know so much. Then, to work with somebody so remarkably attractive a person as Mrs. Gandhi: it was a very great opportunity, the opportunity of my life; it enlarged my life immensely. It also gave me an insight into what life at the top was like.

AMBASSADORIAL ASSIGNMENTS: OUR MAN IN POLAND, ZAMBIA AND PAKISTAN

I married in '67, married the daughter of the maharaja of Patiala; Mrs Gandhi was our principal witness at the wedding. We had a civil wedding, and then a Sikh ceremony.

Then, from '71 to '73 I did a spell as Ambassador to Poland, then went as Deputy High Commissioner to London. While I was still there, the Janata got very annoyed with me and I was asked to go on leave.... I was supposed to be Mrs. Gandhi's man in London. Well, I used this period of leave to write a book on Maharaja Suraj Mal. I did research for four months, at the India Office Library. Suraj Mal got a good reception; last year, my latest book, *Curtain Raisers,* came out.

Then from '77 to '80 I was in Zambia. It was fascinating to be in Zambia. I had known President Kaunda for many years. From Zambia I was posted to Pakistan.

The '80s: Achievements, and Recognition from the National Press

Now, since I went to Pakistan, I started getting some attention in the National Press. And after the NAM, of which I was Secretary General, and CHOGM where I was Chief Co-ordinator, I got an unusually extensive coverage for a civil servant—this was mainly from the Television. Well, the success of the conference can't be attributed to anyone man, it was team-work, but I got the credit. But if things had gone wrong I would also have got the chop. And then the Padma Bhushan came and that was also rather unusual for a serving civil servant to get.

Joining Politics: with Mrs. Gandhi's Confidence and Blessings

My recent successes I owe to the fact that I had Mrs. Gandhi's confidence; I was, and am, deeply devoted to her and to her family. It was during this period that I began considering joining politics. I had always been attracted by politics, right from my school days. By the time I was 14 I had read Gandhiji's autobiography, Panditji's autobiography. Even as a young man in school I used to wear a Gandhi cap on Sundays.

So I had been toying with the idea of joining politics for some time; then, about a year ago, I discussed this matter with Mrs. Gandhi. Actually, it was during the Goa Retreat that this first came up.

At first, no one took it very seriously. People said, why should a chap who's got another five years to go give it all up. But I stuck to my decision because of the PM's blessings and secondly, because I thought, you know, there are so many of us, educated people, people in various professions who've opted out of the political mainstream and having done so, we sit down as armchair critics and say: this is wrong and that is wrong and blame it all on the politicians. And really we don't have any moral right to do so unless we're prepared to chuck up something. So I've made my decision to enter politics five years before retirement. If I'd done it five years later, people would have said: All right, so you've had a nice time for 36 years in the civil service, now you're coming to have a nice time here.

LOOKING AHEAD: TO A BRAVE, NOW INDIA

I think that Rajiv Gandhi has already set the stamp on the kind of government he wants and on what India should be in the 21st century. There will have to be a change of style. This entire chamcha culture has to go; and he's going to look for people who have something to offer, who understand the running of a modern, complex, country, whose emphasis is on efficiency, hard work, education, and not on having hangers-on, asking for privileges all the time. You know, I find it outrageous that responsible people should be reluctant to go to the bank to draw out money themselves or object to standing in a queue in a hospital or to buying their own railway tickets. It's totally outrageous.

ENVISAGING A POLITICAL CAREER: THE CAMPAIGN AND BEYOND

In my political career, as an individual, I can set some kind of example by not expecting people to make way for me just because I hold a certain position. Really, in no other country do you find this kind of thing. I remember, when I was in Zambia as High Commissioner Zambian Ministers would stand in a queue; President Kaunda's son would stand in a queue at the hospital: I've seen it with my own eyes.

Our whole attitude needs changing. We are trying to establish a socialistic pattern of Society, we are a thoroughly democratic country, but people in authority seem to acquire certain angularities and certain habits which are anything but democratic.

As for my election campaign - well, I'm a complete novice. You know, I do as the party wishes me to, having selected me as a candidate to contest for a seat in parliament. Yes, there does seem to be a lot of feeling of goodwill towards me in my constituency, Bharatpur. There's some local pride in the fact that the local boy has made good. And then, the fact that I've given up a good job five years in advance should have some appeal in the Indian mind. If I win, I see myself as an ordinary member of parliament, specialising in foreign affairs.

Indo-Pak Relations: The Future Viewed in the Perspective of the Recent Past

Our relations are accident prone. It is India's basic, fundamental policy to be on good terms with all our neighbours. And it's not for want of trying on our part that relations have deteriorated. Look at the way they've behaved in the Punjab; look at the way they've behaved in the last three-four months, over the processions taken out on Guru Nanak's birth anniversary. It's amazing how their government, with a martial-law administration at the head of it could have allowed such a thing. So while I'm neither unduly pessimistic or optimistic, I'm being realistic. Let's say, we are going through a lean period in our relations with Pakistan.

For President Zia, I have great regard personally, he's always been very considerate to me. But we're talking here about national policies.

India's Image in the World: 'We Are Always in the News'

Well you know, India is like a bug: some people get it, some don't. Then there are those who come back again and again. There are, I think, a vast number of people who are deeply interested in Indian culture. We have, too, our remarkable figures who have attracted world-wide attention. You can see the kind of media coverage Mrs. Gandhi's death had throughout the world, the kind of emotion, world-wide, the tragedy evoked: sorrow, anger...

We are always in the news, not always favourably, but I think we're over-sensitive to what, other people think about us, and we shouldn't be. We're an original people in every way, we're not a cultural extension of any country. In fact, culture and religion went from India to other parts of the world. Our great sages, in ancient times, have addressed themselves to the most intricate human problems and found some answers for them.

Pleasures and Pursuits: An Eclectic Taste

I read a lot: biography, history; from Gandhiji to Julius Caesar. Recently I've read Gopal's book on Pandit Nehru. I've read a great deal of Churchill. I'm not over-fond of poetry, but while I was in

Hanoi recently I bought Ho Chin Minh's poems which I gave to Mrs. Gandhi. But we never got the chance to discuss it.

I'm very keen on cricket, though tennis is really my first game. I used to be the Delhi University Champion and the Delhi State Junior Champion. I like reading books about mountaineering, though my own trekking experience is confined just to the Rohtang Pass. I have a great admiration for mountaineers, I like people who accept challenges, and are not afraid of taking risks to achieve a goal. And I have, in my own modest way, tried to live dangerously.

November 1984.

23

50th Anniversary of 1947
Lonely in a Crowded Beach

A united, Independent India would have been a world power in her own right. A divided India was required to work overtime to play any effective part in world affairs. Jawaharlal Nehru's authority and eminence ensured that the Indian point of view was heard with a certain amount of, albeit grudging, respect in world capitals. It is a great tribute to the foresight and wisdom of Jawaharlal Nehru that the foreign policy framework crafted and created by him has stood the test of time. For 50 years, a broad national consensus has existed on India's foreign policy. The non-Congress Governments of Morarji Desai, Charan Singh, V.P. Singh, Chandra Shekhar, Atal Behari Vajpayee and Deve Gowda have followed the foreign policy parameters laid down by Nehru and Indira Gandhi. Why? Simply because there was and there is no better or more honourable course to follow, unless we wish to become a client State or a camp follower. This the proud people of India will not countenance.

Nehru was ideally equipped to be Foreign Minister of India. From his early youth, he was a diligent student of international affairs. After his return in 1927 from his second visit to Europe, he drafted the foreign policy resolutions of the Indian National Congress at its annual Sessions. He made the Congress party take interest in foreign affairs. In his Presidential address at the 1929 Session at Lahore, he pronounced his vision of India's foreign policy:

> *India today is a part of the world movement. Not only China, Turkey, Persia and Egypt but also Russia and countries of the West are taking part in this movement. We have our own problems—difficult and intricate—and we cannot run away from them and take shelter in the wider problems that affect the world. But if we ignore the world, we do so at our peril ... If India has a message to give to the world, as I hope she has, she has also to receive and learn ...*

It is generally believed that non-alignment was a post-1947 phenomenon. Not so. The principle of non-alignment was accepted by the Congress at the Haripura Session in 1938. The resolution of foreign affairs said that a free India would keep aloof from both imperialism and fascism. The resolution stated:

> *India was resolved to maintain friendly and cooperative relations with all nations and avoid entanglement in military and similar alliances which tend to divide up the world in rival groups and thus endanger world peace.*

By the time Nehru became Vice-President of the Interim Government on September 2, 1946, he had, between 1927 and 1946 visited the USSR, Germany, France, Switzerland, Czechoslovakia, Hungary, Spain, Egypt, Malaya, Ceylon, Burma, China and England. No other Indian politician could match this record. He, therefore, lost no time in articulating the features of free India's foreign policy. This he did in his first broadcast to the nation on September 7, 1946:

> *We propose, as far as possible, to keep away from the power politics or groups aligned against one another which has led in the past to world wars and which may again lead to disasters on an even vaster scale. We believe that peace and freedom are indivisible and the denial of freedom anywhere must endanger it elsewhere and lead to conflict and war. We are particularly interested in the emancipation of colonial and dependent countries and peoples and in the recognition in theory and practice of equal opportunities for all races. We repudiate utterly the Nazi doctrine of racialism wherever and in whatever form it may be practised. We seek no domination over others and we claim no privileged position over other peoples, but we claim equal and honourable treatment for our people wherever they may go, and cannot accept any discrimination against them.*

India's Independence in August 1947 was a world event. The era of colonialism and imperialism was nearing its final phase. India's freedom movement had inspired other people under foreign rule. They now looked to India to fight for their cause at the United Nations and the Commonwealth.

If Nehru had died in 1960 instead of 1964, he would have gone out on a triumphant heroic wave. The perfect symmetry of his life was disfigured in 1962 by the Sino-Indian border clash. Nevertheless, for half a decade, 1950-55, Nehru achieved something unique. He lit the international sky and the glow raised the sights of humankind. He passionately believed in peace, peaceful co-existence, in cooperation, in creative non-alignment, in nuclear and conventional disarmament and development. He was no starry-eyed ivory tower idealist. He had his feet firmly on the ground. More importantly India meant something very special to him. It was something more than a country or a nation. Out of his historical awareness emerged certain fundamental elements of our foreign policy which he spelt out from time to time. He was acutely aware of the nexus between foreign policy and internal cohesion:

Foreign policies depend ultimately on internal conditions and developments. Internal progress for us, therefore, becomes essential if we are to play any effective part in world affairs.

Few examples of his success will suffice—Korea, Indo-China, Congo, Cyprus, Gaza. His call for nuclear disarmament, his assault at the United Nations and the Commonwealth on Apartheid and Colonialism. The birth of NAM at Brioni and its launching at Belgrade owe much to Nehru. Without him there would have been no Bandung, no Panchsheel. How ironical it is that Nehru who pushed for an invitation to China at Colombo to Bandung should, towards the end of his life was broken on the Sino-Indian frontier.

In 1947, India's GNP was not worth calculating. Yet India was a factor in world affairs. Till 1962, India was undoubtedly the most important UN member from the countries of Asia, Africa and Latin America. At the end of World War II, an exhausted humanity looked to India to give the lead, a moral lead. The distinctive character of our freedom movement under Gandhi was much admired. The absence of Mao's China from world bodies went in favour of. India. By 1964, more than 60 per cent of Africa was free of colonialism. The UN beach began to be crowded. We were no longer the only country opposing colonialism and apartheid at the UN, the NAM or the Commonwealth. If we had been a bit more worldly-wise we might have got a permanent seat in the Security Council between 1955 and

1960, because the Americans were at that time on a crusade against Mao's China.

Nehru did not subscribe to the assumptions of the Cold War. There was an Indian way of looking at issues and events and if that meant standing alone. He was unambiguous about this:

> *I can understand some of the smaller countries of Europe or some of the smaller countries of Asia being forced by circumstances to bow down before some of the great powers and becoming practically satellites of those powers, because they cannot help it. The power opposed to this is so great that they have nowhere to turn. But I do not think that consideration applies to India ... India is too big a country herself to be bound down to any country, however big it may be.*

On another occasion he was equally specific:

> *The world seems to be divided into two mighty camps, the Communist and the anti-Communist, and either party cannot understand how anyone can be foolish enough not to link up with itself. That just shows what little understanding these people have of the mind of Asia. Talking of India only, and not at all of Asia, we have fairly clear ideas about political and economic structure. We function in this country under a Constitution which may be described as a parliamentary democracy. It has not been imposed upon us. We propose to continue with it.... We have no intention to turn Communists. At the same time, we have no intention of being dragooned in any other direction.... We have chosen our path and we propose to go along it and to vary it as and when we choose, not at anybody's dictate or pressure, and we are not afraid of any other country imposing its will upon us by military methods or any other methods.... Our thinking and approach do not fit in with the crusade of Communism or crusade of anti-Communism.*

From the very beginning, Nehru's approach to the USSR and USA was friendly. He paid three visits to the USA. The outcome was mixed. The US military aid to Pakistan adversely affected Indo-US relations. Kennedy admired Nehru and spoke of his "soaring idealism." In spite of his partial disillusionment after the 1961 visit of Nehru to the USA, Kennedy promptly responded to the call for help from Nehru in 1962.

The USSR had, during Stalin's time, not been at all friendly towards India. After his death there was a change. Nehru's visit to the USSR in 1955 was a spectacular triumph. Bulganin and Khruschev came to India in December 1955 and met with a tumultuous welcome. It was during this visit when Khruschev announced that Kashmir was an integral part of India. Indo-Soviet relations intensified in every field. From then on, the Soviet Union could be depended upon not to permit any resolution unfair or hostile to India to be passed in the Security Council.

Nehru was both Prime Minister and Foreign Minister for 17 years. Throughout he relied on Krishna Menon and a few civil servants. Girija Shankar Bajpai was by all accounts outstanding. N.R. Pillai had his good points. S. Dutt was sensible, sound and unflappable. But it was Krishna Menon who had the last word. No institution could cope with so erratic, abrasive, unreasonable and demanding an individual. Instead of managing our foreign policy, our diplomats in London and New York were spending time and energy to manage Krishna Menon. B.K Nehru in his recently published *Memoirs* has, in great detail, described the harm Menon did to Indo-US relations. The first serious doubts on our non-alignment were expressed when Menon disregarded instructions and voted the way he did in the debate on Hungary in the Security Council. The good that Menon had done on Korea and Indo-China was soon forgotten. Next came his Kashmir performance. His nine-hour speech did one thing—it internationalised the issue. It also made people ask—if your case needs nine hours of advocacy it must be weak. In India he became a hero, but we had lost the Kashmir round at the UN. When we analyse and examine the totality of Nehru's achievement, we cannot bypass his handling of the Kashmir situation and our relations with China.

It is now generally agreed that it was an error to refer Kashmir to the Security Council and that too under Chapter VI of the UN Charter. Nehru approached the UN in good faith. He expected justice. All he got was a very cold, cold-war shower. Over the years, the Kashmir question sapped the energies of our diplomats. Too much time had to be devoted just to Kashmir. It must be said in defence of Nehru, that he got Gandhiji's and the Cabinet's approval, for taking the matter to the UN. It must also be remembered that if India had not taken Kashmir to the UN, Pakistan would have.

Nehru with his great knowledge of history, his faith in international goodwill and cooperation, misread the minds of the Chinese Communists. They were a new breed in China, arrogant, confident, ruthless. China as a nation was familiar with statecraft. We were not. Nehru took them at face value. An indepth examination of the 1962 events cannot be made till the People's Republic of China opens its archives.

What we do know is that even on so vital a matter adhocism ruled. Ambassador K.M. Panikkar at Peking carried on his own brand of diplomacy and misinformed the Chinese of our position. At Delhi, there was no integrated or well-thought out plan or policy. K. Subramanyam has written that there were plenty of anecdotal accounts but not "a comprehensive hypothesis" of what went wrong and why. The April 1960 visit of Chou En-lai was grossly mishandled by us. His meeting with Morarji Desai was a disaster. Chou En-lai, the suavest of men, was so put out that he actually walked out of the meeting. It was not a happy chapter in Indian diplomacy. As a young diplomat, I was aghast at Desai's performance. I was the note taker!!

The 1962 decade lowered India's prestige and hastened Nehru's death. In 1961, he had been severely, but unjustly, criticised by the USA and the West for liberating Goa. In 1962, he had to swallow his pride and ask Kennedy and Macmillan for military help. Nehru was a big enough man to concede that we had been living in a world of make-believe. He even invoked the name of Churchill, who had in the 1950s called Nehru the "Light of Asia". When he passed away on May 27, 1964, even his most vocal critics conceded that he was a great man, a good man. Adlai Stevenson said on Nehru's death, "Only a tiny handful of men have influenced the implacable forces of our time. To this small company of the truly great, Pandit Jawaharlal Nehru belongs."

It was not an easy act to follow Nehru as Prime Minister. Lal Bahadur Shastri's tenure was far too short to make a lasting impact on international affairs. He shed the external affairs portfolio and appointed Swaran Singh to the job, who had cut his diplomatic teeth during Chou En-lai's fateful visit to Delhi in April 1960. Shastri himself proved a man of courage, when he responded to Pakistan's aggression in 1965 with vigour and a clear head. His Tashkent foray has been excessively praised. By accepting Soviet brokerage he departed from the established pattern. However, he deserves much credit for allowing Swaran Singh and his delegation to walk out of the Security Council in October 1965, when Bhutto resorted to abuse. Thereafter, the Security Council did not take up Kashmir again.

Mrs Gandhi succeeded Lal Bahadur Shastri in January 1966. She had no direct experience of Government but her name was well known. It did not take her long to get on top of her job and make her presence felt in world fora. On the home front she made sure that India became self-sufficient in foodgrains. India's relations with the USSR had been greatly improved during Nehru's lifetime and she carried the process further, without in any way compromising on any aspect of our foreign policy. With the USA, relations remained strained due to differences over Vietnam, Pakistan, Southern Africa and West Asia.

Three events in her 16 years as Prime Minister assured her a high place in history. There would have been no Bangladesh without her. For almost nine months she showed extreme restraint under massive provocation. She went on a seven-nation tour in September-October 1971, to explain what was happening in East Pakistan and the burden it placed on India.

Her diplomacy was eminently successful. The USA was isolated as even her NATO allies supported the Indian view of the crisis in East Pakistan. In her talks with Western leaders and Nixon and Kissinger, she made it clear that there was no Indo-Pak dispute involved—the quarrel was between Pakistan's two wings—between the freely elected Awami League leadership and Yahya Khan's ruthless military dictatorship.

After the surrender of the Pakistani army in Bangladesh on December 16, 1971, she did not extend the war to West Pakistan—

93,000 officers and men of the Pakistan Army surrendered. In the aftermath, she acted in a statesman-like manner. She did not humiliate a defeated Pakistan. By signing the Simla Agreement in July 1972, she ensured durable peace between the two countries. Her world stature grew. She had altered the map of the subcontinent and the geopolitics of the region. Having signed a treaty of friendship with the Soviet Union in August 1971, she ensured that China would not intervene on behalf of Pakistan. The Americans were too busy courting China clandestinely to do anything till it was too late. Even the Seventh Fleet was rendered useless by the speed with which India acted in December 1971.

The next great event was the Pokhran nuclear test. Mrs Gandhi broke the atomic barrier and told the world that Indian scientists were second to none. Why she did not go on to a nuclear weapons programme remains a mystery. Had she done so, we would have been spared the pressures put on us for signing the NPT and the CTBT now.

Finally, she took a significant step in raising the level of our diplomatic representation in China, from Charge d'Affaires to Ambassador. She wanted a non-adverserial relationship with China. This step eventually led to Rajiv Gandhi's successful visit to China in 1988.

Her second tenure (1980-84), though less eventful, was marked by an improvement in Indo-US relations. She also made her displeasure on the Soviet intervention in Afghanistan known to Brezhnev in no uncertain terms.

When she was assassinated, India's foreign policy and diplomacy were in a healthy state. There was internal unity and political stability, social and economic progress and a defence capability not to be scoffed at. She had proved that India had an independent foreign policy. She achieved a broad balance in our relations with the major nations. She gave our policy a certain and desirable flexibility. She also put new life in the NAM during her Chairmanship following the 7th Summit in New Delhi. She was without doubt the most respected Head of Government in the Commonwealth and her presidency over the Commonwealth Summit in November 1983 was the culmination of her ascendency on the world stage.

From March 1977 to January 1980, the Governments of Morarji Desai and Charan Singh were too busy reconciling contradictions to have much time for conducting a meaningful diplomacy and a forceful foreign policy. It is noteworthy that there was no U-turn in the foreign policy arena. The phrase "genuine non-alignment", when used by the Desai Government, invited derision and Atal Behari Vajpayee soon dropped it. He, it must be said to his credit, invoked the names of Gandhiji and Pandit Nehru in several of his foreign policy pronouncements. His serious attempt to further improve relations with China was aborted by China attacking Vietnam during his visit to China.

In a celebrated article that Mrs Gandhi wrote in the October 1972 issue of Foreign Affairs, she outlined for her American audience the tenets of our foreign policy, and what made us tick:

> *India's foreign policy is a projection of the values which we have cherished through the centuries as well as our current concerns. We are not tied to the traditional concepts of foreign policy designed to safeguard overseas possessions, investments, the carving out of areas of influence, the erection of Cordon's Sanitaires. We are not interested in exporting ideologies.*

She further stated:

> *Our first concern was to prevent the erosion of our Independence. Therefore, we could not be camp followers of any power, however rich and strong. We had equal interest in the maintenance and safeguarding of international peace as an essential condition of India's economic, social and political development. In the bipolar world which existed in the immediate post-war era, Jawaharlal Nehru refused to join either block. He decided to remain non-aligned as a means of safeguarding of our Independence and contributing to the maintenance of world peace. Non-alignment implied neither non-involvement nor neutrality. It was an assertion of our freedom of judgement and action. We have not hesitated to express our views on any major controversy or support just causes.*

Such was the high-minded yet practical legacy Rajiv Gandhi inherited when he became Prime Minister on October 31, 1984. He took to foreign affairs as a duck takes to water. He had brio, flair and relished the sophistication that made diplomacy both an art and a craft. His first real exposure on the world scene was at the Nassau Commonwealth Summit in the Bahamas in October 1985. His debut was memorable. He spoke after Margaret Thatcher and came out with flying colours. He got on first names with Hawke, Kaunda, Mugabe, David Lange, Brian Mulrooney, etc. On South Africa he took on Thatcher, who in her autobiography has given a totally one-sided account of the acrimonious discussions on South Africa. A compromise was worked out with Rajiv Gandhi's help and it was decided to send an Eminent Persons Group to South Africa under the Chairmanship of General Obasanjo and Malcolm Fraser. Mrs Thatcher did not agree to sanctions and did herself no good by appearing as a quasi supporter of the racist regime. Her harassed Foreign Minister, Geoffrey Howe, could hardly conceal his embarrassment.

At Nassau, Rajiv Gandhi earned his spurs and Lee Kuan Yew, the seniormost member of the Commonwealth Club, told him, "We now have a fresh young voice on the international horizon. Listening to you, I was reminded of your grandfather."

At the Harare NAM Summit in September 1986, Rajiv Gandhi played a crucial role in reconciling opposing positions, establishing the Africa Fund and preventing a 'local war' between Iran and Iraq at the Summit. He and Fidel Castro were the two Heads who made the Summit a business-like gathering, to bring back those colleagues gently to earth when their flights of fancy made them abandon ground reality, even on South Africa.

Rajiv Gandhi may not be remembered for the NAM and CHOGM Summits he attended. He will be remembered with gratitude for the Delhi Declaration which he signed with Mikhail Gorbachev in November 1986. This was a historic document, which gave new hope to humankind. In his *Memoirs* Gorbachev writes:

> *I established a warm personal rapport with Rajiv Gandhi. I was deeply impressed by the way he organically combined the profound philosophical tradition of India and the East with a perfect knowledge and*

comprehension of European culture. He had great personal charm and was endowed with many human virtues. Rajiv was devoted to the cause of his grandfather, Jawaharlal Nehru, and his mother, Indira Gandhi—his life's aim was the renaissance of India.

This vision of a new world order of the two leaders was reflected in the Delhi Declaration signed by the two of them at Rashtrapati Bhavan on November 27, 1986:

In the nuclear age, mankind must develop a new political thinking and a new concept of the world which provides sound guarantees for the survival of mankind. The world we have inherited belongs to present and future generations alike—hence, we must give priority to universal human values. Human life must be acknowledged as the supreme value. Non-violence must become the basis for human co-existence.

Here was the leader of the Communist Party of the Soviet Union putting his signatures on a document extolling non-violence. Nothing even remotely similar had happened in the history of Communism.

At the Vancouver CHOGM in October 1987, Rajiv Gandhi again played a primary role. He got a unanimous approval of the Commonwealth for the Indo-Sri Lanka Agreement. And 1988 was his best year. In June, he presented his Action Plan for ushering in a Nuclear Weapon Free and Non-Violent World to the UN at New York. This was, in fact, a charter for peace. Unfortunately, it did not suit the Super Powers to let India take the lead in this field and the plan remained a passionate exhortation.

In December 1988, Rajiv Gandhi paid his trail-blazing visit to China, the first by an Indian Prime Minister in 34 years. I personally held the view that he should have gone to Peking in 1985 or 1986, when his authority and popularity was at its peak. But our anti-China lobby still had considerable say. When he brought me as Minister of State in the Ministry of External Affairs in October 1986, I told him that top priority should be given to improving our relations with China. And only the grandson of Nehru and the son of Mrs Gandhi could de-freeze Sino-Indian relations. What kind of a foreign policy were we conducting? Our relations with Pakistan were strained, with the USA uncertain and with China in deep freeze. He immediately gave me full authority to go ahead and plan the China visit: "I have no 1962 hang-ups. Go ahead full speed." This was leadership. We worked on the visit for almost 18 months, preparing the country, Parliament and the Opposition for it. When he embarked on his passage to Peking, he had the country behind him. After his talks with Deng Xiaoping, a breakthrough was achieved. A message went round that the confrontational phase was giving place to a period of cooperation and reconciliation. No concessions were made by either side. The border question was not skirted. The atmosphere changed. That was no small achievement. Addressing the Qinghua University on December 21, 1988 in Peking, he said:

> *I see optimism in both India and China today: optimism about the progress our countries can make, optimism about realising our goals of development, optimism about the levels of cooperation we can reach, optimism about the work we can do together to restore our countries to their traditional position in the vanguard of human civilization, optimism about the contribution we can make to rebuilding the world order nearer our heart's desire.*
>
> *We are summoned by the past to the tasks which the future holds. We have a mutual obligation to a common humanity. India and China can together give the world new perspectives on a new world order, which will ensure peace among nations.*

The border issue remains unresolved, but both countries have accepted that a final settlement will be a negotiated one.

He took special interest in our relations with Pakistan. Had President Zia-ul-Haq not died in an aircrash in 1988, he and the Indian Prime Minister would have reached an agreement on Siachin. His visit to Islamabad in December 1988, the first by an Indian Prime Minister in 28 years, did much to reduce tension between the two countries.

Rajiv Gandhi believed that India had a distinctive role to play in world affairs. We could only do so because we were economically strong, technologically up-to-date and politically cohesive. He repeatedly asserted that the region extending from the Pamirs to the Mekong was of special relevance to India.

It is one of the great tragedies of our times that his life was cut short when India and the world were in sore need of his services.

Foreign policy between 1990 and 1996 received low priority in our national agenda. The Governments of V. P. Singh and Chandra Shekhar had inbuilt limitations and were too shortlived to make any impact. Narasimha Rao in his five years travelled much, spoke frequently but the results were not spectacular. For almost four years of his five-year tenure, he did not deem it necessary to have a full-time foreign minister. The collapse of the Soviet Union in 1991 removed from the map of the world a staunch friend and benefactor of India. No deep analysis was attempted to analyse this profound, world-shaking development and the security implications that India faced with the USSR were no longer there.

The Cabinet seldom discussed foreign policy, the Cabinet Committee on foreign affairs never met. Worst of all, Kashmir was allowed to be internationalised and low level functionaries of the US State Department were fawned upon and feted by the Rao Government. Narasimha Rao did, however, dramatically improve India's economic standing by his liberalisation policy. At NAM and the UN India appeared as an absentee. It must in fairness be noted that Rao carried forward Rajiv Gandhi's China policy. In 1993, India and China signed a Sino-Indian Agreement on Maintaining Peace and Tranquillity along the Line of Actual Control and Reducing Military Forces in the Border Areas pending a final solution.

When the Deve Gowda Government took over in May 1996, it was feared that a coalition of 13-14 parties could neither survive long nor could it conduct a meaningful foreign policy. The extraordinary fact is that Minister I.K. Gujral achieved considerable success in his quiet way. His speech at the UN General Assembly on October 4, 1996, had distinct Nehruite content. Relations with Bangladesh, Nepal, ASEAN (Association of South-East Asian Nations) have been strengthened. There is now hope for improvement on our relations with Pakistan.

Thus, at the end of 50 years, Jawaharlal Nehru's vision remains intact, relevant and indispensable. We must now look ahead. What choices do we have in a rapidly changing world which throws up new challenges with unprecedented speed? All over the world voices are clamouring to proclaim their version of the future. On one side we have Henry Kissinger, who writes in *Diplomacy*:

The international system of the twenty-first century will be marked by a seeming contradiction: on the one hand, fragmentation, on the other, growing globalisation. On the level of the relations among States, the new order will be more like the European State System of the eighteenth and nineteenth centuries than the rigid patterns of the Cold War. It will consist at least of six major powers—the United States, Europe, China, Japan, Russia and probably India.

Professor Samuel Huntington in his book, *The Clash of Civilizations and the Remaking of the World Order*, tells us, "In the post-Cold War world, the most important distinctions among people are not ideological, political or economic. They are cultural. People and nations are attempting to answer the most basic questions humans can face: Who are we? ... The most important groupings of States are no longer the three blocs of the Cold War, but rather the seven or eight major civilizations." These he lists as the Chinese, the Japanese, the Hindu, the Islamic, the Western, the Latin American, the Orthodox and the African (possibly). His view is that future wars will be between civilisations. One can't help reminding the Professor that civilisations have neither armies nor foreign policies.

Americans are rather adept at producing well-packaged formulas (quick-fixes if you wish to be colloquial). These they promote with Messianic fervour or Evangelical zeal, even when the authors have Jewish names. After being ardently isolationist for one hundred and twenty-five years, the United States have for the past fifty years been crusading interventionists. No less a Guru than George Kennan has written with compelling candour about his great country's foreign policy assumptions and presumptions in his best selling book, *Around The Cragged Hill* thus:

I should make it clear that I am wholly and emphatically rejecting any and all Messionic concepts of America's role in the world: rejecting the illusions of unique and superior virtue on our part, the prattle about Manifest Destiny or the "American Century" ... And if there were any qualities that lie within our ability to cultivate that might set us off from the rest of the world, there would be the virtues of modesty and humility; and of these we have never exhibited any exceptional abundance....

We Indians are long suffering but also cussed. We don't like being pushed around. We don't seek confrontation or conflict. At the same time, India will accept no one's hegemony. The world needs *Pax Planitica*, not *Pax Americana*.

We are all ignorant about the future. Yet, each one of us has a vital stake in it, for the simple reason that we are all going to spend the rest of our lives there. Ignorance of the future, however, does not relieve us from the responsibility of chartering a path of action. Life compels us to plan for the future. Nations are doomed if they do not resort to contingency planning. Certain trends, some straws in the wind, past precedents, the lesions of history act as guides and warnings. The choice so often, as Nehru said, is not between good and evil, it is between the lesser and the greater evil, between one-fourth good and the rest three-fourths between bad and worse. There is no blueprint for the future. After thousands of years we are still groping.

If I had my way, I would postpone the twenty-first century. Alas! no one can. I think it was Harold R. Isaacs, the American author who made the telling observation, "We have entered the post-industrial age before two-thirds of the world had barely begun to emerge from the pre-industrial era...." Deng Xiaoping also observed that his goal was to bring the majority of his people to the twentieth century before taking them to the twenty-first!

We now have several studies about organising the world order of the next century. Paul Kennedy gave us his book, *Preparing for the Twenty-First Century.* In more recent times, three important reports have appeared. *Uncommon Opportunities,* an agenda for Peace and Equitable Development, was prepared by the International Commission on Peace and Food which was chaired by Dr. M.S. Swaminathan. This was followed by *Our Global Neighbourhood,* the report of the Commission on Global Governance, headed by Ingvar

Carlson of Sweden and Shridath Ramphal, Secretary General of the Commonwealth. In 1996 appeared, *Caring for the Future,* the report of the Independent Commission on Population and the Quality of Life. This was chaired by Maria de Lourdes Pintasilgo of Portugal. All list the challenges and offer choices. These can be broadly identified: Preserving peace, reforming democracy and the United Nation's ensuring economic growth accompanied by equity and social justice. In other words, a just world order committed to just means. Environment and ecology, science and technology should be used to uplift humanity, not exploit or expropriate. Population control is of paramount importance in China, India, Brazil, Africa. Finally, the need to emphasise that any new order must have an ethical underpinning so that ends do not justify the means.

This is the global scenario. Now we come to India. In the post-Cold War era, the USA is pre-eminent but not supreme. We do riot live in a unipolar world. With the break-up of the Soviet Union, an alternative point of view has disappeared. There is much talk of a homogenised world. This India must resist. Our diversity is our strength. Our variety, our glory. India is perhaps the only country which can act as a bridge between the industrialised West (G7) and the developing world.

There is growing dissatisfaction with the functioning of NAM and since December 1989, India's passive role has invited adverse comment. Much is heard of the irrelevance of non-alignment. Why do we need NAM? One might ask, why do we need NATO? It must, nevertheless be conceded that NAM has performed poorly on several issues—the Iran-Iraq war, PLO-Israeli issues (Norway, not NAM took the lead to find solutions), Yugoslavia, Afghanistan, Bosnia, NPT, CTBT, WTO. The movement showed lack of solidarity on all these issues, as also on the reform of the UN. It is imperative that India shows more interest in NAM and comes out with new ideas. If the movement could speak with one voice on colonialism, racialism, disarmament, then why can it not do so on environment, terrorism, drugs, etc.? Narasimha Rao was right when he said in Tokyo in 1992, "That the pursuit of a non-aligned foreign policy is even more relevant in the post-Cold War period than even before ... regardless of the bloc phenomenon ... the chimera of hegemonism must not be pursued."

That the movement is relevant is proved by its growing membership. Russia, China and Germany obtained Observer Status. NAM needs blood transfusion, it needs energising. India must reassert itself and tell fellow members that self-reliance is more realistic than running after the industrialised world, where growth is down, unemployment up (12 per cent in Germany). We should think carefully before tying up our economic and foreign policies to an area which is showing weakness. NAM countries are being pushed around by the new international Maharajas—the IMF and the World Bank. We are being manipulated by multinationals. This is not to suggest that we give up liberalisation of our economy. Our macro management had been wrong and, therefore, what the Finance Minister Manmohan Singh did in 1991 was necessary. But the market philosophy is not the whole answer. In ASEAN countries, growth and development was spearheaded by the State, not the shopfloor. The market can never be a substitute for the State. Given our pluralistic, humanistic democracy, we and so many non-aligned States cannot abandon the role of the State. The market has not offered any evidence that it is capable by itself of responding to fundamental human needs. One billion people live on one dollar a day. What is the market doing for them?

What should our foreign policy/diplomatic priorities be? Our voice will carry greater weight if there is an improvement in our relations with Pakistan. For 50 years, the two countries have spent astronomical amounts on defence, on arms race in the Indian subcontinent—in today's world it is a luxury we cannot afford. Within the five principles of Panchsheel and the Simla Agreement, we should start a sustained peace process and lower tensions. We must stop apportioning blame, but work for constructive cooperation. Don't we see what is happening in the rest of the world? Agreed, that no two situations are identical or similar; we cannot run away from the fact that yesterday's enemies are today's friends—USA and Japan,

France and Germany, Russia and America, China and Russia, China and Japan, the PLO and Israel, America and Vietnam. Mandela has produced a near miracle in South Africa. I am not being starry-eyed, sentimental or unrealistic when I ask—Cannot the land of the Buddha, Ashoka and Gandhi give the lead in diffusing permanent turbulence and tensions in our subcontinent? The Gowda Government deserves support for its foreign policy initiatives. Once the message goes round that India and Pakistan are genuinely seeking peaceful solutions, other things will begin to fall in place. Let us dare to think the unthinkable, make the impossible happen. War is not the answer. Acceptable compromise is. Begin serious negotiations with Pakistan on all issues; including Kashmir without pre-conditions. We now have in Srinagar a Government with a three-fourths majority. Use Farooq Abdullah as Gowda and Gujral used Jyoti Basu. The people in both countries are tired of this issue, which was not made an election issue by Nawaz Sharif. That is a dramatic change in Pakistan's mood.

Next, India should make SAARC (South Asian Association for Regional Cooperation) the pivot of her foreign policy. We should aim at the establishment of a SAARC common market. The economic potential of SAARC is greater than that of ASEAN. Even India's GNP will be twice that of ASEAN, once we reach 8 per cent growth.

With China, we should have even closer relations. Our economics are similar and so are our needs. I am aware of the hurdles we face while trading with China. These can be overcome. In the past, some people talked of an India-Soviet axis opposed to the Peking-Pakistan-Pentagon axis. This is outmoded thinking.

The State visit to India of China's President Jiang Zemin was the first ever by the Head of State and Party. The agreement signed in New Delhi on November 29, 1996, by the two countries, 'On confidence-building measures in the military field along the Line of Actual Control in the India-China border areas,' is a significant positive step forward in maintaining peace and tranquillity on the India-China border. The agreement accords with the fundamental interests of the two peoples and will also contribute to the ultimate solution of the boundary question. The dark clouds are finally dispersing and both countries are now set on the path of a stable and friendly relationship.

We should not alter our principled stand either on NPT or the CTBT unless the treaties take into account our concerns and make these documents truly democratic. Efforts will be made to pressurise us, these must be resisted. Similarly, we should make no concessions on our nuclear programme and policy. We should make it clear that India is in no way influenced by what Pakistan does on the nuclear question. If Pakistan wants to produce a nuclear bomb, it is for that country to decide. It really is extraordinary that the Permanent Five in the Security Council should preach nuclear disarmament to the world, having themselves violated every single rule in the book. They have no moral right to do so. Their hands are not clean. We should never dilute the intensity of our opposition to such double standards.

The Charter of the United Nations is one of this century's noblest and high-minded documents in many respects. After 52 years of wear and tear, it is in urgent need of revision. The fiftieth anniversary of the UN in 1995, provided a good opportunity for having a fresh look at the inadequacies of the Charter. This opportunity was allowed to pass without any serious effort to reform, renovate, restructure the UN system. The veto power bestowed on the five Permanent Members of the Security Council is an affront to all other members. It was insisted upon by the USA in 1945.

The 1945 euphoria led a generally unenthusiastic man like Cordell Hull, the US Secretary of State at that time, to make the following astounding observation:

There will no longer be need for spheres of influence, for alliances, balances of power, or any other special arrangements through which, in the unhappy past, the nations strove to safeguard their security or to promote their interests.

Subsequent events have shown how misplaced was Hull's optimism.

In the 1930s, Britain and France all but killed the League of Nations by condoning the aggressions of Japan, Italy and Germany.

Today, the US is busy strangulating the UN by starving it financially. Today, that body inspires neither confidence nor hope. It evokes derision. It has become a graveyard of new ideas. The Security Council is the most undemocratic body in the world. It needs drastic reform. India cannot turn its back on the UN, but we should not invest too much in such a body, till the Charter is revised. It was a monumental folly to have contested the non-permanent seat against Japan in 1996.

With the USA, Western Europe, the UK (still an influential country), Japan, Russia, we should expand and enlarge our relations in all areas. We should modernise, not Westernise. We should be among the winners and not losers in this game. The Arab world, Africa and Latin America have been our traditional friends. These ties need renewal and restructuring.

On a more practical note, we need to have many more of our diplomats fluent in Chinese, Japanese, Russian, Korean, Vietnamese languages, so that they can compete and interact linguistically with the nationals of these countries. The Government should also utilise the experience and wisdom of our retired diplomats. Other countries do so with great success.

If India has a message, and I believe she has, it is the message of Gandhi as spelt out in the Delhi Declaration by Rajiv Gandhi and Mikhail Gorbachev. The fundamental question is, can the new century encourage an appreciation of the revolutionary potential of Gandhi's creed of non-violence? Humankind needs a non-violent approach to international security and disarmament. The traditional mind-set has to be discarded. The much-touted globalisation must work from below and not be imposed from above. The information highways should provide space for ethical roadways too. Knowledge and information must be tempered by wisdom.

India can play a creative part in making and shaping the twenty-first century, provided we have unity, stability and cohesion. We are good at reconciling contradictions in society, adept at converting our diversities into assets. For the political, economic and social transformation of our polity we need faithful agents (Gandhi's phrase) and strong institutions. Both are in short supply. Democracy is being degraded in several States of the Union. This needs immediate and effective correctives.

There is a lot going for us. A mood of gloom and doom is unworthy of us. Let us never forget the words of Iqbal:

Yunano Misr Ruma Sab Mit Gaye Jahan Se,
Abtak Magar Hai Baqi Namo Nishan Hamara
Kuch Bat Hai Ki Hasti Mitti Nahain Hamari
Sadiyon Raha Hai Dushman Daure-zaman Hamara.

(Ancient Greece, Egypt and Rome have all lost their traces. But India survives as a unity. There is something in our country, that though for centuries we have been besieged by enemies, we still retain our identity.)

24

The Widening Inequality Gap in India

The annual Oxfam survey was discussed during the recently held World Economic Forum held in Davos, Switzerland. At Davos, it is said, the billionaires tell the millionaires what to do and where to get off.

The Oxfam survey, in parts, gave some figures about India: 73% of the wealth India generated went to 1% of the richest. The country's richest 1% held 58% of its total wealth. During the last twelve months the rich became richer. The gap between the haves and the have nuts grew further. India has 101 billionaires. 37% of this elite have inherited their wealth. 57% of India's wealth is owned by 37% billionaires. Only four women are billionaires.

The number of those living below the poverty line is two hundred and fifty million, equal to the combined population of Germany, U.K., France and Italy.

Coming as I do from Rajasthan, I obviously keenly follow what goes on and what does not go on in my home state. I was more than surprised by the annihilation of the B.J.P in Alwar, Ajmer and Mandalgarh. The political consequences for this electoral set back cannot be ignored. The B.J.P has 158 M.L.As in a House of two hundred. But politics is not only about numbers. Perception is equally important. In Bengal too the B.J.P could find no comfort. The party is facing hostile head winds.

The Congress had got a shot in the arm, to use a tired cliché. One can notice a spring in the walk of Congressmen. Sonia Gandhi is too astute a politician to allow her party to succumb to syrupy smugness.

In January 1953 I was interviewed by the U.P.S.C at Dholpur House near India Gate. The interview was followed by a group discussion. The subject was "Untouchability having been abolished, the caste system too should follow." The participants, besides me were three other aspirants. The discussion was conducted a minor deity of the U.P.S.C.

Sixty five years later there is no sign of caste disappearing. In the castrating words of diplomat turned politician, Pavan Verma, over the years the cast system remains "the most inflexible institutionalized tyrannies of any society."

Lok Sabha and Assembly elections are conducted on caste lines. In December 1984 I fought my first Lok Sabha election as a Congress candidate. I was in for an unpleasant surprise. Caste was omnipresent. Even gotras were scrutinized and used as weapons to defeat a particular candidate. Caste in today's elections is even more decisive a factor than it was over thirty years back.

Apart from legislative action, technology too has played a role in knocking down several caste barriers. One example will prove my point. In planes and railways an upper class (whatever that means) cannot decide who will sit next to him.

Will the cast menace totally ever disappear. No, is my answer. I try not to mix hopes with facts.

When the India-U.S nuclear deal bill was passed in the Lok Sabha a decade ago there was ostentations chest thumping and unseemly back slapping. This was touted as the biggest feather in Dr. Manmohan Singh's turban. The Nuclear deal was not his number one achievement. That was his electrifying a dead economy. This alone has ensured him his niche in history. For all practical purposes the "deal" is dead. A new deal is not yet in sight.

For the next few days Delhi will pay a multiplicity of tributes to Mirza Ghalib, who is a national treasure. Life had not treated him kindly. He was man enough to write – *mushquilen mujh par padi itni ke aasaan ho gayeen*.

I have been thinking about M.F. Husain these past few days. For decades we were intimate friends. He died aged 97 in 2012. A few days back an illustrated book of his poetic letters—all in English, turned up. It is inscribed to my wife Hem and Myself. 10. XII '67. I had no recollection of it till its rediscovery.

25

A.I.C.C Plenary and not Evoke Emotions

The plenary session of the A.I.C.C concluded earlier in the week. The Indira Gandhi Stadium was the right venue. The mosquitos kept the delegates alert and awake. Minister Navjot Sidhu enlivened the proceedings. He is, to use a, not so elegant phrase, a man for all seasons. I have met him only once. I doubt if he remembers. I was reminded of it when I saw him greeting Sonia Gandhi by touching her feet. His blue outfit was an excellent example of sartorial elegance.

I have attended several such sessions. The most memorable was the centenary session held in December 1985 held in Bombay. Prime Minister Rajiv Gandhi's speech left all present spell bound. It was not only inspiring. It was a clarion call to the organisation to prepare itself for the 21st century. And do so with dedication, resolution and vigour. He denounced the power brokers.

Regrettably the implementation was derailed by them. They felt at unease. They distrusted change. They were stuck in out dated political grooves.

I shall not comment on the speeches made at this week's session, except to say that these were serviceable. The resolutions did not make me think nor warmed my heart. If I remember rightly, in one of the resolutions the words, "Congress doctrine" were used. This astonished me. The Congress has always shunned doctrine and dogma. Its traditions are Gandhian. Its ideological and intellectual moorings are Nehruite.

The absence of creative, newly minted and uplifting ideas was all too evident. John F. Kennedy in his inaugural address in January 1961 mentioned "Nehru's soaring" vision. Vision was missing at the Indira Gandhi Stadium. Rahul Gandhi has his work cut out.

Two important elections were held in the past two weeks. President XI Jinping was re-elected to a second term, with no time limit. He could serve a third or fourth term. His is the fifth generation of the leadership of the Communist Party of the Peoples Republic of China. Mao Tse Tung was the pioneer—the great helmsman-second generation leader was Deng Xiaoping. The third generation leader was Jiang Zemin. Fourth generation was led by Hu Jintao.

President Vladimir Putin has already been at the top for eighteen years. He was elected for another six years term. That will make him the longest serving Russian leader after Joseph who was the supremo from 1924 to 1953.

I met President Hu Jintao twice. Putin three times. Last time in Leningrad in 2005. I had accompanied Sonia Gandhi. She was Putin's personal guest. We saw much of him. Even his worst critics will concede that he is immensely popular in Russia.

President Ronal Trump is a very original kind of occupant of the White House. He acts like a Chief Executive Officer of his business empire. Firing his senior advisors at will. There now number twenty eight. More are in the White House exit tunnel. His private life is quite something. A number of women have accused him of.... You know what I mean. The extensive adverse media coverage in this regard only, does not bother the President. It bothers the World. Past Presidents have had enterprising private lives. President John F. Kennedy had many flings. Not a word leaked out as long as he was alive.

President Franklin D Roosevelt died in April 1945. His mistress was with him. Not a whisper was heard.

In the early summer of May 1978 I got on the wrong side of Morarjibhai Desai. He was Prime Minister. I was High Commissioner of India in Lusaka, Zambia. President Kaunda had written to the Prime Minister in very lauditary terms. Morarji Desai did not share Kenneth Kaunda's assessment of K. Natwar Singh. I wrote the following letter to the Prime Minister on 15th May 1978:

High Commission of India,
Lusaka

Dear Prime Minister,

On my return to Lusaka, I saw your reply to President's letter opf 18th December 1977. The President had referred to my work in generous terms. Normally Government should have welcome this warmly, but the extreme austerity of your reply must make my task in Lusaka infinitely more difficult. I am sure it was not your intention to be belittle or undermine the position of your High Commissioner in Zambia, but such an inference can be drawn and is being drawn. This is not a personal matter.

Having been claeed a, "distinguished and trusted citizen of India" in my letters of credence, I continue to hope that I have your full trust and confidence, without which no diplomate can discharge his duties and responsibilities.

With respects,

Yours Sincerely
(K. Natwar Singh)

Shri Morarji Desai,
Prime Minister's Office,
New Delhi

Prime Minister Desai's reply will appear in my next column.

26

Engaging Ideas, Picking Best Title for Book

My autobiography, "One Life is Not Enough" was published in August 2014. Its success came as a surprise to me and the publishers. We had expected a sale of about fifteen thousand. It sold many more. Perhaps the timing was propitious.

"One Life is Not Enough" has been translated into Hindi, Gujarati, Bengali and Marathi. For some time friends have been asking me, "Are you writing another book." My answer has been straight forward. I tell them that after the success of "One Life is Not Enough," I felt that the next book could be a flop. That is why I hesitated.

Over the months doubts began to recede. Last Sunday I took the plunge ... What should the book be about. The preliminary title is, "Mentors and Friends." The mentors are Rabindranath Tagore, Mohandas Karamchand Gandhi, Jawaharlal Nehru, Parmeshwar Narayan Haksar, Indira Gandhi. The friends are E.M Forster, R.K. Narayan, Krishna Kripalani, Amaury de Reincourt, Han Suyin. Drawing the list was far from easy.

Asma Jahangir's death last week attracted much attention in India. She was well known in Delhi and Mumbai. As a human rights crusader Asma was admired and respected. To many she was an inspiration. In her country she had to fight all the way to make Pakistan aware of the rights of women. During Zia-ul-Haq's regime she was arrested. On her release she started where she left off.

In the last decade of her life she became an international entity, particularly at the United Nations. Asma Jahangir sincerely felt that Pakistan should have cordial and good neighbourly relations with India. This made some of her compatriots fume. She did not give up. That needed guts'.

What is common between Robert Mugabe of Zimbabwe and Jacob Juma of South Africa? Both resigned only when impeachment faced them. Mugabe misruled for thirty seven years. Zumba for nine. Jacob Zumba is still remains a member of the A.N.C-African National Congress. This is the party of Nelson Mandela. Nelson Mandela could have ruled South Africa till his death in 2013. He refused a second term in 1999.

Finally Nepal has a prime minister. K.P. Sharma Oli is sixty five years old. This is his second term. Nepal needs a stable government and one that does not collapse on account of squabbles of his partners in the coalition government. This has happened for too often in the past.

Prime Minister Oli has his work cut out. It is not an easy task. His foreign policy and diplomacy will take up much of his time. These will need uncommon adroitness and dexterity. Prime Minister Oli has the reputation of being a leftist, whatever that may mean in a post ideological and fractured world. Even China has shed its Maoist Marxism. It is now under the spell of Xi Jingpingism.

Prime Minister Oli flew to Beijing before electing to come to India. One need not read too much into this, but in diplomacy gestures are an indication. I have little doubt that the Nepalese leader will pay a little more attention to India regardless of his ideological prejudices. Similarly we too should go out of our way to make his task easier, keeping in mind his political inclinations. During the monarchy, Nepal's foreign policy depended on the whims of the Kings, who were surrounded by professional flatterers and sycophants.

The Maldives are no longer on the front page of newspapers. We did well not to undertake a military intervention.

Rajiv Gandhi, got away with his diplomatic adventure in 1988 because China was then not a navigator in the troubled waters of the Maldives. Today it is a major power in the area. The President of the Maldives unnecessarily burnt his fingers by his authoritarian functioning. Fortunately the temperature has now cooled down. We on our part should be vigilant and not sanguine.

If R.S.S Chief Mohan Bhagwat did not exist, it would not be necessary to invent him. His uncalled pronouncement that his outfit could do more for national security in three days what our military would achieve in six months. He has the reputation of a wise and sagacious individual, who normally uses his words carefully. Men of his stature cannot afford lapses of this kind.

27

Nehru Transformed Commonwealth

I have attended five CHOGAM summits, Kingstone, Jamaica 1975, Lusaka, Zambia 1979, New Delhi 1983, Vancouver, Canada 1987, Kaulalampur, Malaysia 1989. Nehru transformed the Commonwealth from a racist white man's club, consisting of the U.K., Canada, South Africa, Australia and New Zealand. Today the membership adds up to fifty three. India's population is twice as much as that of all the other 52 nations. India, Pakistan and Sri Lanka were till 1950 members of the old Commonwealth. On becoming republic in 1950, Nehru made it clear that India could not remain a member unless the Commonwealth made itself relevant to the second half of the 20th century. King was no longer to be Emperor of India.

Prime Minister Modi was the most important and sought after Head at the London Summit. The next Summit will see Prince Charles as Head of the Commonwealth. His mother has occupied that post since 1952.

I was Chief Co-ordinator of the 7th CHOGAM Summit held in New Delhi in November 1983.

To my delight and surprise I received the following letter from her:

PRIME MINISTER'S HOUSE
NEW DELHI

14 December 1983

Dear Natwar,

I have been meaning to write ever since the Commonwealth Heads of Governments left but each day has been busier than the last.

CHOGAM was another successful demonstration of our organisational capability and of the team spirit which we are able to muster on special occasions. As Chief Coordinator, you shouldered the bulk of the responsibility. I want to congratulate you on the smooth functioning of the meetings at all levels and for the excellent arrangements. Please convey my congratulations to all the members of your team.

With good wishes,

Yours Sincerely
(Indira Gandhi)

Shri Natwar Singh
Secretary (PC),
Ministry of External Affairs,
New Delhi

I read the full text of Dr. Manmohan Singh's Rangnekar Memorial Lecture which he delivered in Chandigarh last week. I read it carefully and with deep interest. Prof. Rangnekar was one of the founders of the Department of Economics of the Punjab University after the partition of India in 1947. Manmohan Singh joined the department as an M.A student in 1952. "He was a great teacher who inspired me to go to Cambridge."

In his lecture he has addressed fundamental questions that are of concern to all thinking and alert people. He quotes Dr. Ambedkar, "It is not that India was never an independent country. The point is that she once lost the independence she had. Will she lose it a second time? Will Indians place the country above their creed or will they place creed above the Country? I do not know...."

I am in agreement with most of what he said. I differ from his preaching the Gospel of equality. The world is an unequal place. Nature is not known for equality Human beings lead appallingly unequal lives. The Almighty is not a democrat. Manmohan Singh was born to become an economist of genius. His driver is less fortunate. Duffers rule, the wealthy look down on the poor, not all elected representatives respect equality. Criminals get elected to the Lok Sabha while in jail. We are rightly proud of our one man one vote. Who got elected and how. Of the present members of the Lok Sabha almost 70% have not spoken even once. That probably is a blessing in disguise. Heaven knows what verbal outrages they would have committed. Having said this, I like E.M. Forster give "Two Cheers for Democracy." One because it admits variety and two because it permits criticism.

I have been re-reading Amrit Rai's biography of his father, Munshi Prem Chand 1880-1936. The book is in Hindi, over 600 pages long. Prem Chand remains the most creative, talented and inspiring Hindi novelist and story writer of all time. He wrote his earliest stories in Urdu, shifting to Hindi when Gandhiji arrived on the scene.

A few months before his death Prem Chand was invited by the Hindu Prachar Sabha to address its annual convocation. The broad subject was the spreading of Hindi in a non-Hindi speaking state.

Addressing himself to the Muslim diehards Prem Chand said:

"I ask you, why do you feel so murderously towards Hindi? Do you know—and if not, then you very well ought to know—that the first poet in Hindi, who sowed the seed of literary Hindi ... was [a Muslim] Amir Khusro? Do you know that upwards of five hundred Muslim poets have so far enriched Hindi with their works and that some of them rank among the top poets in the language? Do you know that Akbar and Jahangir and even Aurangzeb had a taste for Hindi poetry and that it was Aurangzeb who had given to new varieties of mangoes [pure Sanskrit] names such as Rasana-vilas and Sudha-ras? Do you know that even today poets such as Hasrat and Hafeez Jalandhari occasionally try their poetic prowess in Hindi? Do you know that thousands of nouns and verbs in Hindi have originally come from Arabic and Persian and are now completely at home in it? And if you know all this and still discriminate between Urdu and Hindi, then you do an injustice to your country and to yourselves.... I have a complaint against my Muslim friends, that they shun even the most easily understood Hindi words."

28

Bypoll Results have Altered Political Landscape

The electoral guillotine is merciless. The ubiquitous Amit Shah is for once observing *monvrat*. This is wise of him. Phulpur and Gorakhpur results are no routine political events. The ramifications are country wide. These adverse results will most certainly influence the outcome of the election in Karnataka.

Gorakhpur was for the B.J.P a devastating outcome. It has been pocket borough of the Chief Minister, who won the seat five times consecutively. Politics is a blood sport. It is also an unpredictable enterprise.

It is certainly a wakeup call. It is something more. The ruling party should realise that Phulpur and Gorakhpur have altered the political landscape. Normally defeats in two constituencies is, to use a tired cliche, no big deal. Phulpur and Gorakhpur are. The leadership of the B.J.P failed to feel the mood of the people and totally misread the temper of the times. Anticipation and institution are important elements of politics. So is sixth sense. Stamina is the sine qua non of politics. What the B.J.P has been doing is to leap before looking. It is legitimate to ask—is a personality cult on the horizon.

The B.J.P, no doubt not short of resilience. It has many months to repair the damage.

Full marks to young Akhilesh Yadav. As in foreign policy, in politics there are no permanent friends nor permanent enemies. He had the political savvy to do a deal with the B.S.P. He took a big risk. It paid off. Will the S.P-B.S. P combination hold. Let's wait and see.

The glee of the Congress party is entirely misplaced. It will remain irrelevant unless it puts its house in order. Neither in U.P nor in Bihar had it crossed the twenty thousand mark. The dinner held by the

Congress President for seventeen or was it twenty opposition parties (all loosers) was an exercise in futility.

Jaya Bachchan is a dignified, likable person. That a political shuttlecock should call her names is not only disgraceful but shameful. What is even more reprehensible is that as soon as N. Aggarwal resigned, B.J.P embraced him. Here is a party which prides itself on propagating political integrity and ethical conduct.

By not responding to the vulgarity of N. Aggarwal, Jaya has shown grace and refinement of character.

The Budget was passed in Lok Sabha without a debate. This, if I am not mistaken is unprecedented. Both the government and the opposition have done is to damage and inflict wounds on our democracy. For a whole week Parliament was not functional. This unparliamentary behaviour is not happening in slow motion. It is going ahead at galloping speed.

I was ambassador to Pakistan in the early eighties of the last century. Our staff was, from time to time harassed. One day, a junior official and his wife were watching a film in an Islamabad cinema house. Suddenly, the film was stopped. An announcement was made that the son of X (who was present) had been badly wounded in a car accident. The panic stricken parents reached their home in no time. Their son was playing with his young sister. Only second rate people can behave in such a manner.

We should deal with the present crisis firmly and decisively.

On 21 May 1964, I received a letter from Vijayalakshmi Pandit. She was at the time governor of Maharashtra. I quote a portion:

"Ever since I came home from the U.S. I have been worried sick about the P.M.'s health. He looked so ill. I could hardly bear to look at him. It was obvious he was heading for a breakdown and was driving himself mercilessly inspite of it. He was alone in the house due to Indu's absence and though he was accompanied by a doctor, the poor little man was so junior he literally trembles every time he had to approach the P.M. there is question of advice or assistance....

Affectionately
Masi

29

Necessity of Order and Laws for Citizens

On 21 March 2018, former Vice-President, Hamid Ansari, addressed Australian National University, Canberra. His subject was, "India and Islamic Civilization: Contributions and Challenges."

Here I give two excerpts, "The classic text on the medieval Indian theory of Kingship is Ziauddin Barani's 14th century work, *Fatwa-I-Jahandari,* on the techniques and rules of government. It is based on an examination of the working of the institutions of Delhi Kingship for over ninety five years. Its based postulates were amplified and re-enunciated in the 16th century by Moghul Emperor Akbar's chief secretary Abul-Fazl Allami in his monumental work *The Ain-I-Akbar,* which itself is a part of a larger work *The Akbar Nama*."

"Barani's principal dictum was that the institution of monarchy was necessary for social order and the enforcement of justice and that, 'the King should have the power to make state-laws even if in extreme cases had to *override the shariat*'. Barani defined Zawabit or state-laws as rules of action which a King imposes on an obligatory duty on himself for realizing the welfare of the state and from which he never deviates. Abul Fazal's observations on the subject followed and amplified a line of thought no different from the earlier. Indian prescriptions of Kautalya's *Arthashastra*."

Hamid Ansari is one of the three Vice-Presidents who added lustre to the job. He is a product of the Indian Foreign Service, for which he qualified in 1961. He served for thirty six years. He was ambassador to Iran, Saudi Arabia, High Commissioner to Australia, and Permanent Representative of India to the United Nations. He served as Vice-Chancellor of Aligarh Muslim University and finally Chairman of the Minority Commission. A carrier, few can surpass.

The other day I met former governor Jagmohan in the Library of the India International Centre, surrounded by books and documents. The Library is his second home. There he spends six to seven hours a day. He is now in his early nineties. He is the author often books, including "My Frozen Turbulence in Kashmir." It is now in its eleventh print.

He gave me a copy of his latest book, "Triumphs and Tragedies of Ninth Delhi." He, as Lt. Governor of Delhi, beautified several parts of the capital and repaired and reconstructed many old and dilapidated monuments. I find it strange that no enclave, lane or road has not been named after Jagmohan.

The West, led by President Donald Trump is committing a grave folly. The British Prime Minister T. May is also in the Trump team. Once upon a time the America was the most isolationist country in the World. Today it is the most interventionist.

The U.S.A President is in a belligerent mood, threatening Syria with dire consequences. George W. Bush destroyed Iraq. Trump is planning to do so in Syria. President Assad is no angel but he has the backing of Russia and Iran. President Trump should abandon warlike brinkmanship and resort to diplomacy. It is unfortunately true that a sneeze in the White House makes the world catch a cold, except the People's Republic of China.

In our political culture a fast was an ethical and moral undertaking. Gandhiji's is the finest example of self-purification. Once in a while he fasted for political reasons which were always of the highest importance. Today fasting and fasts by politicians are treated with derision. The one at Rajghat was both laughable and farcical. The principle leader apparently arrived late, leaving early.

Parliament does not function, the Prime Minister and his colleagues go on a day's fast. Most seeking publicity. One worthy declared he was expressing his agony and pain for Parliament not being allowed to function. He obviously was suffering from amnesia. He was, himself one of the main disrupters.

Each day newspapers report of gruesome murders of children, some below the age often being gang raped. Does any leader fast? Of course not. We are reputed as a country that is civilized, culturally rich. We are also totally insensitive to cruelty inflicted on those who are both innocent and unable to defend themselves. The Nirbhaya case is a glaring example. How many of us recall that horror of horrors.

Pratap Bhanu Mehta, Vice-Chancellor of Ashoka University, wrote in his column in *The Indian Express* on last Friday, about the Kathua. "What do we say for a country that converts the gang-rape and death of a child into a political weapon? What *locus standi* does one have left to even extend genuine sympathy to her family? What language are we left with, that has not been denuded of meaning? I wish we could say with confidence of the Kathua case will morally haunt us for a long time to come: our conduct as a society has shown how easily we can brush it off. But we can say this: Our conduct in this case is already an indication of the moral black hole we have now entered."

30

The Art of Love and Hate—The Hindu Contradiction

The Rigveda is perhaps the oldest book ever composed or written. Dates vary from 2500 BC to 500 BC. It is one of our most revered texts.

It is a profound work of great literary excellence. Nirad C. Chaudhury refers to it in his book "The Continent of Circe." From the Rigveda to the epics, especially the Mahabharata, one faces a consistent attitude towards sex life. I shall give only one example of the frankness, and that from our most venerated book, the first and foremost of our most revealed scriptures, the *Rigveda*. In it Indirani, the Queen Goddess, defies the virility of her lord, Indira the King God and thunder-bearer, in these words: "he achieves not, he whose ... hangs limp between the thighs: achieves he alone whose hairy.... Swells when he lies." The dots are my contribution.

As a contrast I quote from "Megaduta" by Kalidas. Every time I read him I am overwhelmed by his genius and poetical sublimity.

I quote stanza III, page III of Chandra Rajan's translation:

"And further he said this: once in bed asleep, still clinging to my neck you wake up on a sudden, weeping a little and when I asked why again and again, ah you cheat. I saw you in my dream playing with another woman."

Broadly speaking 95% Hindus are not only hypocritical about sex and sexual activity, they are also full of contradictions. Boys and girls, even today cannot mix freely. Yet, they accompany their parents to temples where the linga and yoni are worshipped.

Even ascetics cannot deny that sex is universal. Human being and animals cannot do without it. 1.3 billion Indians did not descend from the sky, They came into the world because their parents shared the same bed.

I have this been re-reading the Kamasutra and the Rigveda. So far none has dared to ban the former. Why? Because it is in great demand, particularly the grotesquely illustrated editions. The exact date of its seeing the light is not known. K.M. Panikkar claims it was composed in 4th century A.D. It is generally agreed that it is perhaps among the oldest treatise on sex. Chinese sexology is even older. Japan is not far away.

Most parts of the Kamasutra are neither vulgar not obscene. Taken as a whole Vatsyayana's creation is in some ways an eulogy of love. He was free from deception and literary cant.

The second half is dull, repetitive and often hilarious. The chapters on "Sexual Union", "The Embrace" and "Kissing" etc are laughable.

Sheila Dikshit and I have been known each other for a quarter of a century. She is the third longest serving Chief Minister—fifteen years. The two with longer spells are Jyoti Basu of West Bengal—twenty two years and Mohan Lal Sukhadia of Rajasthan seventeen years.

Sheila Dikshit in her quiet way in her own unobtrusive manner changed Delhi in several areas. That is not in dispute. The most visible are the fly overs, but Bhagidari has been a game changer.

Her 173 page autobiography, "Citizen Delhi" was published last month. It is as unassuming and understated as she is herself. No self-promotion, no showing off, no ideological hang-ups, no adjectival over dose, no claptrap, no name dropping.

What the reader can learn from Sheila's book is how to manage human beings, how to understand their political and social behaviour and how to renovate Delhi.

Earlier in the week I spent a couple of hours in the central hall of Parliament. If one wants to know what is happening in the country this is the place to be in. Political education is instance. The place combines caution and verbal recklessness, irony and humour, melancholy and effervescence.

The delegate's lounge of the U.N. building is a larger international arena and the best location for an instant crash course on what is happening on the globe. Members of 193 countries are seen in lively discussions, texts of resolutions to be tables are scrutinized with utmost care and caution. The outcome of their deliberation largely acceptable.

The Time of India on February 8, carried an item which drew the reader's attention to alleged remarks made by B.J.P M.P. Vinay Katiyar who suggested that the Muslims should either go to Bangladesh or Pakistan. What business did they have being in India.

Could the M.P arrange for the transportation of eighteen crore Muslims to Pakistan and Bangladesh.

31

A Visit Enveloped in Controversy

The visit of Canadian Prime Minister Justin Trudeau had been enveloped in controversy. Official visits by heads of government do not nonnally last seven days. Trudeau and his attractive family gave the impression that they had come on a holiday jaunt. The three children were adorable, but why was it necessary to bring them to the Rashtrapati Bhawan. The Canadian Prime Minister was being formally received and inspected the three services general of honour. Children were out of place there.

It was a bit odd for the Trudeau's to be seen in colourful Indian garments on a number of occasions. The Prime Minister went overboard by performing a Bhangra in Amritsar. It is one thing to be unconventional, another to be undignified.

His meeting with the Chief Minister of Punjab was business like. The Chief Minister informed the prime minister of his government giving free reign to khalistani terrorists in Canada. This caused concern and resentment in the Punjab. He gave Trudeau their names.

The Canadian High Commissioner had egg on his face by inviting the notorious Atwal to his dinner for his prime minister.

On our part it would have been gracious of Prime Minister Modi to have receive his distinguished guest in Ahmedabad.

I have been a member of the Delhi Gymkhana Club for sixty three years. I was President of the c1ub-1984-85.

The Gymkhana started bringing out a monthly news letter some years back. The February issue has an amusing snippet about Jawaharlal Nehru. The author is R.K. Puri, a member. 1 give an abbreviated version. A young probationer of the Audit and Accounts service was deputed to carry out the audit of the accounts of Teen Murti House, the official residence of the Prime Minister—Jawaharlal Nehru.

The young man and his team of auditors were given full access to the accounts. These were meticulously kept. No errors were detected. The intrepid probationer did not give up. He took a tour of the extensive lawns and fruit garden at the back of Teen Murti House. He suddenly spotted trees laden with fruit. When asked the gardener who consumed them and who paid for them, the loyal gardener was put out, saying Prime Minister relished them at breakfast each day. The probationer persisted, "Who pays". By now the indignant gardener said there was no question of the Prime Minister paying.

The probationer in his report to the bosses recommended that the dues of fruits consumed be recovered from the staff. The Deputy Controller of audit, noted on the file, that the young probationer "should be advised to be more careful in the future."

The file (bureaucratise at its best) moved up. The noting of the superior official was that the probationer exercise discretion in sensitive cases. Finally it went up to the Comptroller General, who noted, "I agree with the probationer's findings."

The file than moved further of the bureaucratic ladder. The Private Secretary to the Prime Minister was incensed, he sent it to the Prime Minister. Nehru returned it. A cheque of Rs. 5000 was attached to the file for fruits consumed by him.

Jayaram Ramesh has written a biography of P.N. Haksar, the most accomplished diplomat India has produced. To him 1 attribute most of the achievements of Indira Gandhi, whose Principal Secretary he was between 1967-1973, especially the birth of Bangladesh.

Jairam's book will be published in London and New Delhi in June.

P.N. Haksar's five hundred files are in the Nehru Memorial Library. Jairam has meticulously studied them. Earlier in the week he dropped into see me. He brought a copy of a note. I had put up to the prime minister. I had no recollection of it. It is dated 13.5.1970. It relates to a two minute meeting of our charge 'de affairs, Brajesh Mishra (later Atal Bihari Vajpyee's National security Advisor) and Chairman Mao in Peking. It was not an earth-shaking event, but what Mao said could not be ignored.

In my one thousand word note I wrote, "1 mentioned to P.M. yesterday that it had fallen to my lot to be present and take notes of Chou-En-Lai's meeting with Shri Morarji Desai, who treated the Chinese Prime Minister, as if he was the Chairman of the Broach or the Nasik Municipal Committee."

Jairam is a sophisticated man of letters. I look forward to reading his Haksar biography.

32

Shame as Statues are Defaced, Pulled Down

Prime Minister Narendra Modi did well to condemn the pulling down of the statue of Vladimir Lenin and the vandalizing of the busts of B.R. Ambedkar, Syama Prasad Mukerjee, E.V. Ramasamy aka Periyar, Gandhiji and Prime Minister Modi.

Those who committed these outrages bring to their parties no credit. They are vicious lumpens, who inflict wounds on our civilization, culture, commitment to tolerance, rational behaviour. Its far as I can remember such barbarism has seldom been witnessed before.

Statues have been pulled down and trampled in the erstwhile Soviet Union. The statue of Saddam Hussain was brought down in Baghdad in the presence of T.V. crews. Other examples exist.

The news of the desecration of statues in different parts of our country were seen on T.V. in various parts of the world. These acts do great harm to our democracy. Why? Because on domestic cohesion depends the strength and success of foreign policy. Jawaharlal Nehru the architect of modern India, wrote, "Foreign policies depend ultimately on internal conditions and developments. Internal progress for us, therefore, becomes essential if we are to play an effective part in world affairs."

During the past four years scores of Heads of State, government, Vice-Presidents, Kings, princes, foreign ministers have come to India. These visits have resulted in enhancing mutual goodwill and respect. Dozens of agreements have been signed. This is fine as far as it goes. But how far does it go. How many of these agreements have produced concrete results or benefits. These are valid questions which need answers.

For some time the diplomacy and foreign policy of the Modi government have appeared wobbly. I will start with Nepal. The Prime Minister of Pakistan was in Kathmandu last week. One of the subjects he discussed with Prime Minister Oli was Kashmir. Yes. Kashmir. China is spreading its influence and wings in Sri Lanka, the Maldives and Myanmar at our cost. Our decision to set up a defence outfit in the Seychelles has run into trouble. Pakistan is in a different category. It has a chronic antipathy towards India.

Our economy is apparently doing well. Does G.D.P alone ensure salvation? How about employment! What about equality. Do we have a well thought through educational policy? Is justice denied to millions or is it not. Are all economic explanations of development faultless? I am not an economist. But I do earnestly hold that economics is only a small part of human life and human activity.

P.N. Haksar, the most cerebral and foresighted civil servant India has produced, concluded his convocation address delivered on October 29, 1979 at the University of Bombay thus., "I began by saying that if we wish to understand development, and not merely understand but do something meaningful about it, economics is not enough."

On 7.3.2008 fell the 35th anniversary of the seventh NAM Summit held in New Delhi under the Chairmanship of Indira Gandhi. Non-Aligned is today considered out of date. You can discard the name, not its contents, which emphasised that nations practice independent foreign policies. NAM needs to be reinvented for dealing with international problems facing us in the 21st century.

For the last eight weeks President Trump and the North Korean leader Kim Jong-Un were abusing each other in unbridled language. The world was startled on Friday by the U.S. President accepting the invitation of Kim Jong-Un to meet. Apparently even the White staff was unaware of Trump's changing his mind. If he succeeds in finding a way to lower the peninsular heat, he would be strong candidate for this year's Nobel Peace Prize.

33

Martin Luther King Jr's Legacy Lives On

Dr. Martin Luther King Jr. was shot dead by a raving racist bigot on 4 April 1968 in Memphis Tennessee. He was thirty nine years old.

He became an international inspiration after delivering a speech on 28 August 1963, one of the unforgettable orations of the 20th century.

The words, "I have a Dream" resonate today even after fifty years of his death. "It is a dream deeply rooted in the American dream that one day this nation will rise up and live out the true meaning of its creed—we hold these truths to be self-evident, that all men are created equal.... I have a dream, my four children will one day live in a nation where they will not be judged by the colour of their skin but by the content of their character.... And when we allow freedom to ring, when we let it ring from every village and hamlet, from every state and city, we will be able to speed up that day when all God's children-black men and white men, Jews and Gentiles, Catholics and Protestants—will be able to join hands and sing in the words of the old Negro spiritual. "Free at last, free at last; thank God Almighty, we are free at last."

I met Martin Luther King Jr. only once, at a reception given by the U.S. Ambassador to the United Nations in New York. He was on his way to Oslo to receive the Nobel Peace Prize. The time. Early December 1964.

Earlier in the year I was busy putting together a volume of tributes to Jawaharlal Nehru, to be published on 27.5.1965. The first anniversary of his death. I wrote Dr. King, requesting him to contribute to the book. I had no response. I had given up on him when I received his tribute to Nehru. He had written from his cell in Selma jail. He called Nehru a, "towering world force skillfully inserting the peace will of India between the raging antagonisms of the great powers of the East and West.... In all these struggles of mankind to rise to true state of civilization, the towering figure of Nehru sits unseen but felt at all council tables. He is missed by the world, and because he is so wanted, he is a living force in the tremulous world of today."

The Tributes volume, "The Legacy of Nehru" was published on his death anniversary. The other contributors included, Clement Attlee, Pearl Buck, Bertrand Russell, Arnold Toynbee, U. Thant....

Winnie Madikizela Mandela died earlier in the week in a Johannesburg hospital, aged 81.

With-Rajiv Gandhi I attended the celebrations heralding the birth of an independent Namibia on 22.3.1990. The capital, Windhock was host to dozens of Presidents, Vice-Presidents and Foreign Ministers. Rajiv Gandhi was, not at the time prime minister but was treated as one. Nelson Mandela and his wife, Winnie were the stars, over shadowing all others.

It had been arranged by President Kenneth Kaunda of Zambia that Nelson Mandela would receive Rajiv on 23.3.1990. I have written at some length of the Mandela-Rajiv Gandhi meeting. Hence I will not repeat myself. I had taken with me, "No Easy Walk to Freedom" by Nelson Mandela. I asked the two to sign on the inner cover of the book. Nelson Mandela wrote, "With my complements and best wishes." Winnie Mandela wrote, "With Much Love."

Winnie Mandela was beautiful, ebullient, charming, erratic, temperamental and gutsy. She will be remembered for her virtues. Not for her shortcomings.

Prime Minister Narendra Modi acted with alacrity to put his thoughtless minister of Information and Broadcasting, the elegant and attractive Smriti Irani in her place. Her attempt to muzzle the media was an astonishing lack of sound judgment. It was the duty of the senior officials of her ministry to tell her of the *faux pas* she would be committing. Obviously they did not do so.

A revolution is taking place in Saudi Arabia. The Crown Prince, Muhammed Bin Salman is leading it. Finally the Kingdom is knocking at the doors of the 21st Century. The Crown Prince during his visit to the U.S.A said, "I believe that each people, anywhere, has a right to live in their peaceful nation.... I believe the Palestine's and Israelis have the right to have their own land." This has drastically altered the economic, political contours of the Middle East and beyond.

Last Sunday Dr. Manmohan Singh released Ashwani Kumar's book, *Ehsas-o-Izhar.* The evening was enjoyable and entertaining.

Part II:
Speeches

If you would make a speech or write one
Or get an artist to indite one
Think not because it's understood
By men of sense, it's therefore good
Make it so clear and simply planned
No blockhead can misunderstand

Adlai Stevenson
1900-1965

1

Indira Gandhi Conference 1991

Albert Einstein, wrote eloquently of the human predicament when he said, "Strange is our situation here upon earth. Each one of us comes for a short visit, not knowing why, yet sometimes seeming to divine a purpose." He then goes on to say, "To ponder interminably over the reason of one's own existence or the meaning of life in general seems to me, from the objective point of view, to be sheer folly. And yet everyone holds certain ideals by which he guides his aspirations and his judgement. The ideals which have always shone before me and filled me with joy of living are good-ness, beauty and truth. To make a goal of comfort or happiness has never appealed to me. A system of ethics built on that basis would be sufficient for a heard of cattle."

Each one of us here possess his or her own philosophy of life and being reasonably intelligent individuals we have to link that philosophy to a worthy public purpose. Not to do so would be an act of irresponsibility.

When I reflect on what the human race has done to itself and what it might have done, I sometimes wonder if humankind will make it. When I contemplate the immediate future of our turbulent and fascinating planet, I am divided between hope and gloom.

While the spiritual springs of human kind have not dried up, they have too frequently been poisoned. One ism after another has left its blood soaked debris and wreckage of broken innocent lives. What armistice can console a mother bereaved of her son, or a wife who cremated her young husband or for a man who buries his friend.

We all live under the dictatorship of fate, something the activists of the dictatorship of the proletariat neglected to account for. All political and economic dogmas and doctrines lie discredited, even those with encyclopedic pretensions promising so much, delivering so little.

Science and technology provide hope, but so often they have been used and misused as takers of life, not savers of life. The process began long before the dropping of atom bombs on Hiroshima and Nagasaki. If 10% of what is today spent on armaments is diverted to development, the end of poverty might be in sight before the end of the century.

What will the 21st century make of the 20th century? Will it admire it, emulate it, or will it despise and reject it ?

The Third Indira Gandhi Conference will for the next four days discuss the challenges of the 21st century. We can make the conference a creative enterprise by the courage of our convictions, the wisdom of our answers, and by trying to comprehend the unprecedented and momentous changes taking place around the world. Ideology is dead, but not history despite Fukuyama.

When Rajiv Gandhi, selected this subject, he was not unaware of the fact that vast numbers of human beings in Asia, Africa, Latin America and some parts of Europe had yet to arrive in the 20th, let alone in the 21st century.

If this conference were being held in 1891, then its agenda would have been entirely different, as would be the agenda of a similar conference in 2091. The message is that change is a fact of life. But change cannot be left to chance, it has to be conceptualised, structured and managed. This is where human ingenuity comes into play.

Humankind was, in the 1890s, rather pleased with itself, over optimistic and complacent about the future. Both optimism and complacency got hammered by 1914.

We of the 1990s are more realistic and cautious. Our agenda is an unembroidered one. We need to discuss the disorders that are likely to pose the most serious problems: The new international order, economic organisation, individual freedom and collective responsibility, population, environment, science and technology, religion and enduring peace.

Today problems respect no national boundaries.

The world is truly a global glasshouse. Throwing stones or apportioning blame or indulging in monetary one upmanship is likely to land us in a greater mess.

It is also time we democratised our diplomatic vocabulary. Great powers-grea:t for lacing our lives with blood and drugs and armaments. It is the responsibility of great states to serve, not dominate humanity, to heal, not inflict wounds.

The growing surplus of human beings is a stupendous global problem, which is at the root of all others. How do we best utilise the energy, the talent, of these human beings and do so creatively? Unprecedented speed of population growth has created new imbalances and vulnerabilities which endanger future sustainability. 72% of the world's poor live in Asia. The number of educated unemployed is a growing spectre.

At the global level we are witnessing an amazing phenomenon - gross imbalance created by the concentration of economic growth in the industrialised countries and population growth in the developing countries. If this imbalance is not corrected then security, environment, economic growth, political stability, and peace will be under constant threat. Effecting peaceful, creative, change through cooperation must be the principal challenge of the 21st century. Joyful confidence in attaining this goal would be out of place, but chronic melancholy is certainly not the answer.

And here I would like to turn to my own country. We may be a young nation state but as a civilization we have been around a long time. We have generally chosen our own path, rejecting dogma and doctrine. The ideal has been to attain harmony. Mahatma Gandhi's life and. teachings kept tugging at my sleeve while I was preparing for this conference.

To me he is the authentic spiritual spokesman of the 20th century. He showed, what a single human being can achieve, through spiritual force and personal example.

His life glows. He proved that it was possible to exercise mercy without cheating justice, and that goodness was indivisible. By applying his non-violent action plan on a mass scale he gave the world the one and only original political idea to come out of Asia, Africa, Latin America, in the last 200 years. In the process, he changed the world and enlarged our moral and spiritual horizons.

I do not wish to appear smug or sanctimonious, but it really is a great solace and comfort to announce to the world that no Indian appears in the crowded monster gallery of the 20th century.

There has never been a time in the annals of history when humanity has been free of one crisis or another, or a time when the minds of men were not troubled by doubt, when our passions pulled one way and our duties another. Human beings have always encountered dilemmas. Cvilizations and societies do not perish because of contradictions, they often perish because of their inability to find solutions for them. One way of not resolving them is to place ends before means. Can we or should we build a just society through unjust means. For Gandhi and Nehru the means justified the end, not the other way round. To the crisis in the spirit of man moral and ethical dimensions have to be applied and here again I turn to Gandhi and his emphasis on righteousness – quite separate from self-righteousness.

There is at the moment discernable, mostly in the west, a wait and watch attitude towards India. In current Americanese, the jury is out. The verdict is awaited.

All I wish to say to our critics and cynics is – look around the world and see where else do you find 850 million, individualistic people, following six religions, speaking 14 major languages, living in different climatic zones, engaged in so tremendous and exciting an adventure of change through peaceful, democratic means.

The Indian experiment—democracy, secularism, humanistic socialism—was masterminded by Jawaharlal Nehru. Such an experiment on so large a scale has not been tried in the history of humanity. I am only too aware of its short-comigs, but that it works is one of the political miracles of the 20th Century. Give it a chance. Try to help. Try to understand. Don't sit in judgement.

How does this amazing democratic enterprise work? It works because 840 million people out of 850 are not involved in wrecking it but strengthening it. Tens of millions of ordinary, decent, upright, hardworking, self-effacing, dedicated, enterprising, resourceful, courageous Indians in villages and cities go about their daily business, without fuss. They, the unrecognised mass of human beings, they keep India going. No, this country is not falling apart. See for yourself in the next few days and you might be lucky to discover what makes us tick.

I thank you P.M. for your joining us this morning and for your inaugural address. May I also congratulate you on getting into the Guidness Book of Records. You came to the helm in a sad year. Rajiv Gandhi's assassination broke my life into two. I know how shattered you were. In five months you have done much that is good and much that is praiseworthy. You have cooled the political temperature and healed wounds. You have with some visible success put the derailed economic and political system of India back on the rails. I wish you luck and success. You will need both.

May I on behalf of the Chairperson thank all our delegates for responding to our invitation. Once in two years, Indira Gandhi's name, fame and work brings eminent thinkers together in Delhi. For that and so much more we thank her. She worked tirelessly for peace, harmony, for goodwill. She brightened our lives.

New Delhi – 19 November 1991

2

Remembering Indira Gandhi

We are assembled here on Indira Gandhi's 73rd birth anniversary. I have a powerful feeling that her benign spirit is at this moment hovering over these hallowed grounds and approving of this award to UNICEF. She took keen interest in the activities of UNICEF and the good work it was doing to bring cheer and light into the lives of children throughout the world.

Grant, may I, on behalf of the Chairman, Rajiv Gandhi and the Trustees of the Indira Gandhi Memorial Trust, congratulate you and welcome you.

As I stand here, affectionate memories of Indira Gandhi come rusning to my mind. I do not wish to drive them away. When she was assassinated the spring went out of my life. But I do not wish to introduce a maudlin, lachrymose or melancholy note into our proceedings.

In India, functions such as this, tend to become excessively formal, solemn, severe, impersonal. And so often Indira Gandhi is depicted as solemn, severe, silent. I am not suggesting that we trivialize such occasions, but I do submit that it is possible and desirable to combine formality with informality, gaiety with dignity, rejoicing with restraint and humour with homage.

Of course Indira Gandhi was a great Prime Minister. Of course she was a powerful, influential political leader, of course she was a world figure of very high standing. We all know that.

What is seldom mentioned is that this supremely beautiful, sparkling human being was a great lover of books, a voracious reader, a great humanist, having wide ranging non-political interests, that she had exquisite taste, a distinct style, uncommon elegence, davastating charm and a marvellous sense of humour.

I shall close my remarks by very briefly quoting from her letters to me which have relevance—her striking humanism and her humour—on 3 August 1981 she wrote,

"Dear Natwar,

I have read some of the interviews in the book you left me and I am depressed. I feel isolated, not because of policies, the correctness of which will be seen in time as it has been before. But while the earth spins on, in beauty and with method, the world of men is a hollow one, where words have no meaning and sentiments no feeling, the young have lost wonder, Elan and even hope. What can a leaden eyed civilization do? Can a flame of idealism or a vision of a better man be protected from all this cynicism, hypocrisy and hatred?"

Fifteen months later, in November 1982, her mood was different:

"Dear Natwar,

Thank you for your birthday greetings. But I am disappointed that there was no good story to enliven my day. Have you read Norman Cousin's book on his illness, giving positive proof that laughter is the best and sometimes the only medicine?"

When I last saw her couple of days before she was so tragically snatched away from us, I told her that having quit the foreign service I was leaving for Bharatpur to start politicking. But my first priority would be to acquire a new ward rope , khadi kurta, pyajama, Jawahar jacket, the Congress livery. She heard me and did not respond. Just as I was getting up to leave, with a twinkle in her eyes and the faint beginnings of a smile she said, "Now that you are coming into politics, a thicker skin would be more useful."

Speech delivered by K. Natwar Singh at Teen Murti House on 19.11.1990.

3

Address at International Publishers Convention

"Humanism, International Politics And Nehru's Thought"

We had decided some time ago that in connection with the Nehru Centenary we would have a seminar on "Humanism, International Politics and Nehru's Thought" in Delhi beginning on the 2nd of October. We are very grateful to the distinguished delegates who have come from various parts of the world and I am particularly happy to mention that we have two Noble laureates, Esquivel from Argentina, a disciple of Mahatma Gandhi who was awarded the Noble Peace Prize in 1980, and we have N.G. Basov who received the Noble Prize for Physics in the year 1964. We are very grateful to the Director General of ILO and to Koirala and to all the other delegates who have come.

We will be meeting this afternoon and tomorrow in smaller groups to discuss the issues that are facing humankind at the moment. We had hoped very much that Mother Teresa would have been with us today. Unfortunately. she has been very unwell and I am sure all of you will join me in sending her our very good wishes for a rapid recovery.

A very large number of people not only in India but the world over are conditioned by what Nehru did, thought and wrote. How do we define a great man? My criteria is very simple. Did his life change the world? I think Nehru's life did. That is why we are assembled here on this auspicious occasion of Mahatma Gandhi's 120th birth anniversary and the Nehru Centenary. Nehru's influence, even before he became the Prime Minister of India was very widespread and he articulated Mahatma Gandhi's vision, Gandhi's teachings. It is quite clear, even in a country like Argentina, that the impact was felt. I met Esquivel in 1984 and he will tell you this morning how he was influenced by Gandhi as a very young man and attracted to his teachings.

We are very sorry that we have not been able to get UNU. He was to come and we were hoping that he would arrive till last night. But unfortunately, from what I gather, he was not allowed to leave Burma.

I once again welcome you all on behalf of the Nehru Centenary Committee and on behalf of the Government and people of India. Those of you who have come for the first time, I hope will stay for some time in the country after the seminar is over. We will do all we can to make your stay here comfortable.

India is not just a country or a geographic expression; it is an idea, concept, and for many it is a pilgrimage, it is a fulfilment, it is a destination. You have come here as delegates to this Seminar, and I sincerely hope you will go back as friends.

The only important political idea to emerge in the last 150 years from Asia, Africa and Latin America, which has changed the lives of individuals and the world came from Gandhiji: Satyagrah that is Non-Violent Non-Cooperation. That is why the first subject of this Seminar is the current relevance of the legacy of Mahatma Gandhi and Jawaharlal Nehru. Nehru articulated this message in the life he lived and the direction he gave to the Indian freedom movement, and after becoming Prime Minister of India to international relations.

Two years ago, in this city of New Delhi, Gorbachev and Rajiv Gandhi signed a document called the Delhi Declaration. That declaration contains a paragraph which says that the world should be free of nuclear weapons and non-violence should be the basis of life. Here was the leader of the Communist Party of the Soviet Union putting his signature on a document along with the Prime Minister of India, which emphasises the importance of non-violence. I cannot exaggerate the significance of this particular document. See how the world is changing.

Gandhiji was, to my mind, the sole authentic spiritual spokesman of the 20th century and his life is a monument of human achievements. In history, truth, non-violence, humanism, decency and amorality are generally bypassed. More often they are held in abeyance. Gandhiji and Nehru put them centre stage. We need to do so again if we are not to make a mess of our lives and a mess of the world. A society or polity which does not define its moral parameters is asking for trouble. In the political arena for a number of years ideology has become passe. The world is running out of political ideas. But what Gandhiji and Nehru said has universal and everlasting application. If you look at the 20th century and count the number of people who have served humanity, in that distinguished list figure the two Indians we are talking of just now. We have been accustomed for a very long time to read Euro-Centric history. I think Gandhiji and Nehru showed the world that there are other points of view. When Mahatma Gandhi went on his last trip to London in 1931 to attend the Round Table Conference, a British correspondent asked him, "Mr. Gandhi, what do you think of Western civilisation?" Gandhiji replied, "It would be nice." The two world wars that we have had in this century are a testimony to the utter failure of European diplomacy. When we became independent, Pandit Jawaharlal Nehru articulated a vision not only for India, not only for the non-aligned world, but for humanity, that either we co-exist or we co-perish. What I mind in the words of Mikhali Gorbachev is a vision that Jawaharlal Nehru articulated so many decades ago. The problem that the World is going to face in the last decade of this century and the early decades of the next century is not the classical problem of colonialism or imperialism or racialism. The world has run out of colonies and I sincerely hope the policy of apartheid in South Africa will also disappear. We have other problems now. We shall discuss them in these two days.

May I once again thank you all very much for being here this morning, and for those who have come here for the first time, I hope you will be able to see something of this country. I know Esquivel is going to visit some of the places where Gandhiji lived and worked and others who have not been here will also take the opportunity to find out how this wonderful country of ours, with every possible diversity in it, works, functions, survives and makes its contribution to international life, in which we do not look at each other with bloodshed eyes but try to make it safe and friendly for everyone.

Thank you very much.

(Inaugural Speech by K. Natwar Singh Minister of State for External Affairs, New Delhi, October 1989)

4

A Plea for Peace

Were I to express adequately, my feelings at the honour you have done me, and my country, by inviting me to be one of the speakers at this function, I should be tempted to become somewhat long-winded, if not, entirely tedious.

When I look at my fellow speakers on this podium and think of their distinction and eminence, I, for once, realise my own limitations and can only plead, for all the indulgence, which they and you can offer and I very much need. It is indeed a privilege to be in a list that includes Wole Soyinka.

I am by profession a politician. This particular species is not generally associated with the world of books. There are of course strilking exceptions – Lenin, Churchill, Nehru, de Gaulle, Kennedy. It is, however, melancholy to confess that the list of well-known politicians not interested in books is much longer. I am a lover of books, possessing a modest personal library of 8000 volumes into which I disappear whenever I can, to lead an exciting life of the mind.

For a number of years, I was a member of the Indian delegation to the United Nations in New York. The cardinal principle there, was, never attempt a joke – you were likely to be misunderstood in five languages by 100 countries.

Since I believe in living dangerously, I have been selective in following such sound advice. My speech this morning, is being simultaneously translated into five languages. I am about to relate what I think is an amusing anecdote. If you misunderstand it, so much the worse for you.

Some days ago I was invited to speak at a college function in India. I was unwise enough to ask the Principal, "What would you like me to speak about?" He replied, "about five minutes."

I have this morning been allotted more than five minutes and in these few minutes I will attempt to tell you something about what is happening in India with regard to authors, books; and publishing.

I shall speak about India and not the developing world. You will have noticed my not using the phrase, – *the Third World.* I take exception to the term, *the third world.* It carries unacceptable overtones. As Octavio Paz, the Mexican poet said, it is a semantic trap.

Before I come to the publishing scene in India and how it meets our current and future needs and requirements, I thought I might say a few words about the Indian literary tradition.

The well-known Indian philosopher and President of India between 1962 and 1967, Dr. S. Radhakrishnan, wrote in his book, *Eastern Religions and Western Thought,* something which is relevant and pertinent today.

"Now that we have the whole world for our cultural base, the process of recovery and training in classics cannot cease with listening to the voice of Isaiah and Paul, Socrates and Cicero. That would be an academic error, a failure of perspective. There are others also who have participated in the supreme adventure of the ages, the prophets of Egypt, the sages of China and the seers of India, who are guideposts disclosing to us the course of the trail of the living non-European civilisations. The chief are the Islamic, the Chinese and the Hindu."

The *Rig Veda* is probably the earliest monument of Indo-European speech. Dr. Machinol, writing about this most ancient of Hindu texts says, "The brave adventures made so long go and recorded here, of those who seek to discover the significance of our world and of man's life within it ... India here set out on a quest which she has never ceased to follow."

Behind the Rig Veda – 2000 B.C. – itself lay ages of civilised existence and thought. The Rig Veda carries this superb dedication.

"To the seers, our ancestors, the first path-finders." One of the most famous and revered quotations from the *Rig Veda,* is the Gayatri Mantra which hundreds of millions in India recite every morning. The Gayatri Mantra, roughly translated says, "let the light that illuminates the Sun, illuminate our intellect also."

The colonial dictum was, 'if we leave aside the blind forces of nature nothing moves in the world which is not Greek in its origin.' This of course was a load of imperial nonsense, Martin Luther King Jr.'s comment sums it up nicely: "the peculiar genius of imperialism was found in its capacity to delude so much of the world into the belief that it was civilising primitive cultures even though it was grossly exploiting them."

One of the best known, if rather over-generous of these scholars, was Max Mueller who wrote, "If I were asked myself from what literature we have in Europe, we who have been nurtured almost exclusively on the thoughts of Greeks and Romans, and of one semetic race, the Jewish, may draw that corrective which is most wanted in order to make our inner life more perfect, more comprehensive, more universal, in fact more truly human, life, not of this life only, but a transfigured and enternal life, again I should point to India."

We may have fallen short of the expectations of Max Mueller, nevertheless, Indian spiritual thought, literature and culture have endured over four millenia and more.

India is not just a country, not simply a nation. For many it is a pilgrimage. As Rabindranath Tagore wrote, "Come inside India, accept all her good and evil – if there be deformity then try and cure it from within, but see it with your own eyes, understand it, think over it, turn your face towards it, become one with it.

The Indian Constitution recognises 15 national languages and English as an official language. Of these 15 languages, Hindi is used and spoken and understood by about 400 million people living in North of India. The other 14 languages are also used by many millions in their respective regions.

India of course shares with the developing world some common features because of a common colonial past. In most developing countries illiteracy rates are high, the economy in most, not robust, commercial activity involves high risk. In almost all former colonial countries' parallel streams of publishing in the local languages and English are present.

Today the Indian book industry presents a curious picture. It can be called developed in the sense that it ranks seventh in the world and third after the USA and UK in the production of English titles. It has an annual output of 13,000 titles which are on a variety of subjects and in a number of languages. There are over 10,000 publishers in the country and of these nearly 1000 are governmental agencies.

No reliable information is available about reading habits of rural and urban communities in India. 70 per cent of Indians live in 5.5 lakh villages, more than 60 per cent of which now have electricity. Here, I am afraid books are not being bought but television sets. The National Book Trust has conducted several surveys about reading and book-buying habits. I shall not tax your patience with details. Regular book fairs are held in India which are now attracting a large number of international publishers. If any of you have been to the Calcutta Book Fair, you will have noticed the long queues before each book stall. The Bengali is an avid reader and would be an avid buyer, if books were less expensive. Elsewhere in India, reading habits vary. We remain an oral society. Our religious books have come down to us by word of mouth. Illiterate villagers can recite the Ramayana and Mahabharata by heart.

While the population of India has increased, Indian publishing has still to achieve its true potential and dimensions. The total annual turnover of Indian publishing is around $ 50 million. Book imports account for about $ 10 million annually. With nearly 15 per cent of the world's population we produce merely 3 per cent of the world's titles.

It is a fact peculiar to Afro-Asian nations that the greater part of their publishing is carried out in a language foreign to the majority of their people.

In India out of 800 million a little over 50 million use the English language.

Yet this English-speaking elite dominates life and activity in all important spheres and creates unhealthy tensions which, if I am not mistaken, countries like China and Japan do not encounter.

It is not my purpose to make a political speech but fortunately or unfortunately politics and commerce cannot be separated and while colonialism and imperialism in their classical forms have disappeared publishing imperialism continues unabated.

Developing countries are used as dumping grounds by the advanced publishing countries. Once in a while their intellectually inferior crumbs in glossy jackets fall into my hands. Reading them I begin to envy the illiterate.

Even instructural literature, history textbooks continue to project the imperialistic and colonial mentality. It is not yet fully realised that the imperial heroes of Britain, France, Spain and Portugal are not the heroes of India, Nigeria, Zimbabwe and the Carribean.

This attempt to perpetuate intellectual dominance has serious political ramifications, both for the country where the book is published and the country where it is exported and read. Even today we hear the phrase, "metropolitan countries," meaning the rich and advanced, contrasted with the "periphery," meaning developing countries. The value judgement here is implicit. Corrective measures are being taken. Penguins have recently launched their publishing enterprise in India.

The English language publishers have built-in advantages, as they inherited infrastructures from originally British-owned firms. Half a dozen Indian publishers are breaking into international markets in a modest way. But I regret to say that the royalty payments, contractual obligations, editing, proof reading, book reviewing, translation standards, distribution, warehouse facilities leave much to be desired. Piracy is on the increase. A large number of Indian authors are at the mercy of their publishers. Several including R.K. Narayan, publish their own books. The lot of authors in Indian languages is even worse.

The Preacher said, "of making books there is no end and much reading is a weariness of the flesh." As always, the Preacher was right and wrong at the same time. He was right because much of what is being published is trash. You will forgive me for saying this but that is the truth. He was wrong because the mind and the body are not two separate entities. When there is something that lifts you up, it is your whole personality that is, in a basic sense, elevated, made whole. As a famous English poet said, when you read a line of great poetry, you feel a sensation in the pit of your stomach. Therefore, books, millions and millions, are needed to make Indian humanity a lively, throbbing, vital part of world intellectual community. Imagine, 800 million Indians by the turn of the century reading about what the world means to them, in its magnificent diversity, in its intellectual splendour. in its great works of art and literature. Imagine them doing so in English, in French, in Russian but above all in their own languages.

What an exciting enterprise we are talking about. What an adventure of the mind! What an exhibition of the spirit! As historical parallel, there is only one episode I can think of and that is the coming of the Renaissance in Europe. Because of Gandhi, and because of Nehru, India is today experiencing a profound stirring of her ancient tradition. Her mind and spirit are in a flux. They are breaking through the bondage imposed by our colonial experience. What this turbulence will do, nobody can tell. But to support and sustain the profound disturbance of her mind, India needs the knowledge that books bring. And India needs it, not in a narrow, chauvinistic sense. India has always believed in the concept of world civilisation.

Speech Delivered by Shri K. Natwar Singh, Minister of State For External Affairs, at the Opening Session of 23rd International Publishers' Association Congress at queen Elizabeth II Conference Centre, London, on 13 June 1988. Others speakers were Roy Jenkins, Wole Soyinka.

5

Introducing Nobel Laureate Wole Soyinka

According to the printed programme I am to introduce Mr. Wole Soyinka. One might as well try to introduce the Taj Mahal.

A Nobel Laureate, who through his sparkling creative vitality has enriched the Republic of Letters needs no routine, run of the mill introduction.

To begin with, may I, on behalf of the Trustees of the Jawaharlal Nehru Memorial Fund, thank you for accepting our invitation to deliver this year's Jawaharlal Nehru Memorial lecture. This is a memorable and joyous occasion. Tomorrow begin the nationwide, year long activities to celebrate the Centenary of that uncommon statesman, who used an elegant and forceful pen, and fluent flow of language, to lift Indians above their immediate needs and invited them to join him, in framing their hopes and aspirations of freedom, justice, dignity, democracy and humanity in words and phrases that moved the heart, stirred the mind and warmed the spirit.

It is appropriate that a master of language from Africa, a son of Nigeria should be delivering this lecture. Nigeria was the only African country, south of the Sahara that Panditji visited. That was in 1962. Our records show that Mr. Soyinka, then 28 years old met Jawaharlal Nehru in Lagos. As is well known Panditji greatly valued and enjoyed the company of writers.

In Mr. Soyinka's latest Curriculum Vitae, an item caught my eye. The Nigerian Government has appointed him as the Chairman of the Federal Road Safety Corps. For a citizen of Delhi like me, this is a tremendously impressive and necessary post. I have no personal knowledge of the road traffic conditions in Lagos, the capital of Nigeria but my friends tell me that driving in Nigeria can be an exhausting and exciting undertaking. I have heard that to minimise the traffic holdups owners of motorcars with even number plates are allowed to drive on the first three days of the week, and those with odd numbers, the remaining four days. The Nigerians being an ingenious and inventive people have solved this problem by installing revolving number plates on their cars. These can be adjusted by pushing a button on the dashboard.

We, in Delhi have not got that far yet, on our roads, Mr. Soyinka, you will find unfolding that glorious panaroma of the past, present and future of this great country. The 10th century co-exists with the 15th. The 16th is trying to tag on to the 18th. The 20th century showing the way to the 21st.

Driving here, as in Nigeria requires, iron nerves, near artistic skill and a fair amount of luck. I would be most grateful if you could share your perceptions in this field with us so that Nigeria and India can move to the future combining speed with safety.

Mr. Soyinka was awarded the Nobel Prize for Literature in 1986. Just as Rabindra Nath Tagore was the first Indian and first Asian to be awarded the Nobel Prize in 1913. Mr. Soyinka was the first Nigerian and the first African recipient of this Prize. He dedicated his Nobel Lecture which he delivered in Stockholm, to Nelson Mandela. The people of India hold that colossal figure in the highest esteem. We awarded him the Nehru Prize some years ago. Even Mrs. Mandela was refused permission by the racist regime in South Africa to come to India to receive the prize. It will interest you to know that the title of Mr. Mandela's autobiography, "No Easy Walk to Freedom", is a quotation from an essay in Mr. Nehru's book, *The Unity of India.*

I said earlier that I would not formally introduces Mr. Soyinka. What I will do is to read out a few passages from a release issued by the Swedish Academy in 1986. In well chosen words, it highlights Mr. Soyinka's literary genius and creativity.

"His background, upbringing and education have given him unusual conditions for a literary career. He has his roots· in the Yoruba people, myths, rites an cultural patterns, which in their turn have historical links to the Mediterranean region. Through his education in his native land and in Europe he has also acquired deep familiarity with western culture. His collection of essays Myth, Literature and the African World make for clarifying and enriching reading. Soyinka has been characterised as one of the finest poetical playwrights that have written in English.

"Among his plays special mention can be made of *A Dance of the Forests* and *Death and the King's Horseman*. The former is a kind of African *Midsummer Night's Dream* with sprits, ghosts and gods. There is a distinct link here to the indigenous ritual drama and to the Elizabethan drama. A key figure in Soyinka, the god Ogun, also appears in the play. He is both creator and destroyer and as Soyinka sees him has traits that lead one's thoughts to the Dionysian, the Apollonian and the Promethean in European tradition.

"*Death and the King's Horseman* is in the nature of an antique tragedy with the cultic sacrificial death as theme. The relationship between the unborn, the living and the dead, to which Soyinka reverts several times in his works, is fashioned here with very strong effect. Soyinka confirms his position as a centre of force in drama.

"Soyinka's plays have strong poetical elements. In several collections of poems he has also appeared as a poet of great distinction. One of the highlights is *Idanre,* and *Other Poems,* in which a central theme is the very thing that Ogun represents: the conflict, perhaps the union, between destruction and creation.

"The collection of poems A shuttle in the Crypt shows real stature. The poems were written during the writer's two years in prison, to which he was sent because of his attitude in his country's civil war. They are poems about mental survival, human contact, anger and forgiveness. *The same experiences lie behind his prose work The Man Died: Prison Notes, which in itself is a literary work of the first rank."*

I shall conclude by a quotation from Pandit Jawaharlal Nehru which is very relevant. In his great book *Glimpses of World History* which he wrote in prison, he said,

"Benjamin Disraeli, the great English Statesman of the 19th century has written: great men condemned to exile and captivity, if they survive, despair; the man of letters may reckon those days as sweetest of his life." He was writing about Hugo Grotious, a famous Dutch jurist and philosopher of the 17th century, who was condemned to imprisonment for life but managed to escape after two years. He spent these two years in prison in philosophical and literary work. There have been many famous gaolbirds, the two best known perhaps are the Spaniard Cervantes, who wrote Don Quixote, and the Englishman, John Bunyan, the author of The Pilgrims Progress.

Nehru continues, "I am not a man of letters, and I am not prepared to say that the many years I have spent in gaol have been the sweetest in my life, but I must say that reading and writing helped me wonderfully to get through them."

During his imprisonment Mr. Soyinka was kept in solitary confinement for 22 months in an insanitary, 19 x 4 feet cell, in, inhuman conditions. He was denied books, paper and pen. He wrote on toilet paper and between the lines of the books that were smuggled in. He has written about his harrowing experiences in thundering words in his book, "The Man Died." He faced his ordeal with superhuman courage. Hemingway defined Courage as: Grace under pressure. The pressure on Mr. Soyinka was no ordinary pressure. His grace was no ordinary grace.

I am sure, Jawaharlal Nehru would have approved our updating his list of literary gaolbirds by adding Mr. Soyinka's to it. Cervantes and Bunyan are read several centuries after their deaths. I think I will not be proved a false prophet, when I say that the plays, poems and novels of Wale Soyinka will be read in the centuries to come.

Speech at Vigyan Bhawan on 13.11.1989

6

Address of Foreign Ministers Conference on Cambodia, Paris, August 1989

Mr. Co-Chairman, Excellencies, distinguished delegates,

I should like to begin by extending my sincere gratitude to the Government of France for having extended to us and the other delegations their invitation to come to Paris to participate in a conference which might well mark a turning point.

Earlier this month, in this great city, the Bicentenary of the French Revolution was celebrated. So were liberty, equality and fraternity; Also the Rights of Man. The melancholy and adamantine fact is that 200 years after 1789, real liberty, real equality, real fraternity are still on the agenda of humanity.

President Mitterrand and other members of his Government notably Foreign Minister Dumas, the Co-Chairman, have played a vital role in bringing us together for this International Conference on Cambodia.

I should like to extend my delegation's warm wishes for the success of this Conference. H.E. the Co-Chairman of the Conference, the distinguished Foreign Minister of Indonesia, has been in the forefront of his country's efforts to find an equitable solution to this problem, which has faced us for several years. The role played by the Government of Indonesia in organising the informal meetings at Jakarta has indeed paved the way for our presence here today. We would like to thank you also, Mr. Co-Chairman, for your efforts and we would like to express the wish that under the joint chairmanship of both distinguished personalities, this Conference will achieve success.

Mr. Co-Chairman, the presence of the Chairman of the Nonaligned Movement in our midst is a recognition of the collective contribution of its members towards resolving disputes peacefully. In the particular instance of Cambodia, the Nonaligned Movement has been complementing the regional and other initiatives. I sincerely hope that in the near future we in the Nonaligned Movement will have the pleasure of welcoming Cambodia to take its rightful place in the Movement.

As recently as two years ago, it would have been difficult to imagine this Conference taking place. Much has happened since the first direct meeting between Prince Sihanouk and Prime Minister Hun Sen. India was of assistance in initiating this dialogue between these leading personalities in December, 1987. I, myself have kept in close and continuous touch with the leaders in Indo-China and Asean. Several multilateral meetings have been held and important bilateral contacts undertaken between the various parties and countries concerned. The most notable among these have been the Informal Meetings held in Jakarta. The Jakarta Informal Meetings have resulted in the enunciation of a consensus covering many aspects of a comprehensive solution to the Cambodian question, including the withdrawal of Veitnamese troops linked to the cessation of all external interference and military assistance to the Cambodian factions and the non-return of the genocidal policies of the Pol Pot regime. It is our hope that the International Conference on Cambodia will take this process further and enable us to reach agreements on the many aspects involved.

India's historical links with South-East Asia have been long and multi-faceted, involving as they have inter-actions in philosophical, religious, cultural and commercial fields. We have been deeply pained at the tragedy and suffering which have befallen this part of the world in recent years. We have, therefore, striven and will continue to strive to achieve a lasting peace, to bring an end to the agony of the Cambodian people. Several distinguished delegates have alluded to the spirit of the Khmer people as symbolized in the marvellous structures at Angkor. Mr. Chairman, we recognise and admire this spirit and we would be gratified to witness its restoration. The recognition of the symbolic importance of this monument to the Cambodian nation has inspired India to undertake the restoration of the temple complex at Angkor over the last few years.

Mr. Chairman, you and other distinguished Ministers are aware of the role which India played since 1954 as Chairman of the

International Commission for supervision and control in Cambodia. In spite of the many problems which the Commission faced and which have been referred to by my distinguished colleague the Foreign Minister of Canada, India learnt much from this experience, just as we have learnt from our participation in other peace-keeping operations in Korea, the Congo, Gaza, Cyprus and Namibia.

We strongly support the call for an International Control Mechanism to undertake well-defined responsibilities for implementing an agreed solution to the Cambodian question. In order, however, to avoid the difficulties which were experienced in the earlier International Control Commission, we would also lend our strong support to the call for the assignment of specific responsibilities and a clear mandate to the International Control Mechanism which can be, inter alia, expected to monitor the withdrawal of the foreign forces from Cambodia. Equally important would be the functions of supervising the cessation of the inflow of military assistance to the Cambodian factions, the non-return of the genocidal practices of the Pol Pot regime and the supervision of general elections.

We fully support the position stated by many delegations that a comprehensive solution would be the best way to ensure stable peace in Cambodia. We are, however, equally conscious of the fact, which has been repeatedly stated, that a political solution cannot be imposed from outside, because ultimately the Cambodian people must decide for themselves. It is a tribute to the wisdom of the Co-Chairmen of this Conference that they have foreseen the necessity for the discussions among the Cambodians to continue in parallel with the proceedings of the International Conference itself. We urge the Cambodian parties to display the necessary spirit of flexibility and constructive compromise and come to an understanding amongst themselves, so that the International Conference can recognise and guarantee the agreements arrived at among them. At the same time, however, the emphasis should be on the parallel nature of the Conference, which means that we should work hard in the various Committees to be set up, to ensure that the necessary environment is created for the achievement of a comprehensive solution.

Since it is the Cambodian people that will ultimately have to decide their future, it is imperative that fair and free elections are held under international supervision within a reasonable period of time, so that the will of the Cambodian people prevails. Their verdict must be accepted, if Cambodia is to leave behind its winter of discontent, and go forward to a new dawn.

There is general agreement that Cambodia should be a sovereign, independent, neutral and non-ailgned country, at peace with itself and its neighbours. This clearly means that foreign military bases or forces will not be present in Cambodia. We have noted the Declaration of Permanent Neutrality of the National Assembly of the State of Cambodia enshrining these principles.

We have listened with interest and respect to the points made by the distinguished Secretary General of the United Nations which have found general acceptance in the Conference. The details regarding the role that the United Nations can play will be worked out by the Working Committees in the next few days. However, Mr. Co-Chairman, may I emphasis India's view that the effective role of the United Nations can only be based on the broad consensus of the countries members of the organisation and which takes into account the various points of view. The exclusivity of reserving decisions to a small number of countries cannot have the desired results.

Once peace has been restored to Cambodia, it will facilitate the return of Cambodian refugees to their home without let or hinderance. The U.N. High Commissioner for Refugees has the necessary experience and machinery for coordinating this process.

Cambodia will need considerable assistance for its rehabilitation and reconstruction. The international community should be generous in providing means for the rebuilding of Cambodia. We in India have several ongoing programmes, of which the restoration of the Angkor Wat, which I referred to earlier, is among the most important. We have provided other assistance including doctors, medical equipment and technical experts. India, a developing country itself, has the experience and expertise to extend assistance in many fields such as small scale industries, forest and agro-based industries, fisheres etc. We are willing to share them and train Cambodian personnel in agriculture, water resources, manpower planning, irrigation, telecommunications, cooperative sector, rural development, etc.

We have assembled here to try to find a political solution for what is called the Cambodian problem. The tragedy of Cambodia has lasted long enough. While it will take a lot of effort from us all to ensure the success of this important conference, anyone of us, by taking an inflexible approach, can hinder its success. This, we must not allow. We must endeavour to dissipate the blinding mist of misunderstanding and breakthrough the mounting wall of prejudice. The building of peace, the enlarging the areas of agreement, are more important than anything else. Should we not, here ensure that future of Cambodia no longer lies in the past? What we need is good will, understanding. Confidence building takes time, so does healing of wounds. Benjamin Franklin's formula to a diplomat was, 'sleepless tact, immovable calmness and a patience that no folly, no provocation, no blunders can shake.'

For too long the people of Cambodia have looked at dark clouds without a silver lining. That silver lining is now more than discernible. Having come so far we cannot, we must not fail. Diplomacy does not offer salvation, it does offer hope. That is why we are here.

Mr. Chairman, let me conclude with a verse from the *Rig Veda,* which is perhaps the oldest Book known to Humankind dating back to between 2000 - 1500 B.C.:

"Meet together, Talk together;
May your minds comprehend alike;
Common be your action and achievement;
Common be your thoughts and intentions;
Common be the wishes of your hearts
So may there be union amongst you."

7

Thank You Dr. Sagan, Teen Murti Auditorium

SHRIMATI SONIA GANDHI, DR SAGAN, DR KARAN SINGH AND FRIENDS:

After so dazzling, sparkling, stimulating, enchanting and profoundly educative a talk, silence, which Boris Pasternak called, the best of sounds on Earth, would be in order. But human beings are, with some notable exceptions, a loquacious lot, silence does not come to us easily.

Then, on an occasion like this, certain agreeable proprieties have to be observed. I am required to make concluding remarks and thank Professor Sagan.

The Declaration of Independence of the United States pronounced in 1776 that all men are created equal. I have respect for the shrines of other men's minds. Thomas Jefferson, Benjamin Franklin and other authors of this great and inspiring document were not ordinary mortals and one hesitates to take them on. Nevertheless, available evidence, accumulated over 200 years, points in the other direction – that all men are created unequal. Carl Sagan does not have an equal in this room. His I.Q. is superior to 99% of the human race. Being created equal and acquiring or ensuring political or social equality are different propositions and I need not go into them here. Even the dictum – equal opportunities to be equal does not carry us far.

If Professor Sagan and I were to be class mates reading Physics, he would get 99% marks and I would get 9%. No, human beings are not created equal. That is one of the grouses many of us have against the Almighty.

Your lecture, Dr. Sagan, would have pleased and delighted Jawaharlal Nehru. In your book *Cosmos,* you rightly state that science came to India very late and that too, not in excess. That it came at all, is due to Nehru's vision and passion for science and humanising technology. It was therefore entirely appropriate that you should deliver the Nehru Lecture and illuminate and stir our static minds. You are a brilliant popularizer, who commands an expository style of superb ease and clarity. We are grateful to you, Sir, and thank you most sincerely.

May I for a moment come back to your wonderful book, *Cosmos*. In it you make some lively and interesting observations on Astrology. You point out that there are ten times more astrologers than astronomers in the United States. Here we are far in advance of you. In India, for one astronomer we have a hundred astrologers. Lately diplomats from former communist countries, stationed in Delhi, have been seen hovering around astrologers, now that the infallibility of the doctrines of Marx is no longer fashionable. Even scientists in my country are devoted to this amazing branch of human activity. We have all heard of Dr. Homi Bhaba, India's most celebrated Physicist. Pandit Nehru one day cornered him – "Homi, what is this I hear, you of all people believing in this astrological nonsense: What an example to set."

Bhaba's answer was, "Sir, I have become a convert after carefully going through the bio-datas of your cabinet colleagues. The only possible explanation for their inclusion in your Council of Ministers is that they all have powerful horroscopes!!

Finally, I will share with you Mrs. Indira Gandhi's encounter with Niel Armstrong – the first man to land on the moon in June 1969. In 1970 he came to India. I was then working in the Prime Minister's secretariat and took Mr. Armstrong to see Mrs. Gandhi. She told him how she had kept awake almost the whole night, following on the radio (there was no TV in those days) his progress to the moon. She had heard his first words – one step for man, a giant step for mankind. The time was 3.50 a.m. Neil Armstrong's immortal response was, Madam, next time I shall make sure to land on the moon at a less unearthly hour."

13 November 1991

8

Homage to Rajiv Gandhi

I find it both painful and difficult to speak about Rajiv Gandhi in the past tense. My emotional side tells me that any moment he might walk into this room from that door and electrify this meeting. My rational side asks me not to confuse hope with fact.

When on 21 May twelve months ago the cruel hand of fate struck, the ultimate futility of all human arrangements and plans struck me with force. Why him? Why he, who was young, fearless, magnanimous, handsome, charismatic, spontaneous, trusting. My mood was dark and bitter. I felt empty and weary and drained and life seemed nothing more than a meaningless dance of ash and dust.

A few days later, reading Alexander Gladkov's book, *Meetings with Pasternak,* I came across a soul stirring passage on Page 134 – Pasternak says,

"History is life's answer to the challenge of death – it is the conquest of death with the help of memory and time."

Rajiv Gandhi's fragrant memory lives beyond death. The Atma never perishes and conquers time.

He lived a short life long. He achieved so much. His work endures.

To you, Madam, may I just say, how much the people of India admire your quiet courage. your noble serenity, your luminous dignity. Crude assaults have been made on your privacy. Your restraint has been exemplary.

Your loss. your grief, your pain cannot be quantified but your sorrow is shared by millions in the country and the world over.

This volume of Tributes to Shri Rajiv Gandhi is a testimony to that. It is brought out by the Indira Gandhi Memorial Trust, edited by Sharada Prasad and one other person and published by A.H. Wheeler and Co.

We are grateful to you Mr Prime Minister for being present here this evening. 1 now request Shri P. V. Narasimha Rao to release the book, present the first copy to Smt. Sonia Gandhi and say a few words.

Statement at the Indira Gandhi Memorial Trust functon on 21.5.1992

9

Happy Birthday Gamini

I am a great believer in personal relationships. Friendship is one of the great gifts that life offers-friendship enriches life, uplifts life, expands life, enlarges life and makes our passage through this fascinating and disconcerting planet a little less tedious and tiresome than it might otherwise be.

Naturally, I was delighted and excited when Sirima and Gamini invited me to be in Colombo on this very happy and significant occasion. Yours was a very special gesture. It advanced the frontiers of friendship and most sincerely do I thank you both for it. Now that you have attained the age of respectability you must start to listen to sound but unsolicited advice. Your youth, since this morning is behind you, but there is something you can do to look less youthful. Do something to your dark hair. Borrow a few grey ones from me.

Dear Sirima, a word of caution from a man of 61. Keep an extra eye on him. 50 is a dangerous age when men want to have a fling or two before the fire begins to dim. Gamini is handsome, famous and at the moment, like me, unemployed. If you need any help just let me or Lalith know. We will fix him.

Gamini, you and I are politicians. It is the noblest of callings. It is also the most abused and misused. Individuals like you are needed in politics so that private decencies can be transmitted to public affairs. So that the level of the national political dialogue can be raised and maintained. At our ages we also accept that what is desirable is not always possible, and what is possible is often not desirable. This is a dilemma, honest politicians face constantly. They do not create the dilemma, but they are required to deal with it.

The crooked ones just don't bother about it. For them the distinction between right and wrong, permissible and impermissible, the desirable and the possible does not exist. Some of us, very fortunately are still prepared to do our bit for what we consider is right.

The adjective most commonly used for politicians is Ambition. There are different kinds of ambition—the racist ambition of Hitler, the totalitarian ambition of Stalin, the cruel ambitions of Pol Pot and Ceaucescue—the gallery of the mosters of the 20th is over crowed.

Then there is the ambition of a Lincoln, a Gandhi, a Nehru, a Ho Chi Minh—an ambition tempered by love, compassion, magnanimity, free of hate and violence. They do their best to find peaceful and creative answers for the ills of the world. They came to the world with clean hands. They leave it with clean hands.

De Gaulle, one of the towering and majestic figures of the 20th century once said: "Ambitious men of the first order who see no other reason for living than that of stamping their mark on their Time and who from the shore upon which common place times retain them, dream only of History."

So, ambition to serve, to help, to right a wrong, to stand up and be counted, to expose fraud and injustice is not to be scoffed at. And you possess this ambition, the right kind of ambition in abundance. It is convenient and easy to comprise, it is damned hard to defy. But without defiance, no one can aspire to leadership. As someone said the first principle of morality is to disobey.

You, Gamini, have dedicated your life to the service of your people and your country. You attained high public office at a very young age. This beautifully produced volume of tributes is no routine, run of the mill, platitudinous tribute. It is the quintessence of your solid, lasting and wholly praise worthy achievement. It highlights your commitment to unblemished justice, political conduct, and above all your integrity and courage.

Now that I am here, may I say a word or two about Indo-Sri Lanka relations, in the shaping of which you played so significant a part.

Ours are two civilizational countries. We have lived in peace and harmony for thousands of years. Geography, history, religion, culture have played a creative role in our age old friendship. Counter balancing interests make it imperative that we promote mutual goodwill, harmony and good neighbourliness. The contours, of, the international landscape are changing very fast.

Diplomacy is an arena of challenge and response. How shall India and Sri Lanka respond to the challenges of the coming decades—the challenges of terrorism. drugs. violence, ethnicity, sub-nationalism, religious fanaticism and fundamentalism, the challenge of poverty, unemployment and over-population? How will Sri Lanka, for example, use the advantage of India's proximity, which also comprises its huge market etc. to its maximum advantage and to the mutual benefit of both our countries and peoples? What response do we have to the new international political and economic order? How can we rejuvenate the Non-aligned Movement? NAM is not an ideology or an ism, it is a way of looking at things and situations and events. It is as relevant today as it was ten or twenty years ago. The challenge are different. The responses have to be different.

The Cold War has ended. Does that make the U.N. Charter irrelevant.

Prime Minister Narasimha Rao, participating in the Security Council Summit on 31.1.1992, in well chosen and measured words, sounded a warning on behalf of NAM when he said:

"The role of the United Nations must naturally rest on the Charter, which incorporates the vital framework for action for maintenance of international peace and security. But the Charter is only as legitimate and secures as its underpinning by the collective will of the international community. At every step, the interpretation of the Charter as well as the actions by the Security Council must flow from that collective will and not from the views or predilections of a few. A general consensus must always prevail. What is right and just must become transparent. It is as simple as that. Members of the Security Council, whether permanent or elected, should insist on this consensus, scrupulously avoiding the temptation to dictate for quick results. Besides, while prescribing norms and standards for national or international conduct, the Security Council must scrupulously accept those norms for itself."

Sri Lanka is Chairman of SAARC for the rest of this year.

We in SAARC, if we speak with one voice, act jointly, can make a creative and constructive contribution towards finding answers for some of the ills that inflict humankind.

(Speech by K. Nativar Singh at the Gamini Dissanayake's 50th birthday celebration meeting at the Lanka, Oberoi Hotel, Colombo, 20.3.90).

10

A London Dinner

Two days ago, some of us were discussing the arrangements for this dinner. To my horror I discovered that Mr. Michael Foot would speak earlier than myself. My heart sank. Some years ago at the United Nations, his elder brother Hugh and I sat in the same Committee on opposite sides of the fence. It was hard enough dealing with the right Foot but there is no keeping up with the left Foot.

Mr. Eldon Griffiths, M.P. and our Chairman tonight, being the shrewd person he is, must have observed the look of agony on my face and asked me: "Is it absolutely necessary for you to speak?" Now Eldon that is the kind of question a diplomat like me would love to ask a politician like you.

He was in a generous mood and actually told me what I might say. The British and-the Indians are for ever telling each other what to do but have the good sense to ignore that advice.

Had this been a purely British function, I would have followed Mr. Griffith's suggestion. Since it is a happy Indo-British occasion, I shall make a compromise. It is well known that functions connected with India in this country never start on time and having once started never seem to finish. Mr. Griffiths ensured that this function began punctually. It is now left to me to ensure that it does not end punctually.

The British are slaves to petty punctuality. No offence meant. We in India suffer from no such handicaps. But when it suits the British they do not particularly care to look at the clock. For nearly forty years Mahatma Gandhi and Pandit Nehru in a polite non-violent way kept on reminding the British that it was time for them to go home, but our British friends totally ignored the clock of Indian independence. You will, therefore, forgive met his evening if I take an extra minute or two of your time.

We cherish our links with the United Kingdom. No one did more for it than Pandit Nehru after 1947. Obviously you do too; that is why a senior respected Member of the Labour Cabinet is here, as is the shadow Foreign Secretary. From our side, the President of the Indian National Congress Shri D.K. Borooah and the Minister of Commerce Chattopadhayaya have come all the way from India to participate in this function. The Prime Minister has sent a message. As a diplomat, it is my duty to ensure that Indo-British relations are strengthened and misunderstandings removed. It is good to know that these sentiments are reciprocated.

What can I say about Jawaharlal Nehru? I paid my tribute to him elsewhere. I owe him a great deal personally. The world owes him a great deal. It is a better place because he lived. He raised the level and quality of national and international dialogue and proved to us that private decencies can be transmitted to public affairs. A politician, he never cared to tidy his past. There was nothing to tidy up.

Great men more often than not leave behind a trail of blood and bitterness. Others leave different kinds of odours. Jawaharlal Nehru left behind a fragrance and to millions his image still glows. His work endures. His achievement inspires.

May I thank you all for joining this function, particularly Fenner Brockway, 87 years young; Jennie Lee and Sonny Ramphal, Secretary-General of the Commonwealth, and all others who have taken time out to come here tonight.

Good Night, and have a nice week-end.

Speech by Natwar Singh, Acting High Commissioner of India, on Friday, 14 November 1975, at London Hilton Hotel, at a Dinner to commemorate the Birthday of late Prime Minister Jawaharlal Nehru.

11

India and Islam

The Consolidation of a Composite Culture and the Challenge of Contemporary Politics

It is an honour and a privilege for me to deliver the 12th Lal Bahadur Shastri Memorial Lecture. Three months ago, we celebrated the 100th Birth Anniversary of Lal Bahadur Shastri—one of the great sons of India. Of him, Pt. Jawaharlal Nehru had said in Parliament: "No man can wish for a better comrade and colleague than Lal Bahadur. The man of the highest integrity, loyalty, devoted to ideals and a man of conscience is called Lal Bahadur Shastri." Today, we salute this great son of India. His humility and his simplicity endeared him to millions of Indians. He was a tireless champion of the interests of the working class and peasants. The slogan he gave us, 'Jai Jawan Jai Kissan', resonates with us even today.

The Shastri Memorial Lecture has established itself as one of the most important forums for the expression of ideas. That is why I have chosen as the theme for my lecture, 'India and Islam', in which I will talk about the consolidation of a composite culture and the challenge of contemporary politics.

I believe, and I have said this even on the floor of Parliament, that one of the major challenges that the world faces today is how to deal with the Muslim world. I have deliberately not used the word 'Islamic'. There are 1.3 billion Muslims in the world, of which 450 million are in the Sub-continent alone. It is a fact that from Mauritania to Medan, Muslim psyche has been hurt and needs to be healed. We, in India, have a history of co-existence with Islam for more than a thousand years. It is significant that of the 150 million Muslims in India, not one joined the Taliban or *Al-Qaeda*. That is why we are uniquely placed to assist with this process. And for this, it is important that we recognize how Islam has influenced India and how India has influenced Islam.

For over two millennia, the geographical location of India has ensured a continuous, vibrant and enriching encounter with diverse communities beyond our mountains and the oceans. This includes a thriving mercantile and cultural interaction between India and the Arabian Peninsula. Early records speak of Arabs employed in administrative positions by Rashtrakuta rulers, who referred to them as *Tajikas*.[1] Indeed, there was a "historical continuity" and a comfortable familiarity in the encounters and interactions between India and the peoples of West and Central Asia.

With the advent of Islam, there was a transformation in these traditional interactions in the shape of a short-lived Arab military incursion into Sind, followed 300 years later with the arrival of the Turks from Ghazni and Ghor. But, their military incursions did not replace the traditional give-and-take of traders, intellectuals and professionals. Indeed, it could be said that the non-military interaction received a fillip on account of royal patronage, which passed on, over the decades, from Muslim rulers to non-Muslim potentates across India.

While it is customary in modern times to use monolithic terminologies to describe the diverse peoples of the Indian sub-continent as "Hindu" or "Muslim", historical record attests that in India neither of these communities were seen as or saw themselves as monolithic communities.

The Muslim community in India was by no means a monolithic one. It was divided on caste and class lines. Moreover, its various segments interacted with other groups in Indian society, transcending caste and religious boundaries. Sufi Islam, in particular, flourished, binding the different communities on the strength of love, compassion and understanding. Such was the

[1]Thapar, Romila, "Historical Interpretations and the Secularising of Indian Society," Kappen Memorial Lecture, Visthar, Bangalore, pg.18.

message emanating from Ajmer and the Shrine of Nizamuddin Auliya.

The great Mughal Emperor Akbar rejected religious orthodoxy and came up with his own "Religion of God" or *Din-i-Ilahi*, which propounded a creed of harmony among peoples and was a blend of Islam, Hinduism, Christianity, Buddhism, Zoroastrianism and other traditions.

The period from the 16th century onwards saw the flowering of India's composite culture that brought together diverse people in a pervasive composite polity. This was not a particularly difficult or painful process because, for centuries before Islam, the broad Indian ethos had brought together diverse beliefs and peoples. The entry of Muslims into the Indian subcontinent merely required the Indian cultural ethos to broaden its circumference and understand and assimilate the values and traditions which came with these people, who were not strangers and with whom India had interacted for several centuries.

Even as the Central Asians (first the Turks and later the Mughals) made India their home, this encounter in due course reached out to and influenced every part of our Sub-continent. No aspect of Indian life remained untouched, and every aspect of Muslim life came to be influenced by India's traditions. The tapestry of our national culture is so tightly woven that it is indeed difficult to identify the origin of a particular strand or give it a special value above others.

The religion of Islam and its Central Asian protagonists brought a new message of equality and brotherhood and shook to its foundations an indigenous cultural ethos that had got mired in stagnant ritualism, grotesque inequality and a loss of creative drive. After the battles were over, the encounters and dialogue between administrators, scholars, architects and craftsmen began. Ideas and experiences from beyond our borders came to influence urban-planning, monument construction, road making and drainage systems, administration and revenue collection, farming and craftsmanship, and the art of warfare. And, for every idea and experience brought from abroad, there was a counterpart indigenous response. The ruins of Mohenjodaro bear eloquent testimony to this.

The hoary experience of hundreds of thousands of these daily personal encounters gave a fresh shape and character to our ethos and invigorated every aspect of our life. In the face of the challenge of the Islamic *Ulema*, Hindu scholars vigorously recalled their own traditional philosophy and scholarship, and, at the same time, after deep introspection, identified and reviewed that which was wrong in their own order that needed reform. On their part, Muslim divines, orthodox and eclectic, came in time to be influenced by Hindu thought and belief.

Even as these exciting debates took place among philosophers and scholars, a deeper and more profound interaction was taking place among the ordinary people. Both Hindus and Muslims at the popular level recognised that there was much that was common between them: they were small farmers or landless labourers ekeing out a life amidst the vagaries of nature and the impulses of *zamindars* who made no religious distinction in showering favour or wrath; they were targets of rapacious revenue collectors; they were foot-soldiers and cannon fodder in wars fought by princes which meant little to them and brought them no benefit; they were victims of drought and flood; in general, their lives were mired in want and penury. These common fears and dilemmas transcended the gap in religious belief and developed in time a similarity of daily life based on mutual support and broad participation in what the other held dear: the joys of marriages and festivals and the sorrows of loss and death.

From these shared experiences emerged two of the most influential and widespread movements in our country, whose reverberations are still with us—the *Bhakti* movement and the Sufi tradition. Both these movements rejected empty ritualism, outdated custom, and the iniquitous religious order that made material demands upon their followers but provided little spiritual solace or comfort. In their place, came the idea of a personal God who could be approached directly by the meanest of His believers. Religion became not the exclusive preserve of harsh and remote priests, but a warm, happy and satisfying daily experience based on a personal engagement with a God Who understood, loved and forgave.

Over several centuries, Indian Sufis and *bhakts* lived and preached side by side, at times differing from each other, but. generally over time, moving on to co-existence, and finally in tolerance and understanding, as Aziz Ahmad, a well-known writer, has noted.[2] From the mid-17th Century, the *Qadiri* silsilah showed the most tolerance, under the influence of Prince Dara Shikoh and Princess Jahan Ara. In the 18th Century, the *Naqshbandi* silsilah became so liberal that one of them regarded the Vedas as divinely inspired, and Hindus as monotheists who had "their revealed scriptures and prophets" like other people of the book. Though Shah Waliullah espoused the orthodox revival in India in the mid-18th century, his son Shah Abdul Aziz, because of the impact of the *Bhagwad Gita* on him, regarded Lord Krishna among the *auliya.*

The *Bhakt* and the Sufi rejected barriers between religious groups and exalted the God who saw no barriers of religion, region or caste. Today, we do not recall the names of the *Ulema* and temple priests who collectively, with their rigid postures and demands, over the centuries, brought such torment and misery to their followers. We remember instead the names of Khwaja Muinuddin Chisti, Khwaja Nizamuddin Auliya, of Meera Bai, Kabir, Guru Nanak, Krishna Chaitanya, Sant Dyananeshwar, Namdeo and Tukaram. Their simple verses preached love of our fellow beings and love of a personal Almighty. Perhaps, Kabir, with his simple eloquence, put across this message most powerfully when he sang:

मोको कहाँ ढूँढ़े बन्दे,
मैं तो तेरे पास में।
ना मैं देवल ना मैं मस्जिद,
न काबे कैलास में।

[2]Ahmad, Aziz, "Studies in Islamic Culture in the Indian Environment," Oxford University Press, Delhi, 1999, pg.138.

ना तो कौने क्रियाकर्म में,
नहीं योग बैराग में।
खोजी होय तो तुरतै मिलिहौ,
पल भर की तलाश में।

["O Servant, where dost thou seek me?
Lo! I am beside thee.
I am neither in the temple nor in the mosque:
I am neither in Kaaba nor in Kailash:
Neither am I in rites and ceremonies.
Nor in Yoga and .renunciation.
If thou art a true seeker, thou shalt at
once see Me; thou shalt meet Me."]

Beyond the arena of religious belief, our syncretic culture manifested itself in art, architecture, music, apparel and food. Muhammad Mujeeb explains this most succinctly:

> Religion became the religion of the people. Then, the spoken languages of the people became literary languages. We have the beginnings of Hindi, Bengali, Gujarati, Punjabi and Sind hi literature. Further, the city became the centre of culture, tailored clothing came into general use, simplicity was discarded in favour of a life enriched and complicated by a vast increase in the articles of daily use, manners became elaborate and were, so to say, codified in the form of a recognised etiquette. None of these changes, except perhaps the first, can be regarded as due to the influence of Islam, but the changes would not have taken place when they did if Islam had not become one of the religions of India.[3]

Much of the beauty and sophistication of life which could be enjoyed in common by Hindus and Muslims was represented by the emergence of Urdu, which, as Mujeeb has noted, "became a symbol of the common culture that emerged out of the prevailing political chaos of the 18th and 19th Century."[1]

[3]Mujeeb, M., "Islamic Influence on Indian Society," Meenakshi Prakashan, Meerut, 1977, pg. 9-10.

[4]MUjeeb, M., "The Indian Muslims," Munshiram Manoharlal Publishers, New Delhi, 2003, pg.464; henceforth *Indian Muslims*.

This period was replete with extraordinarily gifted writers, but Mirza Ghalib stands out as a stalwart amongst them and in himself exemplifies the best of our composite culture. His poetry, Mujeeb points out, has become a part of our everyday speech and so he can be regarded as a "poet of the people."[5] There is no aspect of human life he did not contemplate and comment upon, whether it be man's encounter with his Creator, the confusion and passion of unrequited love, the pleasure of wine and intellectual contemplation, and the anguish and melancholy informing the human predicament.

Ghalib rejected the ritualism that accompanied most religious people:

हम मुबहिद हैं
हमारा कैश है तर्क-ए-रुसूम
मिल्लतें जब मिट गई
अजज़ा-ए-ईमाँ हो गई।

["God is one, that is our faith; all rituals we abjure.
'Tis only when the symbols vanish that belief is pure."]

Another stalwart who strode across India was Muhammad Iqbal, both a poet and a philosopher. He was a complex individual and thus cannot be identified with a simplistic label. Though in later years Iqbal sought to identify himself with pan- Islamism, then popular in some intellectual circles in the Islamic world, his longing of unity among Indians, as Mujeeb has pointed out, "had a deep spiritual basis and did not derive from any transitory political sentiment."[6] His *Tarana-e-Hindi* resounds in our ears day after day. But, his poem *Naya Shivala* (New Temple) sets out his views most powerfully.

सच कह दूँ ऐ बिरहमन! गर तू बुरा न माने
तंग आके मैंने आखिर
दैरो-हरम को छोड़ा।
वाइज कर वाज छोड़ा

[5]*Indian Muslims,* pg. 467.
[6]*Indian Muslims,* pg. 485.

छोड़े तेरे फसाने।
पत्थर की मूरतों में
समझा है तू खुदा है।
खाके वतन का मुझको
हर ज़र्रा देखता है।
आ गैरियत के पर्दे
इक बार फिर उठा दे।
बिछड़ों को फिर मिला दे
नक्शे-दुई मिटा दे।

[My heart was sick: I turned away both from
the temple and the Ka'bah,
From the sermons of the preacher and from
thy fairy tales, O Brahman.
To Thee images of stone embody the divine –
For me, every particle of my country's
dust is a deity.
Comc, let us remove all that causes estrangement,
Let us reconcile those that have turned away from
each other, remove all signs of division.]

Challenges to the Composite Culture: Communal Politics and Partition

The Indian composite culture, nurtured over several centuries has been repeatedly challenged amidst fears that its all-embracing syncreticism dilutes other more exclusive values and identities which, some believe, should be dominant in the national ethos. The 19th Century was a particularly confusing and even chaotic period since, with the entry of British rule, the traditional political order was overturned, traditional beliefs and practices were questioned and rejected, and India's composite culture was deliberately fractured so that the emerging fault-lines would facilitate imperial rule.

This period of uncertainty and ferment evoked different responses from different sections of the Indian polity. Initially, after 1857, the Muslims were systematically targeted for their participation in the uprising, even as some Hindu elites saw the advantages of pursuing Western education and adopting Western cultural styles. As the 19th century came to a close, the British saw with concern a new political enlightenment manifesting itself in different parts of the country, brought together by the setting up of the Indian National Congress in 1885. The British rulers quickly saw the advantage of dividing the burgeoning Indian national movement by systematically pandering to Muslim fears based on their "minority" status, their loss of political power, and the threat to their religious and cultural identity from a "Hindu" majority. In short, the country came to be deliberately divided on simplistic Hindu-Muslim lines, with broad characteristics and dark motivations being monolithically assigned to each community. The fears and aspirations of one community were set off against the other.

Though the communal divide was deliberately encouraged by British imperialism, it must be accepted that from both the Muslim and Hindu communities of India extremist individuals and movements emerged who confronted the other group, feared and caricatured it, and frequently turned to the British for assistance in their competition with it. Still, in spite of the greatest effort of the British rulers, the mass national movement of India did not reject its composite culture, and fiercely resisted British rule even as it rejected the emotive appeal of the extremists on both sides.

But, the partition of our country on communal lines could not be averted. Controversy still rages in the Sub-continent about who was responsible for this painful vivisection of our nation on communal basis. What it has succeeded in doing is to set the stage for continued confrontation between India and Pakistan even as the latter struggles to develop a national identity and put in place political values and structures that would be in consonance with its people's aspirations.

It is a great tribute to our founding fathers that, in spite of the pain, passion, anger and violence that surrounded the communal politics of early 20th Century India and the partition of our country, they did not swerve from their intense commitment to our composite culture which found expression in our secular Constitution.

The Indian state is not secular in the Western sense of a total separation between Church and State. It recognises the importance of religious belief among Indians, but refuses to give primacy to any particular belief-system. Our Left Wing philosopher, M.N. Roy, wished the state to move away from religion. He wanted the State to afford its citizens "not the freedom to choose from among various religious doctrines, but the freedom of the human spirit from the tyranny of all of them."[7] In contrast, Gandhiji regarded all religions as true; he said: "My veneration for other faiths is the same as for my own."[8]

Our philosopher-President, Dr. Radhakrishnan, disagreed with M.N. Roy, saying: "I want to state authoritatively that secularism does not mean irreligion. It means we respect all faiths and religions. Our State does not identify itself with any particular religion."[9]

Above all, Indian secularism was a cherished faith and belief of Jawaharlal Nehru. He had little tolerance of religion in its communal manifestations, which he referred to as "organised religion." He said:

> The spectacle of what is called religion, or at any rate organised religion, in India and elsewhere has filled me with horror, and I have frequently condemned it and wished to make a clean sweep of it. Almost always it seems to stand for blind belief and reaction, dogma and bigotry, superstition and exploitation, and the preservation of vested interests.[10]

[7]Quoted in: Ayyub, Abu Sayeed, "Secularism and Jawaharlal Nehru," in Sinha, v.v. (Ed): *Secularism in India,* Lalvani Publishing House, Bombay, 1968, pg.127.

[8]*Ibid.*

[9]*Ibid.*

[10]*Ibid.*

At the same time, Nehru understood the role of religious faith in bringing out the best in an individual. In the Discovery of India, he writes:

> While we advance on the external plane, as we must if we are to survive, we have also to win peace with ourselves and between ourselves and our environment, a peace, which brings satisfaction not only to our physical and material needs but also to those inner imaginative urges and adventurous stirrings that have distinguished man ever since be started on his troubled journey in the realms of thought and action.[11]

The founding fathers of the Indian Constitution placed before themselves as their highest constitutional objectives the banishing of poverty, illiteracy and backwardness, and the building of a united nation and an integrated society from the heterogeneous, fragmented and segmented societal structure, traumatised by recent religious strife. They were aware that this nascent Indian nation would flourish not merely on the basis of geographical and economic unity and its long common history but only on the basis of the will of the people to be a nation.

In order to promote fusion amidst contemporary challenges, they reached out to the fundamentals of Indian tradition and enunciated a charter of tolerance, equality and justice which is the essence of the Indian Constitution today. The new Indian nation did not move away from religion or ignore its existence; it understood and articulated the essential meaning of religious faith and belief. Above all, it recognised the religious pluralism of the Indian people which had created a composite culture at the centre of its ethos. As Dr. Ambedkar put it in the Constituent Assembly: "If the Muslims in India are a separate nation, then, of course, India is not a nation."[12]

[11] *Ibid.*pg. 127-28.

[12] Quoted in: Sen, Amartya, "Secularism and its Discontents," in Bhargava, Rajeev (Ed.): *Secularism and its Critics,* Oxford University Press, New Delhi, 1999, pg. 470.

In the post-Independence era, the Indian nation, recovering from the trauma of Partition, has made an extraordinary effort to retrieve, refresh and give a contemporary value to its composite culture, which is given legal form in its Constitution. Overall, the record of the Indian state is laudable. Even as country after country has fallen under the jackboot of military dictatorship or one-party authoritarianism, India's democracy has witnessed the cohesiveness of the national order, the periodic rise and fall of Governments, and an expanding prosperity base that is gradually reaching the poorest levels of our polity. All of these are the essential reality of our 57 years as a free nation.

CONTEMPORARY CHALLENGES: THE "SECULARISM" DEBATE

However, we would be failing our founding fathers if we did not address one of the most serious contemporary threats to India's composite culture, which is represented by the ideology of the BJP and its fraternity. To my mind, the philosophical underpinnings, the national strategies, and the tactical moves of the votaries of this ideology present a grave challenge to our national ethos and our national values. This movement robs the Hindu religion of its philosophy and profundity, and the sense of tolerance and accommodation that its adherents have for people different from themselves. It replaces these cherished values and principles with doctrines of exclusivity and hate, with strategies of confrontation and violence, and tactics that involve mayhem, murder and massacre. It mobilises its supporters through emotive appeals, recalling ancient wrongs, bogus threats and caricatures of entire peoples. It constitutes, to my mind, the gravest perversion of our inherited values. If not confronted, it has within it the capacity to destroy nearly 60 years of our constitutional democracy and 3000 years of our composite culture.

I am aware that, in recent years, there has been a vigorous and often acrimonious debate on the idea of secularism and its continuing relevance to the Indian polity. Though respected academics have also called for a fresh look at this idea, the most vigorous assault upon it has come from what is loosely referred to as the *sangh parivar*, with its different constituent elements either presenting a sober critique or adopting harsh and abusive tones, depending on their character and role assigned to each element within the parivar.

I do believe that nations have a right and even the duty to review the values and principles and the concomitant organisational structures on which the national polity had been set up. Given the experience of other countries, such a debate in India about our core national values is not surprising. Those of us who believe in them and cherish them should not shy away from this debate but face it head-on and expose the weaknesses, fallacies, distortions and lies in the case presented by the other side in the name of Hinduism.

While a critique of our composite culture has different bases, the central feature of the ideology of the BJP and its fraternity is to view the Muslim as "the Other" and, celebrate and even idolise an India which exalts *Hindu* culture and ethos at the expense of other communities and influences in our national polity.

The premises put forward by the BJP and its fraternity in the debate against secularism places the "Hindu" identity at the core of the nation; criticises Muslims for failing to integrate with the nation and even being disloyal to it; and finally, criticises the practice of secularism since Independence as having wounded the Hindu ethos and psyche even as Muslims were given privileged status. In support of these assertions, there are frequent references to Indian history based on a selective reading of old events and episodes.

The presentation I have made so far should make it clear that to see India as a "Hindu" country has little support in our historical and cultural experience, which has seen a continued intermingling of diverse peoples, communities and religions over several centuries.

Again, recollection of ancient wrongs of Muslim rulers is both fallacious and pernicious: first, there is no evidence to suggest the sustained persecution of Hindus by Muslim rulers. Indeed, the picture is quite the opposite. Second, even if certain Muslim rulers were guilty of atrocious conduct, it is difficult to see how one can transfer their guilt over the centuries on to millions of Muslims who are in our midst today.

Our cultural inheritance is the product of a sustained intermingling of Hindu, Islamic and other traditions. As Amartya Sen has noted: "There is in fact no communal line to be drawn through Indian literature and arts, setting Hindus and Muslims on separate lines."[13] Maulana Abul Kalam Azad, who knew his Islam and his history better than most, spoke of 'a notable event in history', the fusion of the Islamic and Hindu cultural currents, and 'eleven hundred years of common history'. This joint wealth, according to him, was the heritage of common nationality. In one of his most eloquent speeches at the Ramgarh Session of the AICC (1940), he declared:

> I am proud of being an Indian. I am a part of the indivisible unity that is Indian nationality. I am indispensable to this noble edifice and without me this splendid structure of India is incomplete. I am an essential element which has gone to build India. I can never surrender this claim.

Azad, who bore the brunt of religious abuse with dignity and fortitude, was overwhelmed by partition. Yet he could envisage an Islam not of sectarian belligerence but of confident partnership with other cultural and religious entities. The founding fathers of our polity, as they framed the Constitution, simply gave legal recognition to our religious pluralism which had been a living reality for centuries and which was not and could not be undermined by the misguided zealots and their imperial masters who pursued the partition of our country.

The anti-secular philosophy of the BJP, the strident assertions of its adherents and the rampages of its cohorts have led some observers to suggest that our record in upholding our core national value is at best mixed and, indeed, there has been an increase in religious bigotry, and that minorities remain insecure while

[13]Sen, Amartya, op.cit., pg. 483.

communal conflicts proliferate. One observer believes that secularism in India "looks pale and exhausted."

I do not agree with the negative assessment put forward in regard to our secular order. I remain convinced that our commitment to pluralism and multi-culturalism remains our core national value and enjoys the support of the overwhelming majority of our people. There have been occasional aberrations and some serious setbacks and failures, but the central commitment of our nation has not wavered. Indeed, it would be correct to assert that no political movement will be able to seize power in our polity on the basis of an exclusivist philosophy and agenda, however emotive its assertions and seductive its appeals. Or, to put it in positive terms, to rule India, a movement or party must necessarily represent and uphold India's rich diversity and include within its agenda the interest, on equitable basis, of the different sections that make it our national tapestry.

Having asserted this, it would be wrong to be complacent and to believe that the future is inevitably rosy. To my mind, our failure so far has been in two areas: political and intellectual. In the political arena, we have not always upheld the essential requirements of a secular order, namely, symmetrical treatment of all groups; defence of the rights and interests of all groups but particularly the weaker and vulnerable elements; and, above all, the rigorous use of the instrument of law to penalise those who have participated in crimes against our vulnerable sections. Instead, from time to time, tokenism has taken the place of genuine commitment to our core national values. But these core national values remain our ideal and those of the Indian National Congress.

However, our more serious failure has been in the intellectual arena. For several years, the critics of secularism, particularly those from within the *sangh parivar*, have honed their philosophical moorings, established political alliances, and have tried to build up a movement to promote their exclusivist ideology and their doctrine of confrontation and abuse. They have not succeeded. The 2004 Lok Sabha elections testify to the fact that bigotry has been shown its place. The people's verdict is for harmony and tolerance rather than discord and disunity.

I would like to reiterate our commitment to our core national values of secularism, democracy and pluralism. At the same time, we will vigorously participate in the debates in defence of our nation's heritage and our national values. We cannot allow our legacy to be frittered away or lost due to complacency, indecisiveness or lack of conviction. The battle is for the soul of our nation and there can be no greater call upon us than this.

PART III:
AMONG BOOKS AND AUTHORS

No one of us is great enough for such a vacation. Yet in all the circumstances of his life, unknown or momentarily famous, bound by tyranny or temporarily free to express himself, the writer can capture the feeling of a living community that will justify him. But only if he accepts as completely as possible the two trusts that constitute the nobility of his calling: the service of truth and the service of freedom. Because his vacation is to unite the greatest possible number of men, it cannot countenance falsehood or slavery, which breed solititudies wherever they prevail. Whatever our personal frailties may be, the nobility of our calling will always be rooted in two commitments difficult to observe: refusal to lie about what we know and resistence to oppression.

Albert Camus
1913-1960

1

Selected Works of Jawaharlal Nehru

SELECTED WORKS OF JAWAHARLAL NEHRU VOL. 12 SECOND SERIES

Selected Works of Jawaharlal Nehru, is a project of the Jawaharlal Nehru Memorial Fund. It is an extensive, rather extended but very major and important publishing undertaking. Nehru wrote well, voluminously and on almost every aspect of life.

The First Series—15 volumes—brought the story of Nehru's extra-ordinary and exemplary life upto August 1947. The Second Series, got to a rather slow start and the 12 volumes that have so far appeared take us only upto 15.8.1949. The entire enterprise is under the scholarly stewardship of our most distinguished and able historian S. Gopal, who first established his reputation with his books on Irwin and Reading. Then crowned his career with his three-volume biography of Nehru and his masterly life of his father. Dr. S. Radhakrishnan.

Each year two volumes appear. By March 2000 A.D. the colossal labour will come to an end. The editing of these books meets the very highest standards of historical research, scholarship and political judgement. The footnotes are complete, the index in each volume, exhaustive, and accurate.

In recent years there have been some determined, some crude, some perverse revisionist assaults on Nehru's ideas, politics and foreign policy. He has been villified in the most unconscionable manner. On the whole the great man's reputation, 26 years after his death, remains more or less intact. No one has so far come up with an alternate vision of India's destiny or fresh framework of India's foreign policy. The BJP at its recent annual conference in Thirruvannathapuram tried, but gave up.

This is not to suggest that Jawaharlal Nehru did not make mistakes. He did. Who did not? Churchill. Roosevelt, Stalin, Maotse Tung. This is not light weight company. Nehru belonged to it. Taken simply as a human being he was superior to them all. There was no blood on his hands and for a brief moment in the 50s he seemed to offer the only salvation to the ills of the world. Albert Camus defined an intellectual as, "someone whose mind watches itself." This is applicable to Nehru.

Now let me turn to Vol. 12 which came out some weeks back. Price Rs. 200, pp. 508. Period covered 21.06.1949 to 15.8.1949. These eight weeks show Nehru dealing with a host of problems, internal, external, provincial. Also the question of language, citizenship rights, food problems, taxation, China, Pakistan, Nepal, Tibet, Afghanistan, Burma, Indonesia, all commanded his attention. His letters to a large number of individuals on all kinds of matters make compelling reading. Nevertheless he could have done without writing some of them and saved his precious energy and time, he had excess of the former but not of the latter. These letters are distinctive for their style and civilized tone. Even when he is adminitory, he is never offensive or rude.

Nehru was both Prime Minister and Foreign Minister. He kept a close watch on what his Ambassadors said and wrote. Here's an elegent, headmasterly ticking off, administered to Dhiru Desai, then Ambassador to Switzerland and concurrently accredited to the Vatican. In his enthusiasm Desai had sent the text of one of his speeches to Nehru whose reply must have pulverised the ambassador, "Your speech was disliked by me for two reasons. It was loose in structure and blatant and ornate and flamboyant. State documents should be restrained. Secondly, the comparison with the Gita seemed to me rather uncalled for and certainly not likely to be appreciated by the Indian public...."

Nehru on his Security is worth quoting. I know we live in most treacherous and dangerous times. But I do feel that except for a couple of dozen or so people in today's India, the others don't need to flaunt their shortlived importance through Black Cats, SPG, paratroopers, AK-47 toting gunmen. Who in the name of heaven would want to waste bullets on tin-pot ayarams and gayarams. Nehru wrote, "I have repeatedly expressed my dissatisfaction with the security arrangements that are made in my house or when I travel. Apparently my observations have no effect at all on those who make these arrangements. I suggest that these gentlemen might be reminded of the fact that I still happen to be the Prime Minister of India and I expect my orders to be obeyed. I do not propose to tolerate the fantastic waste of public money and energy in the way security arrangements are made.

"To line up policemen or troops from Palam to my house or wherever I go, is a sign of extreme lack of intelligence, which has no effect on anybody's security. To have a group of people accompany me wherever I go is almost not a measure of security but of drawing attention to me...." Bravo Panditji! If he did not exist we would, indeed, have had to invent him.

N.B. *In today's world leaders do need security. Terrorists, suicide bombers abound. However, security is not foolproof. The assassination John E. Kennedy proves that.*

2

Two Alone, Two Together

TWO ALONE, TWO TOGETHER Letters Between Indira Gandhi and Jawarharlal Nehru, 1940-1964.
Ed. Sonia Gandhi, Hodder and Stoughton

Unlike most Indians the Nehrus were great preservers of paper. Not a single paper of any significance was destroyed. That such a large number of the pre-1947 letters have survived is indeed fortunate. Some were lost in police raids on the Nehru household in Allahabad but the bulk survived. Sonia Gandhi has done a superb job of editing. I know she spent hundreds of hours sifting vast material. The present volume is a sequel to Freedom's Daughter, published in 1989. In both, we get rare insights into deep family bonds and commitments. Sonia Gandhi, has with rare skill, lovingly put together a unique correspondence recording the public and private lives of two remarkable people.

Nehru wrote elegently and stylishly. Even when he was being didactic he was never dull or dreary. Indira Nehru (as she was till 1942) inherited from her father a profound respect for books. She was exceptionally well read like her father she was a lover of words and phrases. A great stickler for grammar and syntax. Her style was less introspective but more trenchant. It evolved over the years and acquired a distinct pace, tone, rhythm and voice, all its own.

In her introduction Sonia Gandhi, writes "the personal ties which bound father and daughter were reflected, again and again, in a chance phrase or a stray reference. Such a fusion of the public and private world confers on these letters a quality. Indeed, the correspondence bears witness not only to the depth of their relationship but also to shared political and moral values. Jawaharlal Nehru had already made his mark on history, Indira Gandhi was destined to do so before long."

At the end of *Freedom's Daughter* we left Indira ill in a sanatorium in Switzerland, mostly confined to bed. She had pleurisy. She was 22, lonely and somewhat depressed. It was war time. Mail was disrupted.

Letters took weeks to reach. She greatly missed books and asked for some. Nehru who was then out of prison sent her books and observed ... "to suffer from lack of books and papers is something that never struck me. I know well how I would feel if I had to do without books, I could bear almost anything but that."

Then we come across an amazingly candid letter from Nehru, who at this time was, in one of his, to borrow Churchill's phrase, 'black dog' moods. On 11 March 1940 he wrote,

"Public and private life act and react on each other, and this sense of failure has pursued me in almost all I do. With this lack of faith in myself, how can I advise anyone? What right do I have to interfere in another's life? I have not made my own a brilliant success and all my good intentions, or so I imagined they were, have not prevented me often from making a mess of things.... Seven years later he was Prime Minister.

Indira Gandhi, recovered and returned to India via Portugal, England and the Cape of Good Hope. Nehru was back in prison. Their first meeting did not go well and caused Nehru much anguish. The crisis was obviously serious. Daughter to father from the Himaliyan hill station, Mussorie,

"'I am in the throes of remorse and regret... Is it any use saying forgive me? I can only hope and pray that this will be a lesson for me to be less stubborn.... And so the erring child asks for forgiveness, and asks too that you believe her when she says that she loves you ... Tous les jours je t'aime devantage,

Aujou rdhui plus qu'tier et bien moins que demin."

Next we have wonderful letters prior to and following Rajiv Gandhi's birth on 20 August 1944. Nehru was again in jail.

Then came Independence in 1947. Inevitably this brought vast changes in the lives of the family. The rebel and the non-violent revolutionary became the ruler and the reformer, the agitator, the administrator.

These letters, bring back the memories and turmoils of a bygone era and a lost way of life. Their tone is so civilized, the approach to life so daring at one level, so restrained at the other. And what is so appealing is that politics does not consume their entire lives.

Literature, poetry, love of beauty and nature, travel, photography, and a zest for life in the most adverse circumstances, marks them out as exceptional people. They are not dreary, dismal, self-pitying, one dimensional, professional politicians, but sensitive and beautiful human beings, who like to live dangerously. What elan, what sang froid! These letters provide mental exhilaration. Reading them one gets a feeling of sailing in serene waters.

1992

3

Jawaharlal Nehru: Letters to Chief Ministers, 1947-64

JAWAHARLAL NEHRU: LETTERS TO CHIEF MINISTERS, 1947-64 Vol. 3. 1952-54: Editor G. Parthasarathi; Published by Jawaharlal Nehru Fund.

On the one hand these letters bring out Jawaharlal Nehru's sharp awareness of political, economic and social reality on the domestic arena, on the other, they demolish the oft repeated charge of his looking at international affairs through the haze of a vague minded idealism. Nehru's idealism was tempered by realism. He tried to resolve the dilemma all great and good rulers face: how to combine liberty with justice, equality with freedom. Nehru had no time for total solutions.

He was probably the last statesman of a major country to stress the paramount necessity of employing the right means to achieve national goals. He made no moral trade offs. He believed that desirable ends cannot be achieved by undesirable means. He believed that there were no magical answers to devilishly complex problems which cropped up each day in free India.

When one looks at the totality of Nehru's achievement, one is compelled to pause and salute. He never discredited the case of truth and reason.

This volume covers the two years from June 1952 to July 1954. These were years of confidence, some innocence, stability and security. Years in which a pattern was set for balanced and coordinated domestic and foreign policies. Nehru took an integrated look at India. An incoherent domestic scene could hardly produce a coherent or relevant foreign policy that invited the admiration and interest of the world without arousing passionate envy or resentment.

This is a long book. The 68 letters and the editorial notes cover 619 pages, touch on major issues—domestic or international— Planning, the Appleby report, community devlopment, zamindari abolition, the development of the NEFA, linguistic provinces, the Five Year Plan, the conduct of Sheikh Abdullah, education, behaviour in legislatures.

Let me quote him on the last item:

"Another exciting and almost fierce debate was that on the Preventive Detention Bill. In the course of this debate, the House of the People witnessed some scenes which were most regrettable. What pained me very much was an element of vulgarity that sometimes crept into some member's speeches and not only in speeches, but in their gestures also. It would be unfortunate indeed if we cannot behave with restraint and dignity in our legislatures." One of these days, what, indeed what would he say if he were to, "come down" to witness zero hour in the Lok Sabha, dharnas in the well of the House and listen to speeches which transcend grammar and syntax with murderous ease.

The Foreign Office is kept busy. Korea, Kashmir, Tibet, Pakistan, U.S. military aid, Nepal, Sri Lanka, the U.N., Commonwealth, India-China, all are kept under constant review. With hindsight, it is easy to pick holes in Nehru's approach or to put it differently in his faith in Krishna Menon's wisdom and infallibility. At that time, there was no earthly reason to follow any other policy. The phrase Non-Alignment had not become common diplomatic currency. Bandung and Brioni were some months away, but the seeds of non-alignment were already being sown on the fertile Afro-Asian-Latin American soil.

Jawaharlal Nehru's world stature had been recognised long before he became Head of the Indian Government. He had been a great reader and admirer of Bertrand Russell. In November 1953 Russell wrote to Nehru.

"A large part of the world is at present divided between two opposite lunacies. When I call them lunatics, I do not mean that it is a sign of madness to criticise the communist or capitalist regions. What is lunatic is the belief that the evils of either system can be amended by a world war. This belief is not universal anywhere, but controls the most powerful governments. Each side believes that it is contending for a sacred cause, and that therefore, the ordinary give and take of diplomatic negotiations would be unprincipled. In this situation, in which the nations march open-eyed towards disaster but do not see how to stop. The neutrals can play a great part and, among neutrals, India can be the leader." Nehru was not starry eyed. On Russell's letter he commented, "Bertrand Russell makes various suggestions for India and other neutral countries. I doubt if any of them is feasible."

This volume carries several lively letters dealing with Chou En Lai's first ever visit to India and shows him as a masterly performer. Churchill also gets generous references.

Jawaharlal Nehru had phenomenal physical and intellectual energy and never spared himself. He was the great educator. We must remember that the recipients of these letters were not insignificant non-entities or political lightweights but his old comrades in arms, big men, of high intellect, C. Rajagopalachari, Govind Ballabh Pant, B.C. Roy, Sri Krishna Sinha, Ravi Shankar Shukla, B.G. Kher. Nothing trivial or trite could be written. Nothing trivial or trite ever was penned by Jawaharlal Nehru.

G. Parthasarathi is rendering great service by editing these volumes. They are indispensable reading for today's policy makers, parliamentarians, arm chair media critics and the young.

1986

4

Don't Spare Me Shankar

DON'T SPARE ME SHANKAR: Published by the Children's Book Trust, Nehru House, New Delhi. Foreword By Indira Gandhi.

My first hobby was collecting Shankar's cartoons. Miraculously, three scrap books have survived time and travel. The first is dated September 1940. I used to cut the cartoons and paste them carefully and some of them I even subjected to the indigrity of paint and brush. They increased my general knowledge and I was familiar with the names and countenances of Indian and world leaders at an extraordinarily young age.

Nehru was the cartoonist's ultimate delight, not one man but a procession of men, moods and ideas. Shankar captured all these in his cartoons.

This is K. Shankar Pillai's tribute to Jawaharlal Nehru in cartoons. He drew nearly 1500 cartoons of Nehru. In this handsome volume are reproduced, with footnotes, 386 which appeared in *Shankar's Weekly.* My generation will find the footnotes unnecessary as we can without their aid straightaway identify the illustrious contemporaries of Pandit Nehru, Rajaji, Sardar Patel, Maulana Azad, Rajendra Babu, Pandit Govind Ballabh Pant, Shastriji, Dr. Ambedkar, Acharya Kripalani and others. The same applies to the mighty of the world-Churchill, Stalin, Truman, Attlee, Mao Tse-tung, Khrushchev, etc.

Since Nehru was at the helm for nearly two decades, the political dramatis personage change and we have a later crop, still recognisable but belonging to the Second Eleven; Messers Desai, Patil, Krishna Menon, Asok Mehta, Gulzarilal Nanda, Swaran Singh, to name only a few. But to the younger generation, brought up on T.V. these identificatory notes are indispensable.

Shankar's Weekly was an unusual undertaking and served a purpose. There was at the time no other comparable magazine in Asia or Africa. It was a sad day when it ceased publication. Fortunately, Shankar's Children's Painting Competition continues to grow from strength to strength and makes new friends for India in many parts of the world.

Caricature does not have a long history in India. Shankar was a pioneer and a trial blazer. For over two decades no one of higher talent appeared on the cartoonist horizon of India. Shankar has been called the Indian David Low. This is high praise. After India became a Republic, a new generation of gifted cartoonists appeared. Their line was subtler, their draughtsmanship sharper and their subject matter more relevant. They were also endowed with acuter socioeconomic antene. Shankar was a pure political cartoonist and he knew the Indian political game inside out. As such he was very good, but he was by the mid 1950s beginning to appear a little out of date. Just as David Low and Cummings in England were succeeded by Vicky of *New Statesman* and Scarfe of *The Sunday Times,* in India, Shankar's mantle fell on R.K. Laxman, Abu Abraham and Sudhir Dar to name the three best known.

Shankar's cartoons during the independence struggle were eagerly awaited. His political insight and instinct were mature and sure. While after Independence he showed no particular political bias, before 1947 he was openly pro-conqess and many of his weekly cartoons in *The Hindustan Times* were censored during 1942 and 1943.

I do not know whether Shankar got the idea from *New Statesman* or the other way round, but the Man of the Week column in Shankar's Weekly (Pandit Nehru was Man of the Week eleven times) was feebler than the *New Statesman Weekly* profiles which carried Vicky's brilliant sketches. Like Vicky Shankar knew his Indian "victims" well. While Shankar was mildly rebuking, Vicky could be wounding.

It is indeed a happy coincidence that this book should come out a few weeks before the Commonwealth Summit. Jawaharlal Nehru was the Father of the New Commonwealth. It was Nehru's revolutionary formula of a Republic remaining within the Commonwealth that saved that institution and made it relevant to the needs of the times. That the matter aroused strong passions thirty five years ago is abundantly clear from the cartoons that relate to the Commonwealth question and appear on pages 8, 9, 10, 12, 16, 17, 19, 25 and 31.

We know what Shankar thought of Nehru. These cartoons and the essays that went with the *Man of the week* speak for themselves. Let us now recall what Jawaharlal Nehru said about the doyen of Indian cartoonists "Shankar has the rare gift, and rarer in India than elsewhere, and without the least bit of malice or ill-will, he points out, with an artist's skill, the weakness and foibles of those who display themselves on the public stage. This is a service to all of us for which we should be grateful. For we are apt to grow pompous and self-centred and it is good to have the veil of our conceit torn occasionally. So I gladly pay my tribute to Shankar and I hope that he will long continue to enlighten us and amuse us and pull us down a peg or two."

The volume provides a most useful index of each person who appears in the cartoons. It is a thousand pities that M. Chalapati Rau, who was so closely associated with the preparation of this work, did not live to see it in print.

5

The Golden Oriole: Childhood, Family and Friends in India

THE GOLDEN ORIOLE: CHILDHOOD, FAMILY AND FRIENDS IN INDIA BYRALEIGH TREVELYAN. SECKER & WARBURG.

Yet, another Raj book! Yet, another outpouring of the infantile nostalgic fixations of pucca sahibs and insufferable Mem Sahibs. Once more the stale air and saturated smell of unendurable and well forgotten Viceregal balls. Have we not had enough of them? I thought the law of diminishing returns had finally caught up with the Raj industry. Not quite. Raleigh Trevelyan, who was born in India where his father was serving in the Army, has given us an unusual, unpretentious, absorbing, non-pucca sahib book which keeps bias as far as possible out from his recollections. Autobiography, history and geography combine to bring 19th century India alive: ("Sir Charles Metcalfe used to travel out at weekends by elephant as he found it easier for reading.") The Brits of the Raj were indefatigable letter writers and compulsive diarists. Many wrote learned books on obscure subjects. Others discovered Indian history for the Indians. Here full use is made of letters and diaries. We have copious quotations from Metcalfe, Mecaulay, Charles and Hannah Trevelyan. Historian G .M. Trevelyan, grandson of Charles Trevelyan, encouraged Raleigh Trevelyan to write a book about his distinguished relations, several of whom spent long years in India both in this and the last century. This is the book. The Trevelyans were a for midable and durable lot. The author A.L. Rowes is summoned to give a thumb nail character sketch of the tribe.

"Integrity to the point of eccentricity, honesty to the point of rudeness, tactless and rough-handed but of an indubitably aristocratic distinction, devoted public spirit with an equal ability to carry it into action; a marked idiosyncracy held in check by strong common sense, not much sense of humour. That distinguished family was apt to think that they were Trevelyans and then the rest of the human race."

The five journeys undertaken by the author in the late 70s and early 80s took him all over the Indian sub-continent India, Pakistan, Sri Lanka, Burma, including my home town of Bharatpur now known for its bird sanctuary. He is sensitive, restrained, honest and acceptably indignant. He evokes the past with understanding and feeling, relating it to the present with equal sensitivity. Reason and emotion are harmoniously blended even when he recalls the disagreeable and the unpleasant.

For over a hundred years, the fate and fortunes of this family were intimately linked with India. Charles and Humphry Trevelyan rose to high office and are among the better known and better remembered of the 19th and the 20th century British civil servants. Humphry did a stint under Prime Minister Nehru, "who was sorry to lose him." The former married Macaulay's sister and the two men together produced the famous/infamous Minute on Education in 1835 generally known as Macaulay's minute. To this day, it remains a subject of lively controversy. Macaulay spent several years in India, but he was no expert on any aspect of Indian life but that did not prevent him from being cocksure about everything. He was brash enough to declare in the minute:

"I have never found one among them (the Orientalists) who could deny that a single shelf of a good European library was worth the whole native literature of India and Arabia." Here is chauvinistic crap at its best/worst. In fairness it must be noted that Macaulay's vision of English becoming the lingua-france of the world has proved prophetic.

Releigh Trevelyan's compassion marks him out as an uncommon person. Two of his kinsmen were killed at Kanpur during the mutiny in 1857, but there is no bitterness in the author's recounting of those terrible incidents. His mature insights on the Jalianwala Bagh (Amritsar) massacre of 1919, I fully share. He is absolutely right when he says that after Jalianwala Bagh there could be no compromise and no trust between the Indians and the British.

Mr. Trevelyan's 'Fifth Journey' took him to many places visited in 1912-13 by E.M. Forster, Goldsworthy Lowes Dickinson and R.C. Trevelyan. I find this chapter fascinating because it not only recalls Forster's own incomparable work but many conversations I had with Forster himself about his initial passage to India. Dickinson was not as enthusiastic about India as Forster. Actually India made Dickinson uneasy, as is clear from this quotation.

"But it (Hinduism) was the religion of the East, not the West. It refused all significance to the temporal world; it took no account of society and its needs; it sought to destroy not to develop, the sense and the power of individuality. It did not say, but it implied, that creation was a mistake; and if it did not profess pessimism, pessimism was its logical outcome. I do not know whether it is the religion of a wise race; but I am sure that it could never be that of a strong one."

Was it worth writing such a book? Will it do any good? My answer on both counts would be yes. "The Golden Oriole" is not a run of the mill book glorifying maudlin Raj nostalgia; while it lacks cohesion, it is an engaging, tolerant, human document written by an Englishman who does not possess a stiff upper lip and whose love for the Indian sub-continent and its inhabitants is genuine.

6

Tigers, Durbars and Kings: Fenny Eden's Indians Journals 1837-1838

TIGERS, DURBARS AND KINGS: FANNY EDEN'S INDIAN JOURNALS 1837-1838, Edited by Jenet Dunbar, John Murray. $13.95, p. 202

In 1835 Lord Auckland (George Eden) was appointed Governor General of India. Since he was unmarried, his two spinster sisters, Emily and Fanny accompanied him to help in the running of his Calcutta establishment. His tenure as Governor-General was one of the longest-almost 7 years-and also among the least distinguished. Oblivion should rightly have claimed him but for the journals his sisters kept.

Both Emily (1797-1866) and Fanny (1801-49) kept journals of the journey they made with their brother in 1837 travelling from Calcutta to Simla, Lahore and finally to Amritsar to meet Maharaja Ranjit Singh (1780-1839), the Lion of the Punjab.

Few livelier or more engaging accounts of life in early 18th century India exist. Emily Eden's "Up the country" is widely known, Edward Thompson who wrote the foreward to the 1930 edition praised it highly. He was, however, less enthusiastic about Emily's other two literary efforts, *The Semi-Detached House* and *the Semi-Attached Couple.*

Fanny Eden's journal of her tiger-shooting trip to the Rajmahal Hills and the account of her up country expedition have received less attention. Janet Dunbar has ensured that this shall no longer be so. Fanny's book is a collection of letters she wrote from India to her friend, Eleanor Grosvenor. These letters are accompanied by striking sketches Fanny drew on her travels. She was a gifted artist and captured the mood and the atmosphere in writing and in her drawings.

"Tigers, Durbars and Kings," is a charming, amusing, irreverent, care-free book. Emily was respectable. Fanny is vivacious, more spontaneous, more disarmingly candid. No post 1857 Memsahib could have written such a book. 1857 was the great watershed in Indo-British relations right upto 1919 when the Jallianwallah Bagh massacre took place. After 1857 British attitudes to India and Indians changed. Fanny Eden's Journal is as un-Victorian as it could be. Indians of all classes are treated with amused consideration and aristocratic tact, never as lower breeds. Here is a most unmemsahib like observation, "Those people (the Indians) must have been so very magnificent in what they did before we Europeans came here with our bad money making ways."

In October, 1837 Lord Auckland embarked on his famous journey, accompanied by his two sisters and 12000 others. The round trip covered nearly 3000 miles and lasted over 2½ years. The modes of transport were as slow as they were varied, boat, horse, elephant, palanquin, and an assortment of carriages. Discomfort, heat and dust were overcome through pomp and circumstance.

Fanny Eden missed nothing. Ranjit Singh's durbars and court life are described with precision and wit. The sketches that go with the text are very good-men, women, animals, durbar, tents, buildings are well and faithfully drawn. Ranjit Singh could be a tease. At one of his nautch parties he noted his distinguished British guest's long silence. The interpreter translated Maharaja's gentle rebuke thus, "My Lord, the Maharaja says he wishes your Lordship would give him a little more friendly conversation."

Here is Ranjit Singh pulling the Auckland leg, at yet another nautch: "he drank harder himself and got very drunk, and tried hard to make George drink. 'When a man drinks hard enough,' he said, 'he opens his heart and tells all kind of non-sense, and that is right among friends.' He asked if it was true that books were written against drinking, shook his head and said what foolish books they must be." Behind all this fun and games serious business was also being transacted, pacts made and treaties signed.

Fanny Eden's journals have elan and verve, missing in her sister's weighter work on the same subject. If I were asked which of the two books I would take on a holiday, I would pick, "Tigers, Durbars and Kings."

7

No Full Stops in India

NO FULL STOPS IN INDIA By Mark Tully, Viking.

The press release of the publishers poses the question. "Is Mark Tully the most influential man in the world?" Not quite. That he is highly regarded in the Indian sub-continent is dramatically highlighted in a spontaneous exchange he had with Mr. Rajiv Gandhi on 20 May 1991, a day before Mr. Gandhi was so brutally assassinated.

Tully writes, "When Rajiv arrived to cast his vote he, leapt out of his car and walked straight upto the press, grinning from ear to ear. He greeted many of us by name, and said to me, "I hear the B.B.C. thinks we are winning this time, Mark." I replied, "I am not quite sure we've stuck our neck out that far." He laughed, "well, you think it is better than last time." "Oh yes, I said."

That Rajiv Gandhi listened regularly to the B.B.C is well known. He was a thousand miles away from New Delhi on 31.10.1984 when he heard the B.B.C. announce that his mother had been shot.

Mark Tully is an unusual Englishman. He would have irritated Rudyard Kipling but delighted E.M. Forster. He is not a snob. Hypocrisy does not touch him. He is not ashamed to use public transport, or eat in roadside Dhabas. He was born in India and speaks fluent Hindustani. He has represented the B.B.C in India for the past quarter century, without going 'native'. He has established his reputation for a variety of reasons. He knows well the several Indias that exist. He is at home in all of them. In his reporting he is never superficial, supercilious, condescending, patronising. Nothing stereotype about him. That is why he has produced such a very good book, free of stilled pathos, pseudo-profundity and stimulated sensitivity.

No Full Stops in India is a splendid title. The ten essays written with clarity, warmth of feeling and critical balance and understanding provide as lively a view as one can hope for, of the panorama of India. Mark Tully has strung together diverse Indian beads with great skill and disarming candour. "The stories I tell in this book will, I hope serve to illustrate the way in which western thinking has distorted and still distorts Indian life—I might almost say they are parables. They provide no answers to India's poverty, but I do believe they do suggest where we should begin to look for these answers—in India itself." He quotes Mahatma Gandhi to support his contention, "My Swaraj (self-rule, or independence) is to keep intact the genius of our civilisation. I want to write many new things but they must all be written on the Indian slate. I would gladly borrow from the West when I can return the amount with decent interest." The 'stories' touch Indian life in the raw and at levels which hardly any foreigners care to see or examine. The Indian elite, not one of Tully's favourite tribes, never ventures near the India of Tully's book. They worship the tin god called consumerism. They perpetuate Western cultural and intellectual imperialism. Rightly, Tully has little time for this lot of my countrymen.

The first 'story' is about Tully's inscrutable, loyal and possessive domestic servant, Ram Chander. Then we have an energetic and authentic piece on the Kumbh Mela at Allahabad—the largest religious gathering in the world and an administrative and organisational wonder. Next an amusing essay on Ramanand Sagar's TV version of the great epic Ramayana, which brought India for an hour's halt each Sunday morning for nearly two years. "Operation Black Thunder" is again reporting at its best-gripping, no frills, no moralising, just unembridered facts, some observed at first hand, others related by individuals who are not putting on an act.

Tully knows that India's forte is crisis management and that somehow we shall muddle through. Only in Patna, the capital of the State of Bihar, does he begin to despair. In Bihar, to use an Indianism, democracy has degenerated into 'demonocracy', with political thugs calling the shots. Long before the withering away of the State in Moscow, Marx's prophecy had come true in Bihar.

These 'stories' are handmade, shades of Christerpher Isherwood and his Berlin stories. The volume adds up to something very substantial. The spirit of integrity stands out on each page. The book should persuade people in the West not to write India off. As

Mr. Vibha Bhushan told Mark Tully in Allahabad, "All you can do with the materialism of today is to keep your cool, keep your philosophy, and do what you have to do to exist in society. Our ways have survived for thousands of years. You are children of today."

Pay heed, ye of the West!!

1991. Financial Times, London.

8

Thy Hand, Great Anarch! India 1921-1952

THY HAND, GREAT ANARCH! INDIA 1921-1952. by Nirad C. Chaudhuri, Chatto and Windus.

When Chaudhuri's, The Autobiography of An Unknown Indian appeared in 1951, it created a sensation. It catapulted its unknown author into world fame. The book was a masterpiece.

Thy Hand ... too will stir the air. It is an intellectual and literary tour de force. At 90, the Indian Spengler continues to provoke, irritate and annoy the complacent, the thoughtless and the philistines. His is a disturbing view of Indian life and society. His temperament is profound but not amiable. He suffers from chronic indignation. He is not a comfortable writer to be with. His life has not been comfortable. He knows exactly what he is doing. If there was a choice between caution and courage, it was courage that Nirad Babu chose. He was never bothered to count costs. Living dangerously comes naturally to him.

Those who elect to swim against the current invite the wrath of the world. Chaudhuri, in his introduction tells us that at one time he thought of giving the title, *One Man Against his People* to this book. I wish he had. His assertion that he was, "against historical trends, not any people," is not borne out by his writings.

His one big, unending quarrel has been with his people who, in his judgment have no sense of history, no creativity, no vision, are a serile, decadent lot. In this volume he carries further his theory of an "all embracing (Indian) decline," which he enunciated with such startling vigour in 1947: "All that we have learnt, all that we have acquired, and all that we have prized is threatened with extinction. We do not know how this end will come, whether through a catalysmic holocaust or slow putrid decay. But regarding the eventual extinction there does not seem to be any uncertainty."

These are hard words. He has without reservation, without let, turned on his people, who have turned on him with matching ferocity but not matching skill.

Chaudhuri is at his incomparable best while writing about himself, his occupations and preoccupations, his appointments and disappointments, his hopes and his hopelessness. The chapters on Bengali literary life and its ethos make rivetting reading.

The literary style and form could hardly be bettered. We are permitted to peer deep into the abyss of N.C.C's character, into the depth of his feelings, into the wounding degradation of the years he spent in Calcutta in his youth.

The essay on Rabindra Nath Tagore (Nobel Prize for Literature in 1913) deserves special mention. I have come across nothing better on the life, poetic philosophy and artistic genius of Tagore. Chaudhuri writes: "Even if the number of writers from all ages and all countries is reduced to a score by a rigorous scrutiny of merit, Tagore would be one of them ... he would be in the hierarchy limited by Goethe on one side and Victor Hugo on the other."

I am not with Chaudhuri when he tackles politics and politicians. The only Indian (it would be more correct to say Bengali) politicians he knew well was Sarat Bose, the elder brother of the famous Subhas Bose. The two brothers get much attention. Subhas Bose's feud with Mahatma Gandhi is spotlit in a manner which can hardly be termed detached or dispassionate. The men of the Indian National Army (INA) are called, "dirty military prostitutes."

Why such venom against men who put patriotism before allegiance to their oath to an alien King? The INA issue was a political one, nothing less, nothing more. The leaders involved, British and Indian, had no option but the one they chose.

N.C.C's grasp of Indian politics is purely academic and theoretical, as is evident from his total disapproval of the partition of India in 1947. He is negatively servere on Mahatma Gandhi and the Indian freedom movement. He even goes to the extent of lambasting Attenborough's film. Gandhi's achievement is so colossal and so obvious that N.C.C's denigration of him reflects poorly on the author and not the Mahatma. Mountbatten is belittled severely. On Nehru the author is less reckless. Jinnah gets high praise. Hitler gets credit for dismantling the British Empire, not Gandhi and Nehru! The British are roundly condemned for deserting their imperial destiny and ratting on the Empire. Often, Chaudhuri spoils his case by overstating it, and consequently he is least convincing when his assertions degenerate into dogmatism. But all this is done in superb prose. The subtleties of the English language are extended by a Master.

N.C.C. has made his bed and is not afraid to lie on it. So let him have the last world.

"Yet writing as I have done. I have been able to create an interest in my books and earn a livelihood which has been adequate for living a basically civilised life. If on account of that I can be included among the small number of men who have lived by imposing their terms on the world, it does not speak less for the world." That is generous enough.

1987, Financial Times, London.

9

Clive of India by Nirad C. Chaudhuri

CLIVE OF INDIA BY NIRAD C. CHAUDHURI Berrie and Jenkins. Nirad Chaudhuri has been transformed into one of the sacred cows of the English literary establishment. This late arrival on the scene was first sought after by literary high society, then embraced. He is now in the process of being smothered by it. This is a great pity for he is a writer of high distinction, originality, learning, possessing a flinty integrity. There comes a point when even patient English readers must tire of the endless masochistic denunciation of India and Indians by Chaudhuri. Reticence is one British virtue he has offended far too often. That is why for his last four books he has had four different publishers.

His literary affair with the British Empire continues. Who else could write a 446 pages book on Clive, (born 250 years ago) and call it 'a political and psychological essay'. The introduction to the book is its best part and here the author tells us why he has undertaken this labour.

"In regard to the topics included in the biography it will be found that there is a good deal that is not about Clive, and would seem at first sight to belong to history rather than to biography. But these had to be brought in because in this period Clive and British India coincided. The historical situation furnished the setting in which Clive worked and rose to power. His was a dormant nature which was roused and brought to life by India. Without describing all that was happening there, it is impossible to explain him."

"In short, I will say that I have only tried to show Clive as he was and his age as it was with out feeling called upon to pronounce any judgement for or against. But I am not insensible to the fact that the reader might think that I have projected a view of Clive that comes very close to the imperialistic, though with neither boastfulness nor apology. I would not excuse myself for that, for it the view seems to be imperialistic it has been forced on me by the nature of the subject. It is not possible to write about the foundation of an empire without seeming to be imperialistic. For myself, I only claim freedom from preconceptions about Clive and the British Empire, not because I did not have them, but because I have outgrown them."

His feelings for his hero are mixed. Chaudhuri is far too keen a student of history not to know that Clive was in fact Poacher turned gamekeeper, yet he leans backward to put him in the same league as Napoleon and Churchill. No one doubts that Clive was a very remarkable man, a military genius who laid the foundations of the greatest empire in history. His final tenure as Governor of Bengal from 1765 to 1767 was administratively as memorable as his first spell had been militarily spectacular. But by the age of 42, Clive was a 'has been'. He never became a great British statesman. Chaudhuri concedes that his personality, had "no elevated moral element in it." Clive had neither Churchill's or Napoleon's political stamina or imagination. How would he have had fared had he had to face their problems and situations. His melancholy character is not reassuring evidence. Plassey, his great military triumph was not Austerlitz. Clive returned to England a conquering hero and yet he was out maneuvered by a small clique of a second-rate men and got himself in to an aweful mess. Chaudhuri offers us learned and sophisticated reasons for excusing Clive's financial improprieties but surely there were honest Englishmen in England in the 18th century and they should be our touch-stone and not the corrupt many.

Portions of the book are vintage Chaudhuri. He casts his scholastic net wide and well. He knocks the economic interpretation of history on the head. Yet even his mastery of facts and fine style cannot make the narrative of the wars in the Carnatic and Bengal anything but tedious for the general reader. At the same time, Chaudhuri succeeds brilliantly in giving us an arresting and graphic picture of life in 18th century India. Also superb pen-portraits of the leading personalities.

I better say it as no one else in England is likely to. At $7.50 Chaudhuri's tome on Lord Clive recalls to my mind the distinction which Marx drew between price and value. Chaudhuri fans will pay the high price. As biography it has little value. No new blinding insights on the character of Clive are forthcoming. Chaudhuri appears more as an advocate and less as a biographer. Not surprisingly time and again he quotes Macaulay. Like Macaulay he has "his heightened way of telling things." He never ceases to be himself. Lord Melbourne is reported to have said of Macaulay, "I wish I was as cocksure of anything as Macaulay is of everything." For Macaulay read Chaudhuri.

10
A Sparrow's Flight

A Sparrow's Flight by Lord Hailsham

In the normal course I doubt if I would have read the memoirs of Lord Hailsham nee Quinton Hogg. India did not impinge on his life and his two visits to India quite obviously made little or no impact on him. India reciprocated. I vaguely remember ushering him into Indira Gandhi's room in 1970 or early 1971. I remember nothing of the meeting.

I do not confine my reading to "India Books". My reading habits are more eclectic and I drink from varied literary fountains and springs. What matters is the quality of the book – its literary style, form and of course subject matter.

A *Sparrow's Flight* has several merits. It has some very funny bits. Marvellous pen portraits of his political contemporaries and a rather unusual view of British politics. The first half is more gripping than the second. Hailsham or Quinton Hogg, was born in 1907 and had a truly brilliant school and University career. He was top of his form in school and an outstanding scholar at Oxford.

Quinton Hogg shot into fame, when, in 1938 he won a bye-election at Oxford against a formidable candidate, Sandy Lindsay, the Master of Balliol, whom the author calls, "a man to suit all tastes, although not a man for all seasons." Hogg, was, believe it or not a supporter of Chamberlain and Munich. In short an appeaser. Not a nice label to have round one's neck, but it seems to have done him no political damage. His opponents screamed, "A vote for Hogg is a vote for Hitler." Hogg's rejoinder was, "Vote for Hogg and save your bacon." It has an authentic Oxbridge flavour.

Hogg's father was Lord Chancellor. The progeny surpassed pater, Lord Chancellor for over eight years, Cabinet Minister, Conservative Party Chairman and the only man besides Douglas Home, who has been a peer, commoner and peer again. He is, judging from this book an ebullient, effervescent and somewhat rambunctious character, whose political awareness was not as sharp as those of his more ruthless colleagues. He held several Cabinet posts and got on well with Mountbatten during the Suez crisis, one of the more spectacular foul ups of Anglo-French-Israeli diplomacy.

The apogee of his fame was reached at the annual Conservative Party Conference as Brighton in 1957. There he indulged in scarcely concealed pavlonian antics and acquired a reputation for, "self advertising publicity," which he protests he does not deserve. Well! Well! The famous bell incident at the closing of the conference is retold with great panache. It did him no good in the long run and six years later when Harold MacMillan resigned as Prime Minister due to ill-health, he was out manoeuvred by more skillful operators and fixers. He alleges that MacMillian double crossed him.

From 1964 to 1970 he went back to his Law practice and lived contendedly with his second wife and children. She died in a riding accident in Australia and all joy went out of his life. "All that summer," Hailsham Writes, "the sun no longer shone by day. The stars did not shine at night. The flowers did not bloom in the garden. The birds were silent in the tree tops."

Like all political lives Hailsham's has its ups and downs, in his case almost evenly. One set back was followed by a totally unexpected promotion. At least three times he convinced himself that his political life was over, each time a turn of the wheel brought him back to a ring side seat.

Hailsham is not a wheeler dealer, not a fixer. For a front rank politician he is remarkably frank and holds Churchill (whom he otherwise admires) responsible for the July 1945 Tory defeat. It says much about the esteem he acquired in later years, for both Heath and Thatcher asked him to join their cabinets.

For my taste there is too much law in the book. British justice has not really covered itself with glory in recent years. Grave miscarriages of justice have come to light lately. What is attractive about the book and the man is the disarming candour, deprecating self-analysis and a somewhat carefree attitude to power and success. The book has a lot of pep. Free from bile, bitterness or venom.

11
The Diaries of Lord Louis Mountbatten: 1920-1922

The Diaries of Lord Louis Mountbatten: 1920-1922. edited by Philip Ziegler, Collins.

In June 1974 my wife, my brother-in-law, Amarinder Singh of Patiala and I spent an afternoon with Lord Louis Mountbatten at Broadlands. After lunch he took us around to show us his library and archives. Everything was meticulously arranged and documented. 'This is my diary of my first trip to India with the Prince of Wales,' he said. I asked to see it. He pulled it out, turned the pages, 'Ah there we are. Wednesday 22 February. We arrived at Patiala at 8.30 AM....'.

Here I am 13 years later seeing the same entry on page 258 of Ziegler's book. While writing this review affectionate memories of Lord Mountbatten rush to my mind, coming in the way of an objective and dispassionate appraisal of this entertaining book. I don't want to drive those memories away.

My wife's family had known Lord Mountbatten for two generations. The introduction of the third generation in early 1948, when he was Governor-General of independent India, was both novel and memorable. The Mountbattens had gone to stay with their Highnesses the Maharaja and Maharani of Patiala at Chail in the Simla hills. The four little princes, including my wife were trooped in to be introduced to Lord and Lady Mountbatten. My wife's youngest brother, Malvi, aged three, was promptly picked up by Lady Mountbatten and put on her lap. He was equally promptly put down when Lady Mountbatten discovered that the little prince had rather thoughtlessly decided to respond to a pressing call of nature and wet her ladyship's dress. But as usual Edwina handled the situation with unmatched savoir foire.

These diaries have nothing of the sparkle or interest of the tour of India. The Far East and Japan, Australian and New Zealand societies, 70 years ago, were still in the making. The supply of engaging or memorable characters was somewhat limited. The first section of the book is simply a hectic accumulation of rather tiresome dances, balls, parties, reception, polo and conversations which would make one envy the deaf.

India was different, Mountbatten obviously enjoyed his Indian tour. It left a permanent and benign impression on his young mind and heart. He could never have dreamed that a quarter of a century later he would return as Viceroy to preside over the liquidation of the British Indian Empire, or that he would be invited by Jawaharlal Nehru to become the first Governor General of independent India.

The Indian tour of the Prince of Wales was ill-timed, the itinerary questionable and the political returns negligible. While princely Indian welcomed the Prince of Wales, British India did not. Mahatma Gandhi's non-co-operation movement had begun in most places outside the princely states—Hyderabad, Mysore, Kashmir, Baroda, Jaipur, Jodhpur, Patiala, Bharatpur, etc. The royal visit was boycotted by non-co-operators shouting, 'Victory to Mahatma Gandhi.' Mountbatten noticed this and refers to its several times.

Another Englishman was also present in India at the same time to record his impression of the visit. This is what E.M. Forster wrote:

'About the Prince of Wales' visit I might also write much. It is disliked and dreaded by nearly everyone. The chief exception are the motor firms and caterers, who will make fortunes, and the non-co-operators and extremists, who will have an opportunity for protest which they would otherwise have lacked ... the Indian National Congress meets in December at Ahmedabad and it will certainly carry through its resolution in favour of civil disobedience and if there is general response, this expensive royal expedition will look rather foolish.'

These diaries throw much light on Mountbatten, some on the moody Prince of Wales, who generally kept good second-class company, and was totally devoid of any intellectual interests. Mountbatten kept his eyes and ears open and his observations are not trivial. On Benares:

'... too picturesque for words from the river, especially the countless ghats on water-front steps...'

On Nepal:

'... the camp is bounded on one side by the steep and precipitious bank of a river, which is dried up except to a small trickle. The view is simply magnificent. I can't help thinking of Kipling's Jungle Books and fitting Mowgli and all the animals in this jungle.'

on himself:

'... on our way back to the cars one of the Prime Minister's sons, the one who is running this camp and shoot came up to me and said, 'And why should not the noble lord shoot a rhinoceros?' I looked round but as there seemed to be a dearth of noble lords in the immediate neighbourhood I came to the conclusion that he must surely be addressing me and answered, 'Why indeed not'

Again:

'I am afraid that I talked a good deal too much about the whole question ... which was silly of me and I am sure could not have added to my popularity with the others.'

Such modesty was to desert him in later years.

A momentous event occurred during his first passage to India. Lord Mountbatten proposed to Edwina Ashley at a viceregal dance party in Delhi on Tuesday, February 14, 1922. 'I asked her if she would marry me, and she said she would.' Lady Reading, the Viceroy's wife was not too enthusiastic. She wrote to Edwina's father: 'I hoped she cared for someone older, with more of a career before him.'

The diaries are full of fun, frolic and amusing anecdotes. The Kimono shopping expedition in Tokyo is described in hilarious detail, but what I enjoyed most is what happened at King Faud's lunch, at Cairo. It defies paraphrasing and is too long to quote so I suggest the reader borrows or purchases the book and turns to pages 305-6.

These diaries were written by a man who was not quite 22. It would therefore be absurd and unfair to look for profoundities in them. Ziegler has done a fine job of editing. Mountbatten admirer will be grateful.

Financial Times, London.

12

City that Rose from the Dead / Review of 'Traders and Nabobs: The British in Cawnpore 1765-1857'

Traders and Nabobs: The British in Cawnpore 1765-1857 by Zoe Yalland by, Michael Russell.

Zoe Yalland's links with Cawnpore (now Kanpur) go back to the early 19th century. She spent many years in the city before and after 1947 and began collecting material for this book in 1968.

Cities, like those who live in them, have their ups and downs, good years and bad years. Cawnpore is no exception. Perhaps it had more than its share of horrors in 1857 when the British hold over India hung in the balance. We get intimate and detailed accounts of life at Cawnpore at this time. The activities of the European community are both amusing and alarming. Most of the men and women who appear in these pages Indian and British are a mixed and uninspiring lot, but there are exceptions on both sides.

Sir Henry Lawrence was one. He survived 1857 and ended by being Viceroy of India. Nana Sahib and Nawab Majid All Shah of Dude (Avadh) make their sinister and flamboyant presences felt. Wajid Ali Shah was an arresting, though utterly incompetent, man.

The events of 1857 caught the British off-guard and the Indians ill-prepared to wage a full scale war of independence. Cawnpore figures prominently in the annals of the period. Zoe Yalland describes the horrors of the Cawnpore massacre in gory detail, quoting from diaries that survived the upheaval.

But nothing startlingly new on this melancholy and unedifying episode is offered.

According to the author, the decade from 1837 was, for Cawnpore, a golden one. The city grew and expanded, trade flourished, new merchant adventures arrived from Europe adding excitement to a tedious existence. European women began to descend on Cawnpore in significant numbers. They created a fresh set of problem. Petty jealousies resulted, 'one half of the European community was not on speaking terms with the other.' The newly arrived single ladies were in search of husbands. They were called the 'fishing fleet' and they threw their nets far and wide. Some were more fortunate than others. Socialising with Indian women began to decline. The Memsahibs contribution to the downfall of the British Empire is not insignificant.

Zoe Yalland's enthusiasm for the golden decade is not shared by that shrewd and indefatigable diarist—Emily Eden who accompanied her brother, Lord Auckland, to Cawnpore in 1837. She rejected the place: 'Of all the ugly Indian stations I have yet seen, this is the ugliest—a dead flat of course—but not one single blade of grass to be seen-nothing but loose brown dust which rises in clouds upon the least provocation. I have a notion that I really could not live here, but as other people do that may be a delusion.' The other people included Robert Montgonery, who was appointed Collector of Cawnpore in 1846. He did much good. His statistical report of Cawnpore 1849 is a demographer's dream. Among the population of traders and professionals are listed—three bookbinders, two bards, 14 buffoons, four ear-cleaners, 291 pundits, 420 prostitutes, 29 snake-hookah-makers ... nineteenth century Cawnpore certainly took care of almost all human needs of the merchant community. I have no quarrel with the author when she states that, 'this book is a tribute to a city and to the men and women who created it and made it thrive. In a space of 100 years Cawnpore grew from a small army camp into an industrial city, eventually to become the Manchester of the East.'

Today Kanpur is one of India's leading industrial centres. The pioneering work of Hugh Maxwell and Gavin Sibbald Jones, recalled here with such warmth, has not been forgotten.

The Financial Times, London Page XVIII.

13
Among Books

Among Books Jawaharlal Nehru—What a man.

This month we observe his 25th death anniversary. Six months later India and the World celebrate his centenary.

Without Jawaharlal Nehru the history of the 20th century would be incomplete. Nehru the Statesman is well known. Nehru the beloved leader of the masses has few rivals. Nehru the follower of Gandhiji is much admired. Nehru the Prime Minister has left his imprint on India and the World.

Jawaharlal Nehru was much else. He was a great author. Through his writings, he reached out to history. But even in his widely read books the private Nehru remains elusive. The veil is lifted, now and then, in his Autobiography, *Glimpses of World History* and *The Discovery of India,* but suddenly the curtain is drawn and great public issues ease out the intimate and the personal.

So, where do we look for Nehru the obedient son of Motilal, the caring husband, the doting father of his only child, the loving brother, the loyal friend. Does he ever let his hair down, bare his soul? How does he cope with his loneliness, battle with depression, annihilate dejection, conquer despair ?

To discover the very private Jawaharlal Nehru we must turn to his selected works—a project of the Jawaharlal Nehru Memorial Fund. Vol. I of the First Series appeared in 1972 and Volume 15 in 1984. The period covered was from 1903 to 1946. These volumes totaled 9292 pages. Of the 2nd Series seven Volumes have been published – 4436 pages. Another eight are due. The editor is S. Gopal and he has done a superb job as editor, combining painstaking, meticulous research with high professionalism. For those interested in the evolution of Jawaharlal Nehru's thinking and the Indian Freedom Movement, these books are indispensable.

Jawaharlal Nehru spent 10 years in Jail between 1922 and 1945. He occupied his time by keeping his mind and body in good shape. He read voraciously, wrote copiously. He writes exceedingly well. Attention is paid to literary style and literary form. "I am a lover of words and phrases and try to use them appropriately. Whatever my opinions might be, the words I use are meant to express them intelligibly and in ordered sequence."

In jail, he kept a regular diary to keep himself from going to seed. It was a tremendous exercise in self-discipline. Nehru was at his best in adversity, when the flame of life burnt low. There was no external sanctuary to absorb his meloncholy. He had to fall back on his inner strength.

13720 pages free of cliches, free of verbiage, full of stimulating, gripping writing is a remarkable achievement. Here we have a restless spirit, a keen mind, contemplating the human predicament and coming to terms with it, with candour, utter sincerity, and mature understanding.

All is not smooth sailing. (I have the 1930's in mind.) Freedom is nowhere in sight. He is at odds with Gandhiji and the Congress. His wife is terminally ill, his widowed mother has been struck by a paralytic stroke, daughter Indira not in robust health is shifted from one school to another. Himself in jail. Was life going to be one long bereavement, an endless and seering agony? Would there ever be a break in the clouds? One entry will reveal the state of Nehru's mind during this period:

"January 12, 1935. A terrible and unexpected shock. Early in the morning a telegram came from Nan (Vijayalaxmi Pandit) from Allahabad that Jivraj Mehta had telephoned from Bombay to say that mother had a stroke of paralysis and was unconscious.... I collapsed and wept and found some difficulty in pulling myself together."

A lesser man would have gone to pieces or worse, become bitter and brutal, coarse and clawing. Not so our hero. From each sojourn in jail ("I have seldom felt quite so lonely and cut off from the world as I have felt here. It is solitary confinement with a vengeance") he emerged a greater, a nobler, refined man. No self-pity, no quarter to hatred, no concession to political intrigue or underhand manoeuvring. No moral trade-offs. No tidying the past. This was the measure of the man.

With his spoken word, Nehru reached the hearts of men. With his books he penetrated their minds, he enhanced their awareness. He gave us hope. He gave us pride.

It was the lunch hour on a hot summer day in 1961. By an extraordinary coincidence, Pandit Nehru and I met in the first floor corridor of the MEA. He was coming out of his room (now occupied by his grandson), I from my humbler perch in the same row (l shared it with three others on R.K. Nehru's staff). I greeted him with folded hands with a book between my palms. He stopped, returned my greetings and asked me what the book was. I handed it over to him. It was my friend Amaury de Riencourt's, *The Soul of China.* I have read his, *Soul of India,* the Prime Minister announced.

"So, have I, Sir."

He took a few steps towards the staircase of the MEA and remarked,

"Rather Spenglarian, I thought."

Having never read Spengler, all I could do was to give a nervous smile.

14
Sardar Patel

By any reckoning Sardar Vallabhbhai Patel is one the three greatest Indian political leaders of the 20th century. Born October 31, 1875, died December 15,1950. He was six years younger than Gandhiji and fourteen years older than Pandit Jawaharlal Nehru. He was a practical and realistic man with a superb political temperament. Just the instrument Gandhiji needed to take care of the Congress Party machine. He had, what the Romans called *GRAVITAS.* He was a man of few words. Neither before 1947 nor after, no one fooled around with him. Not one Indian Prince stood upto him. Once they had fallen in line and deprived of real power, Sardar Patel was generous in letting have them the trappings of slamaur, friuility.

While the lives of Gandhiji and Pandit Nehru are fully and minutely documented, the same cannot be said about Sardar Patel. In 1953 appeared Narahari Parikh's two volume Biography of the Sardar. In 1964 The Bharatiya Vidya Bhawan published K.L. Panjabi's *The Indomitable Sardar.* In 1970 Allen and Unwin of London brought out D.V. Thamankar's, *Sardar Patel,* with a Foreword by Lord Mountbatten, V.P. Menon's book is perhaps the most reliable on the integration of the Princely States. Then we have the ten volumes of Sardar Patel's correspondence between 1945-1950, ably edited by the late Durga Das between 1971 and 1974.

Sardar Patel's centenary in 1975 produced no work of consequence on him. This is a pity. His is a great life and needs a S. Gopal or M.J. Akbar to write a worthwhile biography, warts and all.

Forty years after his death it has been decided to bring out his collection works. The Advisory Board is headed by Shri S. Nijalingappa and includes Chaudhuri Devi Lal. The Chief Editor is Dr. P.N. Chopra, one time editor of *The Indian Gazatteers.* Vol. 1. which has recently been released to the period 1918-1925. Shri

Nijalingappa's Foreward offers no fresh insight or overview into Sardar Patel's life and remarkable achievement.

There are less convoluted and more grammatical ways of saying it.

Dr. P.N. Chopra's twenty five page Introduction is useful and informative but shows signs of literary exhaustion and poor proof reading. On page X, Dr. Chopra writes, "The son of a sturdy *Kisan* Vallabhbhai had...." On page XII, "But Vallabhbhai knew that he belonged to a middle class family...." Yet on page XIV we are informed that, "As a peasant, Vallabhbhai was eager to go to villages around London and acquire first hand knowledge....' We all have our limitations and shortcomings, but this is a bit much. Then on page XXVI, "Sir Leslie Wilson, Governor of Bombay, in his letter of 21st July 1925, to Lord Lytton,* the Viceroy...." Heaven's above, the Viceroy in 1925 was Lord Reading and not Lord Lytton.

All major publishing undertakings have their teething troubles. I am confident that Dr. Chopra and his team will in the months and years to come do full justice to the exciting and important work that they have undertaken. There is a lot of valuable material in the first volume on the Kheda non co-operation Movement, The Flag Agitation in Nagpur and the Borsad Satyagrah. In all three Sardar Vallabhbhai Patel provided inspiring leadership. Even more valuable and moving are accounts of Sardar Patel's personal life, the death of his young wife, the plight of his son Dayabhai and daughter Manibhen. She was constantly in her father's thoughts and he was sufficiently worried about her to take Gandhiji's advice.

The early pages of this book lift a curtain or two on Sardar Patel's entry into politics and his coming under the spell of Gandhiji after a short period of his playing the England return barrister. But once he joined the Mahatma there was no looking back. Patel gave Gandhi his total and unflinching loyalty. Of the Sardar's stay in London between 1910-1912, there are only a few skimpy letters and they tell us next to nothing about his London stay. He passed his Bar Examination in 1912, standing first and left for home right away to look after his impoverished family. He was then 37 years old. During that very

*The Viceroy was Lord Reading.

period Jawaharlal Nehru was also doing his Bar at Law in London, but obviously the two never met there.

In all ten volumes will be brought out. Volume II will take the Patel story to from 1926 to 1930. During these four years Vallabhbhai Patel and his brother Vitthalbhai attain national stature.

India Today.

15
Scholar Extraordinary

On March 3, 1990, Nirad C. Chaudhuri became the fifth Indian to be presented the Honorary Degree of Doctor of Letters by the Oxford University. The others are, Rabindra Nath Tagore, S. Radhakrishnan, Indira Gandhi and Satyajit Ray. Three Bengalis out of five.

Nirad C. Chaudhuri has been residing in Oxford since 1970. It was only after, *Thy Hand: Great Anarch,* appeared in 1987 that people in England woke up to the fact that NCC was not only alive but in full command of his richly endowed and powerful intellect. Thy *Hand* is nearly 1000 pages long. When he sent the manuscript to Chatto and Windus they threw up their hands. Who would read a book that long. They asked NCC to reduce the book to 350 pages. The answer from the author was characteristically unambiguous—not one page would be cut. That was that. The book was not to be published and NCC would not go to another publisher.

I got to know off this melancholy development and took up the matter with Graham Greene, a senior Director of Chatto and nephew of the novelist. Greene had come to India with a delegation of British publishers. On his return he reversed the earlier decision and the book was published without any cuts. It became a literary success without being a financial disaster. In fact the first edition sold out in less than four months. Consequently NCC began to be lauded and discussed in the close knit Oxford establishment. Chatto also brought out a paperback edition of NCC's, *A Passage to England.* All this led to the Hon. Degree. At 93 NCC is perhaps the oldest recipient.

Last month I spent two enthralling hours with Nirad Babu and Mrs. Chaudhuri at their Oxford home. He is in good health. She is not. Our conversation was in danger of becoming wide ranging. I wanted him to talk about himself. For that he needed no great encouragement. NCC possesses considerable verbal ingenuity and is generally ahead of the likes of me. So one has to listen carefully and mostly in silence as NCC's idea of a dialogue is that he speaks for both participants. Having known him for 36 years I have after some effort got used to his ways.

He was delighted with the Degree and showed me colour photographs of the ceremony, taken by his talented son Dhruva. He gave me a copy of the speech delivered by, "The Public Orator in a Congregation held on 3 March 1990, in presenting for the Honorary Degree of D. Litt." The language is archaic. The speech was actually delivered in Latin!

Let me quote from it. "The eminent Bengali whom I now present is thoroughly versed in both English and European poetry and has interpreted Indian society and customs to us with great intellectual ability, illuminating incidentally several aspects off our own society ... Chaudhuri expressed his views on contemporary events with a frankness which was too great to make him popular with his fellow Indians, praising certain aspects of the former Raj, and lacking in the requisite enthusiasm for there birth of New India. But with the passage of time his reputation at home is new restored. The Unknown Indian of his book has deservedly won fame and recognition."

I asked NCC what he was currently writing. "There will be no Vol. III of the autobiography in English." He spoke excitedly about his article in Bengali in *Desh* magazine of Calcutta. The writing project keeping him busy in his Bengali Trilogy. *Atmaghata Bengali.* The book is being published by Mitra and Ghosh of Calcutta. Vol. I deals with Bengali mental life till 1900. Vol. II will tell us much about the decline of Bengali character. Vol. III will explain the process of that decline from 1920 to 1947. Somewhere in these Volumes he will highlight the difference between the Bengali national movement and the national movement led by Gandhiji. Vol. III should be finished by the end of 1990.

I asked him if he was now a determinist or still a free will wallah. "I have become a determinist." When I queried him on Tolstoy's theory of history, at the end of "War and Peace" he replied. "I do agree with Tolstoy, we are not free agents. Some Unseen hand, some cosmic power is responsible for collective human behaviour." He paused. Then, "Take my case. I cannot explain my life on rational grounds. It is a combination of accidents and purpose fullness."

It was getting dark and I had a train to catch to London. He asked me to wait. Slipped into another room, reemerging with the handsome American editions of *Thy Hand* and *The Autobiography of An Unknown Indian.*

16
Andrei Sakharov

In one of his essays in his immensely enjoyable book, *Great Contemporaries,* Churchill wrote, "The amount of energy wasted by men and women of first class quality in arriving at their true degree, before they begin to play on the world stage, can never be measured."

This fits Andrei Sakharov, the details of whose brilliant early carrier and later torments are not well known in our country. What has appeared has been lifted from European and American Magazines and newspapers. Nor are his books readily available in our bookshops. Yet it is a life worth examining, because there is a heroic dimension to it.

Andrei Sakharov was born in 1921. His father was a professor of Physics in Moscow. Young Sakharov graduated from Moscow University in 1942 and worked as an engineer during the war. From 1948 to 1968 he worked on the military appliances and later the peaceful uses of thermo-nuclear reactors. He has been called the father of the Soviet Hydrogen Bomb. He was elected full member of the Academy of Sciences in 1953. The youngest man ever to sit in that exclusive club. On him were showered the highest civilian awards of this country. Apart from being a genius he was also an exceptionally sensitive man and not deaf to the whisperings of his conscience. The possibility of the production of the Atom Bomb made Einstein uneasy. The Hydrogen bomb did the same to Sakharov. None knew better than him the dangers of radioactive contamination. In 1957 he began a campaign for halting Nuclear Tests. From then on he was a marked man. Being who he was the authorities were at first cautious in dealing with him. In 1966 he finally broke with the Soviet "Establishment", became an open critic and then a dissident—a non-violent upholder of human rights and after the exiling of Solzhenitsyn in 1974 public enemy number one of the excesses and deficiencies of the Soviet regime.

In 1968 his first book *Reflections on Progress, Peaceful Co-exlstance and Intellectual Freedom* began circulating in *Samizdat.* An enterprising

Dutch journalist telephoned the complete text to ail Amsterdam paper. The New York Times published extracts which made Sakharov known to the West. In 1974 he was awarded the Nobel Peace Prize. That made matters worse. The inner emptiness of the Brezhnev era is only now coming to light. The Sakharovs were its most prominent victims. Sakharov and his second wife, Elena Bonner condemned Soviet intervention in Afghanistan. They were put under house arrest and in 1981 banished to Gorky, 300 miles east of Moscow. The merciless miseries and horrors they bravely suffered aroused world wide sympathy and admiration. They refused to bow and bend before an unjust order. Sakharov displayed the courage of a hero and the endurance of a Martyr. It is impossible to take a charitable view of what totaliatrian regimes have done to free thinking, freedom loving, upright, patriotic, talented, creative, men and women. The list is depressingly long-Djilas, Pasternak, Dubeck, Solznenitsyn, Havel, Sinyavsky to name only a few.

The arrival at the helm of Gorbachev heralded epochal and momenteous changes in the Soviet Union. Three years ago he picked up the phone and called Sakharov in Gorky and told him he was a free man. A more dramatic and symbolic public gesture to right a wrong is hard to imagine. With supreme confidence, unprecedented candour, he is opening doors locked for many decades. He was stirred the air as no one else has in the second half of the 20th century.

But let me get back to Sakharov and his other book, *My Country and the World,* which is a severe and devastating indictment of the Soviet State under Brezhnev and Co. The quality of the man can be measured by this sentence in the preface, "... we have a universal responsibility to use a single standard in judging human misfortune and injustice wherever they may occur." Later he writes, "It is no accident that for many years, in our country, new and promising scientific trends in biology and cybernetics could not develop normally, while on the surface out-and-out demagogy, ignorance, and charlotanism bloomed like gorgeous flowers. It is no accident that all the great scientific discoveries in recent times—quantum mechanics, new elementary particles, uranium fission, anti-biotics and most of the new, highly effective drugs, transistors, electronic computers ... all of them happened outside our country." No wonder the Soviet Union is now so keen for technology transfer from the West.

Writing in the International Herald Tribune of 19.12.1989 William Safire bracketed Sakharov with Gandhi and Einstein, "whose roles he so uniquely combined." One would hesitate to put any individual in the Gandhi—Einstein league but a case can be made for the inclusion of Sakharov.

Andrei Sakharov did that in a communist state adopting Gandhi's methods. There can be no going back. That is Sakharov's fantastic achievement. He embodied the desperation of the victims of a tyrannical system. The Russian people trusted him because he seemed to them an exceptionally steadfast, moral champion of their deepest feelings and interests.

India Today.

17

Zia-Ul-Haq

Three years ago President Zia-ul-Haq of Pakistan was killed in a mysterious plane crash. Three days later, on August 20, 1987, I as part of an all-party delegation was in Islamabad for General Zia's burial. The crowd was enormous, but the coffin was almost empty. Very little of the late President's body could be identified.

Now, his admirers and friends have brought out a book of tributes. *Shaheed-ul-Islam Muhammad Zia ul Haq* is published by Indus Thames Publishers, London. The price tag is £15. It carries a foreword by Salem Azzam, Secretary General of the Islamic Council, London. Contributors include, Zbigniew Brzezmski, President Carter's national Security adviser, General K.M. Arif, President Zia's closest army colleague, Nawaz Sharif, the Chief Minister of Punjab and Benazir Bhutto's principal critic, Z.A. Suleri, who was media adviser to the late President.

I got to know President Zia well during my tenure as Indian ambassador to Pakistan and personally got to like him. St. Stephen's College, Delhi was a special bond. We were both old boys of the college and he greatly valued and fondly remembered his four years there before partition.

One late evening I was walking on the magnificent terrace of our embassy residence in Islamabad (if I remember it was in 1981) and taking in the breathless beauty of the moon above the Margalla hills, when I was interrupted by one of my staff. He had come up on the double and panting announced that President Zia was on the telephone. Another Indo-Pak crisis, I concluded and hurried down.

As soon as I said hello, the President came on the line. "Kanwar Sahib, how are you? Bahut din se mulakat nahin hui." He never addressed me any other way.

"I am very well, President, and how are you Sir?"

"With the grace of Allah, I am well. Very well. Thank you"

"Mr President, it's very gracious of you to call, I am at your disposal. Khariat to hai, Sir."

He laughed. "Janab aap ko raat ke Khane ke dawat de raha hun. Day after tomorrow."

"I am honoured, Sir, I shall be there at the appointed time. Thank you very much."

For an ambassador an invitation of the Head of state is a command and cannot be refused unless the two countries are in a state of high crisis.

He went on, "Give me the names of some of your friends in Pakistan. I shall ask them to join us."

Since I had got to know him well enough I could do a little gentle leg-pulling.

"President, you already know who my Pakistani friends are. Your intelligence set-up is well acquainted with their names and addresses. You can select any of them." He enjoyed this. Now to the book. It is too adulatory, uncritical, almost hagiographic and reverential to bring out his character. His manners were impeccable, his courtesy unmatched, his humility genuine. He learnt the power game quickly and mastered it. No one else has ruled, Pakistan for 11 years.

His attempts to defy geography and make Pakistan a west Asian country. He was deeply religious and much is made of his Islamisation policy in this book, but even here he had his critics. Much is made of his Afghan policy and false claims are made on its behalf. The fact is that he really had no policy, but the Soviet intervention in Afghanistan made him "legal tender," which he was not after hanging Z. A. Bhutto in 1979.

Even in a book of tributes some contributors have not resisted India-bashing. Some of it is both cheap and silly i.e. India, Israel and South Africa are an anti-Pak nuclear gang-up.

President Zia deserved better.

Illustrated Weekly of India.

18
Tricky Dick

Richard Nixon has always been bad news in India. More often than not he has been bad news in the United states also. He has the unique and dubious distinction of being the only President of the USA to have been compelled to resign that high and awesome office. Watergate did him in.

I am perhaps one of the very few people now living in India who watched his 'final' TV Press conference after his 1962 defeat as Governor of California. I was then living in New York. Nixon's parting words were, 'you won't have Dick Nixon to kick around any more.' Having spat those words out he stormed out of the TV Studio. There was near unanimity that his political carrier was over.

It did not quite work out that way. He was, within six years, back on the political landscape with a vengeance. He was now President. But that too ended in disgrace and dishonour. Had he not resigned he would have been impeached and had he not accepted President Ford's pardon he would almost certainly have spent sometime in jail.

When Nixon resigned as President, in 1974, Professor Galbraith had this to say: "Richard Nixon has gone and that is a good thing. To the end he pictured himself as a man of virtue, but he was always given to overstatement, still we've had honest men in our public life and some truly inspired thieves. Nixon may have been the intermediate case but he did not know the difference ... he had a great ability to attract men like himself, although perhaps more those with a talent for public predition as opposed to private greed Nixon, of course, inclined to both."

As he himself acknowledges in his book *A View From the Stands* Galbraith bears some responsibility for bringing Nixon into public life. In 1941 he recruited him to his staff on the wartime price control operations office.

Nixon, in his latest book, *In the Arena,* does not of course mention Galbraith. Nixon's latest offering is an *expost facto* justification of the unjustifiable. His book is evenly divided between self-pity and self-deception, with a generous peppering of lachrymose and wholly unconvincing explaining away of Watergate. He is not a natural writer, with little appreciation of style and form and not overflowing with new ideas. Nevertheless, his books make money. This one will too. And he tells us that short of money he is. Whether it deserves to sell or not in another matter. Whether a man of his flawed character deserved to reach the top of the ladder, makes one begin to have faith in astrology.

In the Arena is a patchy and uneven book. Parts of it, those dealing with current affairs, Eastern Europe, Russia, Gorbachev etc are already out of date and even when he is not out of date he is neither profound nor original. He justifiably claims credit for his China breakthrough. This will remain his single solid achievement. He did change the contours of the diplomatic and political world arena by going to China and thus righting the monumental folly of ignoring the existence of the People's Republic of China. That folly had gone on for a quarter of a century. We have fuller and livelier accounts of the Mao-Nixon and Chou-Nixon talks in Henry Kissinger's two prolix but entertaining books. *The Years of Upheaval* and *The White House Years.*

Nixon held Mao in awe. The greatman not once went to see Nixon. It was the President who went to see Mao. For Chou En Lai, he has a healthy respect, but does not provide the accurate and admiring portrait Kissinger did. Nixon in his vice-presidential avatar had been a virulent anticommunist and an anti Peoples Republic of China Republican. Now, no praise is enough for China and its ageing leadership. The Chinese with their long-term view of history take all this in their stride.

I was particularly keen to see what the 78 year old Nixon had to say about India, Gandhi, Nehru, Indira Gandhi or 1971. Very little and that too en passant. Since resurfacing Nixon has travelled to many parts of the world but not to India. He did well not to. His anti-India policy during 1971 has not be forgiven or forgotten. Mrs. Gandhi dealt with him with cool and calculated severity. And that paid dividents.

The purely family and personal matters take up a fair portion of the book. But the obiter dicta on a variety of subjects-risks, philosophy, causes, privacy, silence etc. is a little short of inspired banality. Even the bits about Vietnam (another Nixon "achievement") are old hat.

At the end he emerged a rather lonely and sad figure. Neither statesman, nor great President, not a visionary, not an idealist, but a competent, resiliant, gritty machine politician who knew when to pull and when to push for most of his active life. But his luck ran out when he got to the White House. A less determined man would have gone under for good, but Nixon fought his personal battles like a man and has at long last become legal tender once again in his country.

He muses on great men: "All the prominent great leaders I have known have had goals greater than themselves. They sought high office not to be great but to do great things. Britain owes its existence to Churchill, France to De Gaulle, West Germany to Adenauer. Italy to de Gasperi, Japan to Yoshida, Israel to Ben-Gurian, and India to Nehru.... The impact such leaders have on the world is incalculably great. They all accomplished their goals through the prosaic nuts and bolts of democratic politics. But none ever made the mistake of thinking of politics as an end rather than a means."

In the Arena: A Memoir of Victory, Defeat and Renewal by Richard Nixon, Simon and Schuster.

19

Gandhian Capitalist

B.R. Nanda is now recognised as a biographer of distinction. His Mahatma Gandhi first appeared in 1958 and has remained in print ever since in several languages. Then came his book on the Nehrus, Moti Lal and Jawaharlal.

Seth Jamnalal Bajaj is one of the unsung heroes of the freedom struggle. He was born at Sikar in Rajasthan in 1889 and died at Sevagram in February 1942. It is a unique life. Our freedom movement is among the most luminous and inspiring events in our long, largely depressing history. Under Mahatma Gandhi's innovative leadership it held the world spell bound. The magic and example of Gandhi mesmerised Bajaj and he became the, "fifth son" of the Mahatma.

Nanda has rightly called his book. *In Gandhi's Footsteps; The Life and Times of Jamnalal Bajaj.* It is as much about Gandhi as it is about Bajaj. Like Jesus Christ, Gandhi collected at Sabarmati and Sevagram his own band of nonpolitical apostles Vinoba Bhave K.G. Masruwala, J.C. Kumaruppa, Gangaprasad Deshpande, Srikrishnadas Jajoo. Mirabehn (Madeleine Slade), Kaka Saheb Kalelkar and Jamnalal Bajaj.

Bajaj was not temperamentally cut out for politics, and in spite of his genuine flair and love for constructive village developmental work he was sucked into high powered political activity. To his astonishment, at 31 he found himself Treasurer of the Congress and member of the Working Committee. By this time he had taken all the ashram vows, including Brahmacharya, which put very severe strain on his young and deeply devoted wife. Their letters are extraordinarily candid and the Bajaj family should be given full marks for preserving them. Nanda has made good use of them, they make the book come alive.

Nanda has performed well the duties of a good biographer. Nanda has done a skillful job of distilling his material, he has retained the essential and discarded the redundent. What to leave out is as important as what to leave in. He does not get lost in the alleys and *galis* of Indian political life and never strays too far from the main highway. Research is very hard work. It can be agonising, frustrating, also rewarding and exciting. Suddenly the discovery of a little known fact will do wonders to tidy up a mass of material and make sense out of non sense. Nanda has tapped a very large number of sources, letters, memoirs. newspapers, periodicals, AICC reports, Congress Working Committee minutes, government files, vicereal correspondence. He has used this vast material to give the reader a coherent account of events in orderly sequence. Clarity is vital and here we have it in good measure.

The author succeeds in luring the reader from page to page. He is undogmatic and educative. He is calm and controlled, except when he writes about the big business names of Indian industry. He gives vivid accounts of the Bajaj household, presents new facts about congress party squabbles at the highest levels, low party morale at one working committee meeting during Gandhiji's Presidentship only Jawaharlal Nehru and Sarojini Naidu turned up.

Bajaj was held in high esteem and affection, not only by Gandhiji, but Nehru, Rajaji, Badshah Khan, Rajen Babu. With Sardar Patel he had tiffs and misunderstandings which the Mahatama resolved. Jamnalal, like all Marwaris, was a financial wizard. He attended to the financial problems of the Nehrus, Rajen Babu and others. He was the only businessman of consequence who threw in his lot with Gandhi and the Congress and who went to jail a number of times. So did his immediate family, including, his teenage son, Ramakrishna.

Nanda is rightly not placid about 'Indian big business' and the freedom movement. He successfully demolish the generally accepted view that Gandhi and the Congress were hand in glove with big business. Not so. Nanda writes, 'The aim (of big business) thus was to secure from the Congress struggle the highest economic dividents for the capitalist class at the smallest cost and if possible, no cost at all. Birla stayed out of the Salt Satyagrah in 1930, as he had done with the

Non-cooperation movement.... Not surprisingly, the industrialist's spirit of nationalism revived again in the late 1930's, during the brief interlude of Congress rule in the provinces. However, after the outbreak of World War II, when the congress was again in the wilderness and its entire leadership in jail, they did not the slightest compunction about making huge profits from war contracts' Jamnalal Bajaj was the one exception.

Nanda's book, a centenary publication, is an appropriate homage to an exceptionally noble human being who gave so much and asked for so little.

In Gandhi's Foot steps: The Life and Times of Jamnalal Bajaj by B.R. Nanda. Oxford. Rs. 225. Published 1990.

20

Maulana Azad

The Indian Council For Cultural Relations and Vikas Publishing House deserve our congratulations for bringing out two handsome volumes on Maulana Abul Kalam Azad. Volume one carries tributes and Appraisals. Vol. two the Maulana's selected speeches and writings. The Editorial Board was chaired by H.Y. Shard a Prasad. Sayeda Saiyidain Hameed is the Editor.

Maulana Azad was one of the great luminaries of our freedom movement and served as Congress President from 1940 to 1946. He was Education Minister from 1947 to his death on 22nd February, 1958. In addition he was a man with a mighty intellect and without doubt one the greatest orators the country has produced. As a college student I first heard him speak at the Jaipur session of the A.I.C.C. in December, 1948. He mesmerized his audience. The chiseled, chiche free, brilliant words and phrases poured out with effortless ease. He extended the scope of language and enriched the already high level of our national political debate.

He was an intellectual child prodigy and was recognized as an original and outstanding Arabic scholar by the time he was twenty years old.

M.A. Jinnah dismissed him as a show boy of the Congress. This showed Jinnah in poor light and did Azad no harm. He is as good and shining a product of India's composite culture as one can find. Unfortunately his autobiography, *India wins Freedom* was something of a disappointment, especially the 30 pages which were held over for publication for 30 years after his death. They were an uncomfortable anti-climax.

Here we have the great essential work of Maulana Azad and its quality is of the highest order. And he could write so splendidly about non-political matters. In "Ghubar-i-Khatir, be writes on, "The pleasures of Tea and Prison Life," which in Ahmednagar Fort prison, he wrote to his friend, Nawab Yar Jung on December 17, 1943.

"On the subject of tea, my difference of opinion with others is not only in respect of its branches and leaves, for in that case there could have been a way of resolving it. My difference is basic, not incidental. It is a difference of kind and not of degree.

"The first question about tea relates to its intrinsic value. I drink tea for its own sake, where as, for others, it is a means to an end. Think about it, I am moving in one direction, while the world is moving in another.

"Tea was born in China, and according to the Chinese, it has been in use for fifteen hundred years. There, it did not occur to anyone that its purity should be corrupted by use of milk. In all the countries to which tea has gone directly from China, i.e. Russia, Turkestan, Iran, it did not strike any one to use tea with milk. But in the 17th century, when the English discovered tea, I do not know what possessed them. They introduced the abominable practice of adding milk. Gradually, this practice degenerated to the extent that people started pouring tea in milk, instead of pouring milk in tea .

"I am a Muslim and profoundly conscious of the fact. I have inherited Islam's glorious traditions of the last thirteen hundred years. I am not prepared to lose even a small part of that legacy. The history and teachings of Islam, its arts and letters, its civilization and culture, are part of my wealth and it is my duty to cherish and guard them. As a Muslim. I have a special identity within the field of religion and culture and I cannot tolerate any undue interference with it. But, with all these feelings, I have another equally deep realization, born out of my life's experience, which is strengthened and not hindered by the spirit of Islam. I am equally proud of the fact that I am an Indian, an essential part of the indivisible unity of Indian nationhood, a vital factor in its total make up without which this noble edifice will remain incomplete...."

1991 Illustrated Weekly of India.